KALU OGBAA

Gods, Oracles and Divination

Folkways in Chinua Achebe's Novels

Africa World Press, Inc.
P.O. Box 1892
Trenton, New Jersey 08607

Africa World Press, Inc.
P.O. Box 1892
Trenton, New Jersey 08607

Copyright © 1992 by Kalu Ogbaa
First Printing 1992

All rights reserved. No part of this publication may
be reproduced, stored in a retrieval system or transmitted
in any form or by any means electronic, mechanical or
otherwise without the prior written permission of the
publisher.

Book design and typesetting by Malcolm Litchfield
This book is composed in ITC Berkeley Oldstyle and ITC Novarese Italic

Cover Illustration by April C. Simmons
Cover Design by Ife Designs/ Ife Nii Owoo

Library of Congress Catalog Card Number: 91-72278

ISBN: 0-86543-256-2 Cloth
        0-86543-257-0 Paper

Contents

	Acknowledgements	v
1	Introduction	1
2	Igbo Cosmology and Traditional Religion	9
3	Gods, Oracles and Divination	25
4	Names and Naming	61
5	Rituals and Ceremonies: The Dramatic Elements	88
6	Proverbs	111
7	Folk Stories	144
8	Folk Songs and Chants	176
9	Language and Imagery	214
10	Conclusion	242
	Bibliography	253
	Index	259

1 | Introduction

> Some of these ways are folktales, proverbs, proper names, rituals and festivals.
> —Achebe in *Morning Yet on Creation Day*

Chinua Achebe's four novels, *Things Fall Apart* (1958), *No Longer at Ease* (1960), *Arrow of God* (1964) and *A Man of the People* (1966)[1], appeared within the eight critical years when most African countries resumed their sovereignty after a century of European rule. How aptly these novels can be interpreted as realizations in fiction of the same spirit which expressed itself politically in the struggle for independence will emerge in the course

---

[1] All four novels were originally published by Heinemann Educational Books Ltd., London in 1958, 1960, 1964 and 1966 respectively. However, the editions quoted in this study are:

Things Fall Apart (TFA), London: Heinemann Educational Books Ltd., 1966;
No Longer at Ease (NLAE), London: Heinemann Educational Books Ltd., 1978;
Arrow of God (AOG), London: Heinemann Educational Books Ltd., 1977; and
A Man of the People (AMOP), London: Heinemann Educational Books Ltd., 1978.

of this study. Like Leopold Sedar Senghor, Franz Fanon, Okot p'Bitek, and Kofi Awoonor, Achebe often pictured contemporary Africans as cultural mestizos who must first find out the secret of their blood before they could come to their inheritance. Again and again Achebe tells us that his aim as a writer is the emancipation of Africa from the bondage of an alien culture. Speaking at the conference on Commonwealth Literature held in Leeds University in September 1964, he saw his achievements in terms of the cultural re-education of his contemporaries:

> I would be quite satisfied if my novels (especially the ones I set in the past) did no more than teach my readers that their past—with all its imperfections—was not one long night of savagery from which the first Europeans acting on God's behalf delivered them. Perhaps what I write is applied art as distinct from pure. But who cares? Art is important but so is education of the kind I have in mind. And I don't see that the two need be mutually exclusive.[2]

In an interview with Dr. Donatus Nwoga after the Leeds conference, Achebe repeated the idea giving emphasis to the background of devaluation of African aspirations and achievements in the era of imperialism. The African, he felt, suffered from "a colonial complex." So he indicated how he was going to fight it when he said, "You see, a writer has a responsibility to try to stop this because unless our culture begins to take itself seriously it will never sort of get off the ground."[3] And later in the same year, Achebe returned to the topic in an article in *Nigeria Magazine* titled "The Role of the Writer in a New Nation." In it, he drew attention to the search for political legitimacy through the identification of new African nations with the old empires of Ghana, Mali and Songhai. This process might spring from garbled history; but it must be seen in the light of a psycholog-

---

[2] Chinua Achebe, "The Novelist as Teacher," *Morning Yet on Creation Day* (New York: Anchor Press/Doubleday, 1976) p. 58.
[3] D. Duerden & Cosmo Pieterse (eds), *African Writers Talking* (London: Heinemann Educational Books Ltd., 1971), p. 8.

ical need of black peoples. For the image of Africa has been sullied by centuries of misrepresentation in which even the friends of Africa (like "the famous humanitarian, Albert Schweitzer") have participated:

> For me, at any rate there is a clear need to make a statement. This is my answer to those who say that a writer should be writing about contemporary issues—about politics in 1964, about city life, about the last coup d'état. Of course, these are all legitimate themes for the writer but as far as I am concerned the fundamental theme must first be disposed of. This theme—put quite simply—is that African peoples did not hear of culture for the first time from Europeans; that their societies were not mindless but frequently had a philosophy of great depth and beauty, that they had poetry and, above all, they had dignity. It is this dignity that many African people all but lost during the colonial period and it is this that they must now regain.[4]

In April 1973, Chinua Achebe addressed the University of Washington African Studies seminar on the theme of "Africa and her Writers." Here he made his most circumspect statement about the social functions of art. His main illustration was the building of the Mbari house in Igbo culture. But the address contained general reflections on Western and the Soviet traditions in literature: "In the beginning art was good and useful. It always had its airy and magical qualities, of course, but even the magic was often intended to minister to a basic human need...." After making many qualifications, and detours he returned *apropos* of Ayi Kwei Armah, to the artist's "deadly obligation to use his considerable talents in the service of a particular people in a particular place." It was in responding to a question, however, that he again repeated that literature is bound to have a political purpose:

---

[4] Chinua Achebe, "The Role of the Writer in a New Nation", *Nigeria Magazine*, No. 81 (Lagos, Nigeria: Federal Ministry of Culture, 1964), pp. 157-8.

> I believe that writing is very much a political activity. Any kind of writing, any novel, especially in our situation, becomes very much a political action. And I don't buy the idea that there is a separation between politics, public life, public themes, public concerns, and individual artistic concern. I don't see the difference.[5]

In practice, Achebe has used his writing, as a political action, to re-evaluate the African cultures and civilizations; and this study attempts to examine how he deals with Igbo folkways in his novels.

Concerned as he was for the revival of African cultural ideals, Achebe was singularly fortunate in the conception he had of what these ideas are. For the fact is that he did not think of institutions, ideologies or customs, but mainly of African—mainly Igbo—imaginative forms which readily lend themselves to the novelist's art:

> Since Igbo people did not construct a rigid and closely argued system of thought to explain the universe and the place of man in it, preferring the metaphor of myth and poetry, anyone seeking an insight into their world must seek it along their way. Some of these ways are folktales, proverbs, proper names, rituals, and festivals.[6]

Clearly, these are important Igbo folkways that must be mentioned when one is discussing Igbo culture. That is because in the folktales and proverbs are found the people's myths and poetry, world views and folk beliefs, imagery, witticisms, mottoes, wisdom, and general philosophy of life. A careful evaluation of them, therefore, reveals both the linguistic habits and the thought patterns of the Igbo. Furthermore, Achebe's Igbo (indeed, Africa) is the home of myth-makers, priests, moralists, storytellers, public speakers and other men of imagination who shape and reshape the total response

---

[5] Karen Morrel (ed), *In Person: Achebe, Awoonor, and Soyinka* (Washington: The Institute for Comparative and Foreign Area Studies of the University of Washington, 1975), pp. 5, 14, and 30.

[6] Chinua Achebe, "Chi in Igbo Cosmology," *Morning Yet on Creation Day*, p. 132.

of society to life. For that reason, it is inevitable that our appreciation of Achebe's art will focus differently if we pay appropriate attention to the cultural forms and folkways of the Igbo which, on his own testimony, he is so concerned to preserve in his works.

It is not necessary in a study of Igbo folkways in Achebe's novels to take the view that he learned nothing from the European tradition of fiction. There are clear indications that *Things Fall Apart* may have taken a few hints from Hardy's *The Mayor of Casterbridge*.

In fact, a comparative study of the characterizations in *The Mayor of Casterbridge* and *Things Fall Apart* reveals the great extent to which Achebe either was inspired by or borrowed from Hardy. For example, the heroes of both novels are farmers: one a hay trusser and the other a yam grower; as a result of their obscure parentage, both men have an obsession: Henchard suffers the monomania of becoming the Mayor of Casterbridge and Okonkwo, the Lord of Umuofia clan; both have passionate love for their daughters which the daughters know about and attempt to requite: Elizabeth Jane spares no effort in looking for her missing father, whom she gives a decent burial after his corpse is discovered in the forest, and Ezinma "had broken her twenty-eight day visit to the family of her future husband, and returned home when she heard that her father had been imprisoned, and was going to be hanged," as an expression of her love of her father (TFA, p. 177). And in spite of the admirable efforts they make to become great, both heroes die ignoble deaths, partly because of their tragic flaws and partly because of the roles of the gods.

Hardy and Conrad were certainly authors who Achebe knew well. Generally speaking, the realistic tradition of the nineteenth century English novel set the pattern for his works. It is possible too that the particular curve of experience in *Things Fall Apart* and *Arrow of God* have their origin in Achebe's knowledge of Greek tragedians.

The major fact, however, is that Achebe grew up in an Igbo village. What this means is that the first layer of imaginative patterns in his mind is the heritage of Igbo language, literature and other cultural forms. These established the basic structural syntax in terms of which he would encode and retrieve meaning both in life and art.

The assumption made here is that works of art do not have the completeness which some critics attribute to them. Their viability outside their time and place can only be partial. An African folktale, a Hungarian folk song, and a Chinese Noh play can be enjoyed more or less outside their societies. But there is always an effort of historical analogy and reconstruction; and this process could lead to errors in appreciation. Even when the work is apparently simple, cultural exegesis is still needed to clarify the meaning of its elements. Every culturally derived artefact entails in greater or lesser degree the whole of the culture in which it is created. Everything that is said, figured, or symbolized emerges out of an implicit background of ideas the existence of which makes historical elucidation an important part of aesthetic criticism. In reading a play of the English renaissance, for example, we need to tune our ears to the peculiar nuances of Elizabethan word play, to the growing importance of secular humanism over medieval religious values, and to what Tillyard calls the Elizabethan world picture. Similarly, Dmitry Furmanov's haunting portrait of Vasily Ivanovich Chapayev can only be clear if the reader attends to an unavowed Marxist/Leninist dimension in the portraiture; that is, to the fact that Chapayev is seen as an individualist, a heroic individualist, in a collectivist society.

This study of Igbo folkways in Achebe's novels is an examination of the patterns of Igbo thoughts and expressions as elements which bear on structure and significance in Achebe's novels. Again and again in the novels, Achebe's attention rests on the conflict between the traditional order of values and on the conflict between the traditional order of values and Western perspectives. This occurs in *Things Fall Apart* at the end of the novel when, following Okonkwo's death, his friend Obierika turns to the District Commissioner and says angrily: "That man was one of the greatest men in Umuofia"; but the District Commissioner hardly listens as he thinks about the use he will make of the new insight into savage burial customs in his future book, *The Pacification of the Tribes of the Lower Niger*. In *No Longer at Ease* the conflict appears in the very first chapter in which Green's racial dogmatism is contrasted with the more humane comprehension which the novel as a whole embodies. In *Arrow of God*, the very conception of a divine arrow turns upon the ambiguity of Ezeulu's relationship with his god; for, while from his own cultural perspective he is Ulu's victim, there is another perspective in terms of which the tragedy that befalls his household is self-inflicted.

The conflict between Igbo traditional order of values and Western perspectives requires some form of critical explanation. In fact, Robert Wren touched on it in his own study when he remarked:

> With these novels, it is not enough, dictionary-like, to define obscure words or names. That *Umuofia* means "children of the forest" explains little. The reader needs to know as well that *ofia* has connotations in modern Nigeria: *ofia* is bush, uneducated, uncontaminated by European urbanism. The locale of *Things Fall Apart* and *No Longer at Ease* is symbolically named for the bush people who inhabit it. Ironically, their life is civil, ordered—a contradiction to the connotations of *Umuofia*—and this is, in a profound sense, the meaning of the novel; we Nigerians were not what we seemed, what you called us, what in your ignorance you perceived, even you, you Nigerians who have adopted European thought.[7]

While Wren's efforts towards explaining the conflicts and connotations of "obscure words and translation of names" focus on the historical and cultural context of the novels, it is the business of the present study to explain and translate the Igbo folkways as a way of illuminating the novels for enhanced appreciation of them by all categories of readers.

The book is written in ten chapters. The first chapter, in giving insight into the unique contribution the study makes to the existing studies in Achebe's major fiction, puts in historical perspective the novelists's cultural and social commitment and how it bears on the general study of the novel as an art form. The next two chapters together focus on Igbo religion and cosmology as elements in Achebe's artistic form as they also reveal what informs the morality of the Igbo characters. The fourth chapter is devoted to the analysis

---

[7] Robert M. Wren, *Achebe's World: The Historical and Cultural Context of the Novels* (Washington D.C.: Three Continents Press, Inc., 1980), p. 9.

of the use that Achebe makes of names and naming in the novels, but such analysis is not given an onomastic treatment. Chapter five contains the examination of rituals and ceremonies of the Igbo as dramatic elements. Effort is made in the chapter to de-emphasize the religious and metaphysical imports of the folkways, in order to focus on their secular and entertainment values.

The next four chapters are devoted to the examination of the linguistic habits and verbal arts of the Igbo and how effectively Achebe exploits them in the novels to express the culture and civilization of his native Igbo in a foreign artistic medium, the novel. The tenth chapter, which concludes the study, serves as final remarks on Igbo folkways in Chinua Achebe's novels and on the novelist's exploitation of them as important elements in his artistic form and perspective.

Our overall objective in this study is thus two-fold: first, to provide an in-depth critical examination of Igbo folkways in Achebe's novels because they are considered important elements of the rich and dignified Igbo culture. Besides, the folkways serve as useful stylistic and technical devices that Achebe uses expertly in writing the novels which began a new literary tradition in Africa—a tradition which has helped to win a literary independence for the "dark continent" of Africa. And secondly, through our analysis, we have sought to give readers a new approach to the appreciation of Igbo culture and civilization through its literature. It is our sincere hope that the discussion which follows will validate these intended objectives.

2 | Igbo Cosmology and Traditional Religion

> We also believe in Him and call him Chukwu.
> He made all the world and the other gods.
> —Akunna in *Things Fall Apart*.

Igbo Cosmology and traditional religion are important folkways that should be understood by readers of Achebe's novels, because cosmology and religion seem to be the concern of every Igbo character in the old and new orders—the old order in *Things Fall Apart* and *Arrow of God*, and the new order in *No Longer at Ease* and *A Man of the People*.

Also, a background knowledge of Igbo cosmology and traditional religion enables readers to gain useful insights into what informs and shapes the world-view, moral code and ethics of the characters in the novels: namely, the relation of man to other creatures or forces in the universe, to his fellow men, and to the supernatural force behind all creations, variously called cosmic force, God, or as in the case of the Igbo people, *Chukwu* or *Chineke*. It should be noted, however, that cosmology and religion are so interrelated that they are not treated as separate concepts as the title of this chapter seems to suggest. Rather, they are given a holistic treatment, following Achebe's exploitation of them in his novels.

Chukwu/Chineke or Supreme God

Igbo traditional religion begins with the Igbo concept of the Supreme God—Chukwu (translated literally as greater god because of the presence of the lesser gods) or Chineke *(chi[nke] naeke,* god-who-creates or Creator) who is so omnipotent, and ineffable that he is approached by men through lesser gods and deities. Victor C. Uchendu, an Igbo Professor of Sociology, writing on "Igbo Ideas of the High God" says in part:

> The idea of creator of all things is focal to Igbo theology. They believe in a supreme god, a high god, who is all good. The logical implication of the concept of god who is all good is the existence of a devil *(agbara)* to whom all evil must be attributed. This is not peculiar to Igbo thought. It is a characteristic of all known religions which accept the doctrine of a high god who does no evil.[1]

However, Uchendu does not fail to point out the difference between the Christian God and Chukwu of the Igbo:

> The Igbo high god is a withdrawn god. He is a god who has finished all active work of creation and keeps watch over his creatures from a distance. [Hence] The Igbo high god is not worshipped directly. There is neither shrine nor priest dedicated to his service. He gets no direct sacrifice from the living but is conceived as the ultimate receiver of all sacrifice made to the major deities. (In fact, Igbo sacrifice to any unknown and uninvited deities who might be present.) He seldom interferes in the affairs of men, a characteristic which sets him apart from all other deities, spirits, and ancestors. He is a satisfied god who is not jealous of the prosperity of man on earth.[2]

---

[1] Victor C. Uchendu, *The Igbo of Southeast Nigeria* (New York: Holt, Rinehart and Winston, 1965), p. 94.
[2] *Ibid.,* pp. 94-95.

That means that Chukwu is not omnipresent; neither is He worshipped or approached directly except through the minor deities to whom sacrifices are offered for their mediation services to man and Chukwu.

Achebe's exploitation of Igbo concept of Supreme God in his novels can be exemplified with the following friendly argument between an Igbo village head, Akunna, and a white missionary, Mr. Brown:

> "You say that there is one Supreme God who made heaven and earth," said Akunna on one of Mr. Brown's visits. "We also believe in Him and call Him Chukwu. He made all the world and the other gods."
>
> "There are no other gods," said Mr. Brown. "Chukwu is the only God and all others are false. You carve a piece of wood—like that one" (he pointed at the rafters from which Akunna's carved *Ikenga* hung), "and you call it a god. But it is still a piece of wood."
>
> "Yes," said Akunna. "It is indeed a piece of wood. The tree from which it came was made by Chukwu, as indeed all minor gods were. But He made them for His messengers so that we could approach Him through them. It is like yourself. You are the head of your church."
>
> "No," protested Mr. Brown. The head of my church is God Himself."
>
> "I know," said Akunna, "but there must be a head in this world among men. Somebody like yourself must be in the head here."
>
> "The head of my church in that sense is in England."
>
> "That is exactly what I am saying. The head of your church is in your country. He has sent you here as his messenger. And you have also appointed your own messengers and servants. Or let me take another example, the District Commissioner. He is sent by your king."
>
> "They have a queen," said the interpreter on his own account.
>
> "Your queen sends her messenger, the District commissioner. He finds that he cannot do the work alone and so he appoints *kotma* to help him. It is the same with God, or Chukwu. He appoints the smaller gods to help Him because His work is too great for one

person."

"You should not think of Him as a person," said Mr. Brown. "It is because you do so that you imagine He must need helpers. And the worst thing about it is that you give all the worship to the false gods you have created."

"That is not so. We make sacrifices to the little gods, but when they fail and there is no one else to turn to we go to Chukwu. It is right to do so. We approach a great man through his servants. But when his servants fail to help us, then we go to the last source of hope. We appear to pay greater attention to the little gods but that is not so. We worry them more because we are afraid to worry their Master. Our fathers knew that Chukwu was the Overlord and that is why many of them gave their children the name Chukwuka—'Chukwu is Supreme.'"

"You said one interesting thing," said Mr. Brown. "You are afraid of Chukwu. In my religion Chukwu is a loving Father and need not be feared by those who do His will."

"But we must fear Him when we are not doing His will," said Akunna. "And who is to tell His will? It is too great to be known" (TFA, pp. 162-3).

The conversation between Akunna and Brown is a major statement by the author on Igbo religious practices. It reveals another aspect of Igbo folkways which is not understood by an outsider. And that is why Mr. Brown alleges that Chukwu is anthropomorphized by the Igbo. But as Akunna points out, it is to the gods and deities that sacrifices are offered, a religious rite which does not constitute worship *per se*. It is Chukwu, the source of all creation, that is worshipped; but that is done with the assistance of the superhuman agencies. If we may draw an analogy here, the gods and deities are regarded by the Igbo as attorneys-at-law under Chukwu, the Supreme authority, before whom they plead human cases. The fees paid for their services are the sacrifices offered to them. Since the gods and deities possess these human tendencies, it is no wonder then that they are so talked about in human terms.

To emphasize further the human attributes of these gods and deities, the sacrifices they demand through oracles are sometimes negotiated like human attorneys' fees:

> "Some people say the Oracle warned him that he would fall off a palm tree and kill himself," said Akukalia. "Obiako has always been a strange one," said Nwakibie. "I have heard that many years ago, when his father had not been dead very long, he had gone to consult the Oracle. The Oracle said to him, 'Your dead father wants you to sacrifice a goat to him.' Do you know what he told the Oracle? He said, 'Ask my dead father if he ever had a fowl when he was alive'" (TFA, p. 19).

The point is, if the Igbo worshipped false gods, as Mr. Brown asserts, then no one would impugn the authority of the gods and deities or contradict the words of the oracle and go free as Obiako here does, for that would be sacrilege; no one would do the kind of thing that Akunna talks about. That is, "when they (gods and deities) fail and there is no one else to turn to we go to Chukwu." Chukwu is worshipped because He is so just that no sacrifice can influence or obstruct His justice, neither does He need or demand anything at all from man. The relationship of man to the gods and deities is like the relationship between a human employer and his employees. The Igbo believe that the universe is anthropocentric; therefore man can manipulate any other creations of Chukwu, including the gods, to his advantage by offering them some sort of sacrifice, especially kola. The idea of manipulation has become synonymous with bribery, and in the novels some corrupt characters regard kola, one of the items of sacrifice and of entertainment, as metaphor for gifts, bribes and kick-backs.

In the Akunna-Brown argument, Achebe employs the pedagogical technique of analogy, comparison and contrast to teach his readers the traditional religion of his native Igbo. He creates the dramatic moment and atmosphere suitable for the verbal confrontation between representatives of two divergent cultures. Mr. Brown is persuaded that Igbo traditional religion is definitely idle- and idol-worship; therefore he confronts Akunna whom he thinks he could easily persuade, since they are friends. Akunna, acting as the author's mouthpiece, is found prepared to meet any challenges to his religious culture. In answering Mr. Brown's questions, he compares his religion with Mr. Brown's. But Mr. Brown, who sees some sharp contrasts between the two religions, voices his opposition which, on closer examination, borders on form rather than substance. However, by making an analogy between the roles of Igbo gods and the various representatives of the white man's religion and government, Akunna forces Mr. Brown to make a tactical withdrawal and replan the attack that he hopes to carry out somewhere else and at some other times. What we understand from their conversation is that Igbo traditional religion is not inferior to the invading alien religion, Christianity. Both religions have the same essence, although their forms of manifestation differ tremendously.

Chi or Personal God

Next to Chukwu, in order of importance, is *chi* in Igbo cosmology and traditional religion. Before discussing Achebe's use of *chi* in the novels, it is helpful that readers have a general understanding of *chi* and its roles in the lives of traditional Igbo. Like many other phenomena in Igbo life, *chi* has dynamic meanings and roles, depending on given circumstances and the individual lives involved. Hence any reader who depends on the Igbo dictionary for the meaning of *chi* (perhaps linking its etymological relation to Chukwu) may be mistaken in his interpretation or appreciation of the use to which Achebe puts the notion of *chi*.

According to Mazi Elechukwu Nnadibuagha Njaka, *chi* is the manifestation of the individual ego in the spirit of life; it is that being which links its house, man, to the One Soul (Chukwu); *chi* is the sustaining essence of a living man but not the man who dies; *chi* is man's double, linking him to Chukwu, his ancestors, and the unborn, guarding, guiding, and protecting him in his activities during his lifetime; and *chi* is omniscient, can foresee danger, and is concerned only with the person with whom it remains through one lifetime.[3] The point, therefore, is that because the above meanings and functions are ascribed to *chi*, one can conclude that the concept of *chi* is at the root of individualism in Igbo tradition and that *chi* does not help an individual who fails to help himself. Nevertheless, what may appear as contradiction in the meanings and roles of *chi* (as Achebe espouses them in his novels) is, in fact, a difference in the contextual manifestations of *chi*.

Chi as Achebe uses it in the novels is, variously, a personal god or spirit, guardian angel, soul, or spirit double. Defined by its roles in a man's life, *chi* is creator, fate, or destiny.[4] *Chi* assumes its definite and individual meanings and roles according to the context in which it is used. In the following instance, *chi* is a personal god or spirit which functions as fate or destiny.

> Unoka was an ill-fated man. He had a bad *chi* or personal god, and evil fortune followed him to the grave, or rather to his death, for he had no grave (*TFA*, p. 16).

Unoka, Okonkwo's father, is portrayed as a lazy and poor character; nevertheless, he could not have been that way if his *chi* were not as lazy and poor. The Igbo cosmological belief here is that the human being is a reflection of his personal spirit, *chi*.

As spirit double or personal creator of the man, *chi* is stronger or greater than its human double:

> You know more book than I, but I am older and wiser. And I can tell you that a man does not challenge his *chi* to a wrestling match (*NLAE*, p. 37).

Here, one is advised to avoid fighting an enemy when he knows that

---

[3] Mazi Elechukwu Nnadibuagha Njaka, *Igbo Political Culture* (Evanston: Northwestern University Press, 1974), pp. 31-32.

[4] For Achebe's full discussion of *chi* see his "*Chi* in Igbo Cosmology" in *Morning Yet On Creation Day* (New York: Anchor Press/Doubleday, 1976), pp. 131-145.

the enemy is stronger than he, for that spells disaster; but more importantly, the quotation emphasizes the importance of one maintaining order in nature. That is, in the hierarchical order of the universe, spirit comes before human beings. In addition, spirit controls the body, therefore spirit is superior to body.

Chi is also a guardian angel or good fortune:

> Everybody was killed, except the old and the sick who were at home and a handful of men and women whose *chi* were wide awake and brought them out of the market (*TFA*, p. 126).

To the Igbo, good fortune is not a happenstance. It is something brought unto human beings by a benevolent god or guardian angel. Those who have malevolent *chi* are ill-fated and they cannot escape any misfortune coming their way.

Finally, *chi* is an individual ego or initiative:

> But the Igbo people have a proverb that when a man says yes his *chi* says yes also. Okonkwo said yes very strongly; so his *chi* agreed. And not only his *chi* but his clan too, because it judged a man by the work of his hands (*Ibid.* p. 25).

Chi as individual ego or initiative seems to suggest that character is fate. In *Arrow of God*, Achebe's narrator says, "If a man says yes his *chi* also says yes" (p. 28). This notion of *chi* seems at variance with *chi* as fate or destiny; yet the Igbo do not see it so.

The use that Achebe makes of *chi* is very crucial in characterization for it points to the Igbo belief in the notion of predestination and man's apparent helplessness in the face of his being denied gifts such as children, wealth and good health by intransigent *chi* during the process of man's creation in the spirit world. But such a belief in fate and destiny is modified by a corollary belief[5] that the indi-

---

[5] The corollary belief is held by my own people, Ihechiowa in Arochukwu/Ohafia LGA, Imo State of Nigeria. It was explained to me by a village elder, Chief Ogbonnaya Eke, during my research in 1979.

vidual, when still a spirit being, has a say in his creation as he is being made ready for incarnation or reincarnation into the human world. At that stage, the human-to-be is allowed to choose what kind of human life he will lead. The choice he makes is then ratified by Chukwu and *chi* respectively; that choice is his fortune which must "follow" him all the days of his physical life. Those who make bad choices (including Unoka, Okonkwo's father, in *Things Fall Apart*) are said to have *ajo chi* (literally bad *chi*). Since the Igbo believe in this myth of free will and choice at creation, it becomes proper for them to talk of bad *chi* not as a criticism of God's ordination of man's life in a certain way, but as that of the man who makes the bad choice, even if that choice was made in *ala mmo* (the spirit world) before birth.

Achebe's treatment of *chi* is somehow ambiguous, because he neither defends nor condemns the Igbo belief in *chi*. Rather he exploits the various belief as he lets his readers into the inner lives of his major characters. For example, Okonkwo's determination to fight his father's bad *chi*, in *Things Fall Apart*, is a ruling passion in the life of the hero—a passion that derives from the concept of *chi* as individual ego and initiative and accounts for his success. Nevertheless, whenever the ego or initiative is mismanaged, it seriously brings about the hero's alienation from his family:

> ... but his whole life was dominated by fear, the fear of failure and of weakness. It was deeper and more intimate than the fear of evil and capricious gods and of magic.... And so Okonkwo was ruled by one passion—to hate everything that his father Unoka had loved. One of those things was gentleness and another was idleness (*Ibid*. pp. 12-13);

At times *chi* as personal ego makes the hero commit offenses against the earth goddess, Ani:

> You have committed a great evil.... The evil you have done can ruin the whole clan. The earth goddess whom you have insulted may refuse to give us her increase, and we shall all perish (*Ibid*, p. 28);

And finally, it prompts Okonkwo's action against the British Administration in Umuofia:

> In a flash Okonkwo drew his machete. The messenger couched to avoid the blow. It was useless. Okonkwo's machete descended twice and the man's head lay beside his uniformed body (*Ibid*, p. 184).

As Okonkwo fights his father's *chi*, he wrestles with his own. The Igbo's belief in *chi*, coupled with the myth of reincarnation, tends to suggest that the child in the spirit world knows and accepts before hand the family into which he is reincarnating.[6] Once he is born into it, he may strive to improve its lot but not to repudiate totally whatever the family stands for. If he does, there could be disorder. It is one of Okonkwo's problems that while he succeeds in bringing honour to himself, his family, and his clan, he completely rejects the gentleness of his father, whom he fails to accord a decent burial. His failure thus violates a family tradition and hence brings a curse. We are reminded of this in *No Longer at Ease* when Okonkwo's abandonment of his father's ways is indirectly reciprocated by his own son, Nwoye, who leaves him and becomes a Christian convert, Isaac Okonkwo. Isaac in turn abandons his father's ways including his traditional religion. Isaac's son, Obi, disobeys him by deciding to marry Clara, an *osu*. Isaac reminds Obi of the heavy penalties for such disobedience:

> I [Isaac Okonkwo] was no more than a boy when I left my father's house and went with the missionaries. He placed a curse on me. I was not there but my brothers told me it was true. When a man curses his first child it is a terrible thing. And I was his first son. . . . When they brought me word that he had hanged himself I told them that those who live by the sword must perish by the sword. Mr. Braddeley, the white man who was our teacher, said it was not the right thing to say and told me to go home for the burial. I refused to go (*NLAE*, p. 125).

---

[6] Chief Eke is still the source of the Igbo belief.

This boy [Obi Okonkwo] that we are talking about, what has he done? He was told that his mother died and he did not care. It is a strange and surprising thing, but I can tell you that I have seen it before. His father did it (*Ibid*, p. 145).

Unlike his father, Isaac, Obi was born and raised in a wholly Christian home. This may have encouraged him to expect his Christian parents to ignore the "pagan" cult of *osu* and support his marriage proposal to Clara. Maybe the young Nwoye would have done so but not the mature Isaac who is, at this point, lamenting his own adolescent disobedience to his father, Okonkwo. By allowing the traditional practices to triumph over the Christian, the narrator realistically demonstrates that, in spite of the success of Christianity in traditional Igboland, there were some traditional ways, however bad, that the white man's religion could not (and still cannot now) wipe out. The question of *osu* in the first three novels is a case in point.

Honoring the Ancestors

To disobey one's parents and elders is a very serious offense which could earn one a curse, but a worse offense than that is the dishonoring of the ancestors whose importance in Igbo cosmology has made foreign commentators such as David Carroll say that "the Igbo religion transcends local boundaries. It consists of three major categories of belief—the worship of the great public deities, the cult of personal gods, and the worship of ancestors."[7] But, the Igbo know that the ancestors are "honored", not "worshipped" in the strict sense.[8] The importance of the ancestors in Igbo religious life is rooted in the Igbo's belief in life after death, *chi*, reincarnation, and reciprocity.

It is believed that every man in the temporal world has his

---

[7] David Carroll, *Chinua Achebe* (New York: Twayne Publishers, Inc., 1970), p. 29.

[8] Uchendu, *op. cit.*, p. 102.

double in the spirit world. While the living man tries hard to lead a decent life on earth, acquiring wealth and titles as a passport to the spirit world where he hopes to continue his existence, with all his earthly titles and status, his spirit double, at the threshold of reincarnation, makes choices of good or bad things which Chukwu and *chi* will then ratify as his fortune on earth. One of such spirits could be a deceased ancestor, who must be honored and courted by the living relatives in order that he will reincarnate into their family. In fact, young married couples have been observed competing to take very good care of an elder in his death-bed in the hope of having him reciprocate their favors by reincarnating to them as their first child.[9]

After Okonkwo commits a female *ochu*[10] and is banished from his own village of Umuofia, he goes to take refuge in the home of his mother's kinsmen in Mbanta. While there, Okonkwo takes time to reflect on his misfortune. When it dawns on him that "clearly his personal god or *chi* was not made for great things and that a man could not rise beyond the destiny of his *chi*," he seeks to contradict the saying of the elders, "that if a man said yes his *chi* also affirmed" because here he is "a man whose *chi* said nay despite his own affirmation."[11] The narrator reports that "the old man, Uchendu, saw clearly that Okonkwo had yielded to despair and he was greatly troubled."[12] Consequently, Uchendu talks to him, giving him the kind of guidance and protection that he needs to survive the traumas of exile. In this sense, Uchendu becomes the true representative of Okonkwo's deceased ancestors. If Okonkwo never cared for them in the past, Uchendu's present duties to him ought to remind him of the importance of honoring one's ancestors.

In fact, before his exile, it is one of such elders, Nwakibie, that gives Okonkwo some seed yams to sharecrop; the yams he gets from his farm enable him to feed his mother, sister, and his own immedi-

---

[9] Part of Chief Eke's information.

[10] Chinua Achebe, *Things Fall Apart* (London: Heinemann Educational Books Ltd., 1966), pp. 112-113.

[11] *Ibid.*, p. 119.

[12] *Ibid.*, p. 119.

ate family. In such a society, where men are willing to become "their brothers' keepers," it is mandatory to respect old age since there are a lot of material, psychological, and social benefits that one can enjoy, if one respects his elders and works hard. Hence, "age was respected among his people, but achievement was revered,"[13] becomes a germane phrase. Also, since the Igbo traditional society had an oral tradition, no one could bypass his first teachers (parents and elders) to acquire the knowledge he needed; but one could do that in a literate society, where great minds are stored in books or other forms of record. The achiever in Igbo traditional society is one who submits to the instructions and authority of such parents and elders.

Primarily, however, the ubiquitous presence of the ancestors in Igbo life makes them apparently more important than Chukwu or *chi*: they occupy the "three worlds" of the dead, the living, and the unborn and exercise enormous influences in all of them. Trust in their cyclic movement and existence is due to the Igbo's belief "that Chineke (Creator) created this world for man and that man will not die, although individuals may die to be reincarnated to continue on earth."[14]

Ways of honoring the ancestors (which will be discussed in detail in subsequent chapters)[15] include invoking their presence with palm wine, kola nut, and white clay before meals, during meetings, and when one has visitors; naming one's children after them; and according the deceased first and second burials. For instance, before the kola is broken, the oldest man present in the house or in an important gathering invokes, through incantation, the spirit of the ancestors who are believed to live beneath the earth. The libation poured with palm wine not only slakes the ancestors' thirst, but also softens the holes on the ground through which they physically appear in the dead of the night, and the lines drawn with white clay

---

[13] *Ibid*, p. 8.
[14] Njaka, *op. cit.*, p. 21.
[15] The various ways of honoring the ancestors were explained to me by Chief Eke.

symbolize their peaceful welcome.

The wine and kola offered to the ancestors are expected to be taken by them because once they are invited, they can assume human forms and, therefore, can drink and eat as humans. A first burial rite ushers them into *ala mmo* (the land of the dead), and the second puts them among the rich and the titled; hence only the very rich and titled men are given second burials. The spirits of those who are not buried are believed to inhabit the "evil" forests, from where they disturb human beings, and such spirits are encountered especially at night as ghosts. In fact, some of the unexorcised spirits are believed to reincarnate as *ogbanje*[16] in order to torment their ill-fated mothers in a cycle of births and untimely deaths. To exorcise the evil spirits, chase the ghosts away, and prevent the *ogbanje* from further reincarnation, oracles are consulted, sacrifices are offered, and the *Ogbanje's iyiuwa* (evil stone) is exhumed and made impotent by a powerful medicine man. We will come back to all these matters later.

Appropriation

The Igbo people's belief in Chukwu, *chi* and ancestors is their religious imagination which one gleans from the stories of individual men acting among their fellow men. Being familiar with Igbo village storytelling habits—habits which include giving moral tags to each story—Achebe could not have written about Igbo religious life without raising some universal moral issues. In other words, he appropriated the Igbo world-view as a means of asking, in his own way, some ontological and theological questions which have puzzled man for ages. Initially, there is a tendency for readers and critics to localize the tragedies of the major characters, attributing them to Igbo or African problems. But carefully examined, some of the issues Achebe raises prove to be human problems which are presented as

---

[16] *Things Fall Apart*, pp. 69-70.

Igbo Cosmology and Traditional Religion | 23

universal parables.[17]

Death is one of such human problems that people of all cultures have no answers for; therefore, men endure the loss of their loved ones by hoping in the life after death which, for the Christians is realized in paradise or heaven. For the Igbo it comes in the form of reincarnation of the deceased ancestors. Hence the ancestors are accorded impressive first and second funeral rites. Achebe accords such a farewell address to Ezeudu in form of a monody presented by a one-handed spirit, consistent with the Igbo custom, that the deceased ancestor must be addressed only in the language of spirits:

> "Ezeudu!" he called in his guttural voice. "If you had been poor in your last life I would have asked you to be rich when you come again. But you were rich. If you had been a coward, I would have asked you to bring courage. But you were a fearless warrior. If you had died young, I would have asked you to get life. But you lived long. So I shall ask you to come again the way you came before. If your death was the death of nature, go in peace. But if a man caused it, do not allow him a moment's rest" (TFA, p. 112).

Although this passage is prose, it has poetic qualities that make it suitable for the festal occasion: incantatory in tone, repetitive in structure, and choric in its oral performance. No wonder the people danced, following the example of the one-handed spirit who "danced a few more steps and went away." And more importantly, Achebe loads the passage with as many Igbo folk beliefs as he possibly could—the criteria for measuring a fulfilled life are given and they include riches, courage or fearlessness, long life, and peace. Juxtaposed with them are their opposites such as poverty, cowardice, short life, and lack of peace. Both the positive and the negative criteria constitute the Igbo belief in dualities and otherness. In the passage, too, one learns that reincarnation is a sure thing with the Igbo, and they try hard to work for it, thus making each rebirth a

---

[17] C.L. Innes and Bernth Lindfors, *Critical Perspectives on Chinua Achebe* (Washington, D.C.: The Three Continents Press, 1978), p. 24.

higher cyclic movement in the perpetuation of the human race.

The traditional Igbo characters in Achebe's novels, as a result of their belief in Chukwu, *chi*, and the ancestors, show greater piety and less skepticism than people within the urban setting. Unlike the Christians who tend to believe more in life after death, the practitioners of Igbo traditional religion do not distinguish between life here on earth and that lived after death; there is life-in-death and death-in-life. Thus, each of them aspires to live a good moral life which they believe will be the same in the spirit world. Even in these divergent religious attitudes we are introduced to the overall conflicts between the traditional and the modern, the indigenous and the foreign, that the novels dramatize.

With such metaphysical outlook of life, religion seems to be the foundation of the social, political, and legislative institutions of the people; hence the Igbo religious leaders such as priests and their surrogates enjoy a theocratic status and reverence. However, while the Igbo cosmology and traditional religion can make the social control of the people a lot easier, thereby producing unity among villagers and clansmen, too much trust in oracles, gods, and goddesses, in the ordination of *chi*, and in the pronouncements of such divine agents as priests and priestesses, oracle tellers, and powerful medicine men could produce social disaster. Hence, as we shall see later on, twins and their mothers are mercilessly killed because diviners consider them an abomination to the gods, and those who suffer the "swelling" disease known in modern medicine as dropsy are sent away to die miserably in the "evil" forest.

Sometimes superstition is mistaken for piety, wickedness and violence for bravery and manliness, personal aggrandizement for patriotism, and sheer personal dreams for the will of the gods. Aware of these weaknesses in the traditional Igbo society created by individuals in authority, Achebe argues that the success of the white man in establishing his influence in Igboland could not have been without local assistance. One finds such weaknesses in Okonkwo and Ezeulu. They try to fight the fight of their gods instead of functioning only as "arrows of god." How they are punished by the gods is examined in the next chapter.

3 | Gods, Oracles and Divination

> Nothing is absolute. *I am the truth, the way and the life* would be called blasphemous or simply absurd, for is it not well known that a man may worship Ogwugwu to perfection and yet be killed by Udo?
> —Achebe in *Morning Yet on Creation Day*.

In traditional Igbo religion, worshippers approach the Supreme Being, Chukwu, through such divinities as gods, goddesses, and oracles. Because that religion exerts a great deal of influence on the moral and political lives and activities of its present day practitioners, it is one of Achebe's novelistic techniques to appropriate the piety of the people and the influence the divinities have on them in creating the characters in *Things Fall Apart* and *Arrow of God*. Indeed, the religious and patriotic blunders of such characters as Okonkwo and Ezeulu are seen to have some spillover effects on the lives of their children whose characters are delineated in *No Longer at Ease*. Hence, before a person makes moral or philosophical remarks on the characters, he should first of all gain insights into the roles of the divinities as revealed in traditional Igbo religious practices, insights which aid proper understanding of the characters' individual relationships with the divinities.

Origin, Nature and Function of the Deities

Because of their "ontological mode of existence between God and man," no one can accurately trace the origins of Igbo deities, especially the older ones, who may be the "deified heroes and mythological figures."[1] The origins of the latter gods are known, but quite often different narrators give what impartial readers may consider conflicting mythological accounts of the deities. To the worshippers of the deities, what cannot be scientifically proved is accepted without question, through faith and tradition. After all, faith and tradition, they say, are the basic and necessary traits of all religions.[2]

Nevertheless, there are myths that confirm that the deities were created by men possessed and inspired by the spirit of Chukwu[3]; hence, the Igbo believe that their gods, goddesses, and oracles are the sons and daughters of Chukwu. These divinities are powerful and intelligent beings who roam the world but have their permanent homes in the seas, mountains, caves, forests and trees which worshippers regard as the shrines of such deities. Because Chukwu delegated them to be His representatives, the spiritual beings are in active contact with the world of nature and of man. Furthermore, for an absentee landlord like God to establish his presence and influence, he has to have strong representatives to oversee various human activities and departments.

Superior to the man-made gods are the nature gods and goddesses such as Ani, Anyanwu, Idemili and Amadioha whose existence cannot be threatened by human beings. These are the spirits of

---

[1] John S. Mbiti, *African Religions and Philosophy* (New York: Frederick A. Praeger, Publishers, 1969), pp. 76-78.

[2] For details of some of the myths, see Donatus Ibe Nwoga, *The Supreme God As Stranger in Igbo Religious Thought* (Ekwereazu in Imo State, Nigeria: Hawk Press, 1984), pp. 33-48.

[3] Chief Kalu Ogoro of Ihechiowa, himself a creator of latter gods, explained how he was often visited in dreams by spirits who instructed him on how to create some gods for troubled societies.

nature or personifications of natural forces.[4] They cannot be treated with disrespect like the man-made gods when they fail to fulfil human expectations; rather, human beings are always prepared to accept blame for the apparent failure of such gods. For instance, should there be a drought like the one in *Things Fall Apart*, the general belief is that someone must have committed some "abominable" offense against the god or goddess in charge of rain. Therefore, the people will have to consult the oracle to divine the will of the god, a means by which the right items of sacrifice are determined. In other words, some natural disasters are always attributed to offenses that men commit against the gods. The traditional Igbo also believe that however great an offense may be, it can be atoned with a matching sacrifice which may include the sacrifice of human beings.

Achebe's Appropriation of Igbo Belief in the Divinities

In the novels, Achebe uses gods, goddesses, or deities to represent the personifications of spiritual beings in charge of such human interests as protection against wars assigned to Ulu, wealth assigned to Eru (the lord of wealth), and morality and fertility to the Earth-goddess, Ani. Oracles, on the other hand, are deities whose roles are purely prognostic; as agencies of divination, they serve both man and other gods and goddesses. The spirits of the living-dead ancestors are personified as "masked spirits," or the collective *egwugwu*. These latter "spirit beings" come and go whenever there are festivals and court hearings. They do not have shrines like the gods, goddesses, or the oracles. Their homes are beneath the earth from where they are invoked (through incantation, mystic drumming, and ritual dancing) to come and accompany human beings in their ritual performances and legal deliberations.

Like the gods in Igbo world, the gods in Achebe's novels are given specific assignments by their creators. However, inherent in

---

[4] Kofi Asare Opoku, *West African Traditional Religion* (Accra: FEP International Privated Ltd., 1978), p. 55.

the assignments of these deities is the Igbo principle of division of labor. As long as each god, goddess, or oracle does his or her work, there will be harmony or order; but disharmony or disorder occurs whenever any department fails to carry out its function at the right time. One such disorder occurs in *Arrow of God* when Ezeulu fails to eat the sacred yams thereby delaying the announcement of the harvest of the new yam; this failure not only threatens people's lives with starvation, but also turns worshippers away from Ulu to the Christian God:

> Now Mr. Goodcountry saw in the present crisis over the New Yam Feast an opportunity for fruitful intervention. He had planned his church's harvest service for the second Sunday in November the proceeds from which would go into the fund for building a place of worship more worthy of God and Umuaro. His plan was quite simple. The New Yam Festival was the attempt of the misguided heathen to show gratitude to God, the giver of all good things. This was God's hour to save them from their error which was now threatening to ruin them. They must be told that if they made their thank-offering to God they could harvest their crops without fear of Ulu (*AOG*, p. 215).

Quite often, villagers expect the man-made deities to reflect the wishes and temperament of their creators. For instance, Ulu was created by the six villages of Umuachala, Umunneora, Umuagu, Umuezeani, Umuogwugwu, and Umuisiuzo, "who lived as different peoples, and each worshiped its own deity," to protect them against "the hired soldiers of Abam [who] used to strike in the dead of night, set fire to the houses and carry men, women and children into slavery" (pp. 14-15). Ulu helped them to become a clan, and they took the name of Umuaro, "and the priest of Ulu became their Chief Priest." Having been so united against a common enemy, "from that day they were never again beaten by the enemy" (p. 15). In spite of the peace and security Ulu brought to them, the people expect Ulu to be as intransigent as they are; they call him the praise name, "Great Ulu who kills and saves" (p. 72).

As god of security, Ulu was intended to deal with external

aggression against Umuaro, but not necessarily to combat the potentially dangerous internal threats of envy and rivalry between individuals from different villages, between priests, and between gods of the federation of villages that make up Umuaro clan. Umuaro's failure to appreciate the magnitude of such internal weaknesses prevents them from rallying around their Chief Priest to deal with the new external threat, the white man's religion and administration. They erroneously believe that the fight between Ezeulu and the white man's administration is a personal problem of the priest. Although Ezeulu triumphs over the challenges of the white administration, the humiliation he suffers in the process rekindles the traditional Umuaro rivalry; it also strains his relationship with the white man. Ironically, without the support of the people, Ulu, the god that deals with external aggression, cannot save the people from the threats posed by the Christian religion. Thus his presence in Umuaro is already considered irrelevant by such rival elders as Nwaka and Ezidemili who have always insinuated the destruction of the god to the people:

> Let us not listen to anyone [Ezeulu] trying to frighten us with the name of Ulu. If a man says yes his *chi* also says yes. And we have all heard how the people of Aninta dealt with their deity when he failed them. Did they not carry him to the boundary between them and their neighbors and set fire on him? (p. 28)

Judging from Nwaka's speech, the lives of man-made gods like Ulu depend on the whims of the people who own them. Apparently, it seems so only to those who want to make their wills the wills of the gods. But they do, however, receive their rewards. For instance, after Okonkwo settles in Mbanta when he "had begun to play a part in the affairs of his motherland," he stirs up the people against the Christians whom he calls "the abominable gang" that must be "chased out of the village with whips"[5] but a wiser villager reminds

---

[5] Chinua Achebe, *Things Fall Apart* (London: Heinemann Educational Books Ltd., 1966), p. 145.

him of the danger of fighting for their gods:

> "It is not our custom to fight for our gods," said one of them. "Let us not presume to do so now. If a man kills the sacred python in the secrecy of his hut, the matter lies between him and the god. We did not see it. If we put ourselves between the god and his victim we may receive blows intended for the offender" (*Ibid.*).

As will be discussed later in this chapter, Okonkwo and Ezeulu, by putting themselves between the gods and their victims, received blows intended for the offenders.

The Goddess Ani

One of the nature gods in Achebe's novels is Ani the earth goddess, the personified daughter of Chukwu. She is in charge of human morality and fertility as well as the increase of animals and plants. As physical earth, Ani functions metaphorically as the womb which contains the living-dead ancestors during the period of gestation before they are reincarnated from the spirit world of the tomb into the physical and human world. When a child is born, its umbilical cord is buried in the earth where it enjoys the protection of Ani. The child's first hair is cut and buried in family land on which the parents plant a family tree—e.g., orange, *ukwa*, coconut—as a totem. ani keeps in balance the Igbo trinity of the living, the dead, and those yet to be born. Hence, it is fashionable for the Igbo to address Ani as Mother Earth. Her authority over the moral codes of the people is supreme. In fact, one cannot clearly distinguish between Igbo religious morality and Igbo socio-political morality because both forms derive from Ani whose spirit is invoked with white clay (part of the earth) and libation poured on the ground; it is a ritual performance that must precede any meeting, be it a festal or religious occasion. Igbo customs are called *omenani* because they derive from the authority of Ani.

As an agrarian community, the Igbo have daily communion with Ani: as they work their farms the farmers know that the increase of their crops is due to the loving care of Ani. So she deserves all the gratitude of the people which is expressed annually in the form of new yam festivals, ritual dances conducted before and after harvests, as well as the cleansing sacrifices offered to her. Every Igbo is afraid of doing anything that would attract the wrath of Ani, for apart from denying people all the blessings that come from her, Ani is capable of "wiping out whole families."[6] This is why the strongman Okonkwo is as willing as the weakest man in Umuofia to offer a propitiation sacrifice when he offends Ani by beating his wife during the Week of Peace.

In the area of folk-medicine and magic, the influence of Ani is still felt. The one common disease that plagues the traditional Igbo societies of the novels is *iba* (malaria), and a common cure for it is a concoction of boiled barks, leaves and grasses. For example, "when Ezinma lay shivering on a mat beside a huge fire that her mother had kept burning all night," the narrator reports: "'It is *iba*,' said Okonkwo as he took his machete and went into the bush to collect the leaves and grasses and barks of trees that went into making the medicine for *iba*" (p. 73). These medicinal materials grow out of Ani and it is she who grants them their curative efficacy. And when medicine is practiced as magic and occultism, barks and leaves of trees, grasses and clay are used. The narrator refers to this use of nature's flora when he says that "Okeke Onenyi learnt many herbs and much *anwansi* or magic whose name was *Oti-anya afu-uzo*."[7] Because of their importance as health officers and occultists, medicine men occupy a high position in the society. They enjoy the protection and blessings of Ani, the giver of their stock-in-trade, as long as they do not do anything offensive to her or to her children. But when they do offend her, they usually would plead for mercy by offering some sacrifices to Ani; otherwise, they would be stripped of their powers.

---

[6] *Ibid.*, p. 61.

[7] Chinua Achebe, *Arrow of God* (London: Heinemann Educational Books Ltd., 1977), p. 147.

Oracles and Divination

In the traditional Igbo societies of Achebe's novels, one of the people's problems in having several gods is that any allegiance one pays to one god may turn out to be an offense against another god because the man-made gods are as envious as their makers. To avoid offending the gods, citizens must always watch out for signs. Therefore, "omens and premonitions play a large part in the fortunes"[8] of Achebe's people. Ordinary people can interpret ordinary omens: when Ezinma's eye twitches, "That means you [Ezinma] will see something."[9] When the new moon "sits awkwardly" it is "a bad moon.... A bad moon does not leave anyone in doubt. Like the one under which Okuata died. Its legs were up in the air."[10] It is obvious from these examples that anyone with psychic tendencies can recognize some omens and have premonitions of some disasters before they happen. To satisfy that need, priests who divine the will of the gods are constantly consulted.

Oracles and divination have enormous influence on traditional societies of Achebe's novels. That influence is not, however, peculiar to those societies for, according to Ruth A. Firor:

> Divination is the active counterpart to omens and premonitions. It is the *sortilegium* and *augurium* of the ancients, practiced lawfully only by the priests or by the head of a family. Among the Germanic tribes, divination, like the priestly office, was hereditary. It was held unlawful when practiced by any not recognized as priest of a cult. Such a practitioner was believed to use his knowledge chiefly for the selfish benefit or active hurt of individuals rather than for the social weal.[11]

---

[8] Ruth A. Firor, *Folkways in Thomas Hardy* (Philadelphia: University of Pennsylvania Press, 1931), p. 11.

[9] *Things Fall Apart*, p. 37.

[10] *Arrow of God*, p. 2.

[11] Firor, *op. cit.*, p. 41.

Only some of these characteristics that Firor outlines apply specifically to Igbo divination. In *Arrow of God*, Ulu, Umuaro's god of security, functions as an oracle and Ezeulu is his Chief Priest. His office is hereditary and the succession of Ezeulu causes his oldest son, Edogo, a lot of concern (p. 92). Everybody in Umuofia and Umuaro believes that their priests and priestesses practice divination "for the social weal," but what they do not easily detect is that diviners could use their knowledge "chiefly for the selfish benefit or active hurt of individuals" and the community as a whole. Achebe exploits this error or credulity (innocently committed by the people out of religious and patriotic fervor) to point out the weaknesses of the traditional Igbo religious and socio-political practices. In fact, oracles (divine utterances made by god through priests and priestesses in response to inquiries[12]) seem to be the causes of the major calamities that one finds in the novels.

In *Things Fall Apart*, Okonkwo kills Ikemefuna because "the Oracle of the Hills and Caves has pronounced it" (p. 52); the Oracle pronounces that the swelling sickness is an abomination to the earth, therefore Okonkwo's father Unoka who dies of it "could not be buried in her bowels" (p. 17); to remove the shame of being the son of an *àgbàlà*, Okonkwo decides to do anything *manly*, including committing three murders. In the end he commits suicide; again the oracle pronounces his death an abomination to Ani so "he will be buried like a dog ... ," despite the honors he has brought to Umuofia (p. 137). Twins are abandoned in the bush where they are thrown away to die, and their mothers ostracized because the oracle says they are an abomination (p. 141); but most outrageous of these abominations is an *osu*:

> He was a person dedicated to a god, a thing set apart—taboo for forever, and his children after him. He could neither marry nor be married by the free-born. He was in fact an outcast, living in a special area of the village, close to the Great Shrine. Wherever he went he carried with him the mark of his forbidden caste—long,

---

[12] *The Random House College Dictionary* (1975 edition), p. 934.

tangled and dirty hair (p. 142).

It is an irony that people who are chosen by oracles and dedicated to the gods (an act intended to save the community from whatever problems they have) should now become enslaved forever instead of being regarded as saviors. These "outcasts" were the first to join the new religion. When Nwoye joins the Christians, Okonkwo disowns him, thinking to himself: "To abandon the gods of one's father and go about with a lot of effeminate men clucking like old hens was the very depth of abomination" (p. 139). Little does he realize that the white man's religion offered hopes and brotherhood to the *efulefu*, especially as it stopped the human sacrifice of which his adopted son, Ikemefuna, was a victim:

> It was not the mad logic of the Trinity that captivated him [Nwoye]. He did not understand it. It was the poetry of the new religion, something felt in the marrow. The hymn about brothers who sat in darkness and in fear seemed to answer a vague and persistent question that haunted his young soul—the question of the twins crying in the bush and the question of Ikemefuna who was killed (p. 134).

In *No Longer at Ease,* Obi Okonkwo and Clara are not allowed to marry because Clara is an *osu*. The Umuofia men in Lagos and Obi's parents (devout Christians) at home do not endorse the marriage proposal. Obi's (perhaps Achebe's) reaction to the opposition can well be summed up in the words of the narrator:

> It was scandalous that in the middle of the twentieth century a man could be barred from marrying a girl simply because her great-great-great-great-grandfather had been dedicated to serve a god, thereby setting himself apart and turning his descendants into forbidden caste to the end of Time. Quite unbelievable. And here was an educated man telling Obi he did not understand (p. 65).

Obi's failure to gain the support of his people, his eventual breaking of his engagement to Clara, and his effort to arrange an abortion for her cause him mental anguish and financial drain which lead him into taking bribes. Of course, he is caught, convicted, and imprisoned. In a word, Obi and Clara are victims of oracles told four generations earlier.

Yet in *Arrow of God*, Ezeulu suffers because apparently he remains obedient to the oracle, Ulu. When Umuaro men want to go to war with Okperi, he tells them Ulu would not fight an unjust war. They disregard his warning; consequently "Ulu thrashed them, thrashed them enough for today and for tomorrow!" (p. 15). The people are unhappy with him because they believe that "no one ever won judgement against his clan" (p. 230). Ironically, it is the truth Ezeulu tells against his clan that wins him the admiration of the British Administration and leads to their offering him an appointment. At the same time he alienates some of his own people by appearing to be the white man's "friend." On his return to Umuaro, the elders order him to eat the sacred yams in arrears. When he is moved by the people's suffering to change his mind, he is chastised by Ulu. He absolutely pursues the truth as the oracle tells it. He worships Ulu to perfection but he is brought low by another *god*, the will of the people.

Oracles play important roles in the religious lives of the Igbo. They have helped people to appease their gods and ancestors with sacrifices, and such suppliants have thereafter found favor with their *chi*. On the other hand some suppliants have been ruined by oracles told by bad diviners. Achebe maintains an ambivalent attitude towards the usefulness of oracles. Such an attitude is to be expected of any objective reporter, who does not want to influence his readers unduly. Yet judging from the influence of oracles and divination on the lives of his characters, we can say that the novelist does not condemn divination as a folkway but he definitely condemns bad diviners and those who obey the pronouncements of the oracles without the least reflection that the tellers of oracles are human beings who could make their human wills those of their gods.

The Downfalls of Okonkwo and Ezeulu

Our discussion of the downfalls of Okonkwo and Ezeulu begins with answering Achebe's question, "Is it not well known that a man may worship Ogwugwu to perfection and yet be killed by Udo?"[13] To answer the question is to call in question the relationship of man to the myriad of Igbo gods and spirits, the relationship between the tutelary gods of the villages, and the nature and powers of the gods and their priests. But in addition to worshipping the deities, one has to face another formidable authority—the will of the elders who represent the people.

With the coming of the white man to Umuofia and Umuaro, the human authority increased to a point of threatening the divine authority. Since the two kinds of authority are not usually compatible, it becomes very difficult, if not impossible, for a "worshipper" to do the will of the gods while obeying the mundane authorities without offending one or both of them at a time. A man can, however, escape the wrath of the gods or the alienation of the people if he is level-headed enough to review the development of incidents and modify his views of things—a quality that he needs in order to think out right answers to his problems. Unfortunately, Okonkwo's and Ezeulu's pursuit of the absolute are so inflexible that their people fail to support them in their fights against those that the heroes perceive as external enemies of the community. So, when they fail, the voice of the people becomes the voice of their respective gods.

Okonkwo's Suicide

In his article, "A Note on Okonkwo's Suicide," Robert Fraser cites a number of critics and commentators who appear reticent in their response to the question of why Okonkwo committed suicide.[14] It

---

[13] Chinua Achebe, *Morning Yet on Creation Day* (New York: Anchor Press/Doubleday, 1976), p. 133.

[14] Robert Fraser, "A Note on Okonkwo's Suicide," *Kunapipi* 1, 1 (1979), p. 108. Fraser argues that "the reticence of such an impressive battery of critics is perhaps nevertheless hardly surprising since suicide, being the most private of acts, the question of its motivation is especially delicate."

is my belief that the reticence which Fraser refers to is self-imposed by the critics; for instead of simply looking for answers from the novel, they go beyond the text in order to psychoanalyze the character of Okonkwo, and when they fail to come up with an impressive result which befits their hypothesis, they become reticent. In fact, however private and delicate suicide may be in general, the motivation of Okonkwo's particular case is revealed by the narrator. Therefore, a closer examination of the text proves that Okonkwo's suicide is motivated by his failure to achieve his self-imposed leadership of his clan. The immediate but summary motivation of the suicide is hinted at by Obierika when his friend's dangling body is discovered: "That man was one of the greatest men in Umuofia. You drove him to kill himself; and now he will be buried like a dog ..." (p. 187).

Throughout the novel the narrator explains that personal achievements and piety are the basic qualifications that anyone who calls himself a *man* in Umuofia must possess. Piety in the Umuofia context does not just mean "reverence for God or devout fulfillment of religious obligations," its meaning includes "dutiful respect or regard for parents, homeland,"[15] and elders who represent the deceased ancestors. Obviously Okonkwo is an achiever who also shows ostensible signs of piety from time to time. Therefore, he apparently deserves anything but the contemptible death by suicide which leads to his being buried like a dog; but his case is a proof of the maxim, "Character is fate."

> In terms of achievement [that is before his exile], Okonkwo was clearly cut out for great things. He was still young but he had won fame as the greatest wrestler in the nine villages. He was a wealthy farmer and had two barns full of yams, and had just married his third wife. To crown it all he had taken two titles and had shown incredible prowess in two inter-tribal wars. And so although Okonkwo was still young, he was already one of the greatest men of his time. Age was respected among his people, but achievement was

---

[15] *The Random House Dictionary*, p. 1005

revered (pp. 7-8).

Apart from explaining here what things constitute greatness in Umuofia, the narrator gives us another hint at the reason why Okonkwo will eventually choose to die suddenly. That is, since achievement is revered and because his father died without it, Okonkwo's fear of failure motivates him to pursue achievement with a religious fervor. Having tasted the joys and glory of achievements up until the time he goes in exile, he considers his failure to achieve when he returns to Umuofia as failure in life. Thus, achievement is Okonkwo's life-spring; deny him achievement and you put out the life in him:

> His life had been ruled by a great passion—to become one of the lords of the clan. That had been his life-spring. And he had all but achieved it. Then everything had been broken. He had been cast out of his clan like a fish onto a dry, sandy beach, panting (p. 119).

While achievement is what motivates everything Okonkwo does, it also serves as a means of demonstrating his patriotism. His personal victories at wars and wrestling matches earn his clan the epithet, *Umuofia obodo dike,* "Umuofia the land of the brave" (p. 109). Okonkwo's military achievements made it easy for his clan to obtain quick compensation (of the ill-fated lad Ikemefuna and a young virgin) for the wife of Ogbuefi Udo murdered by Mbaino:

> And so when Okonkwo of Umuofia arrived at Mbaino as the proud and imperious emissary of war, he was treated with great honor and respect, and two days later he returned home with a lad of fifteen and a young virgin.... Okonkwo was, therefore, asked on behalf of the clan to look after him in the interim (p. 12).

It is the clan that sends him to Mbaino and after he give his reports, the clan is satisfied with the execution of the mission. Neither the gods nor the people are displeased with his exploits so far.

In contrast, when Okonkwo beats up his wife during the Week of Peace, he is reprimanded by Ezeani, the priest of Ani, for Okonkwo's act is so "abominable" that it "can ruin the whole clan." Having been told the enormity of his thoughtless act, Okonkwo is repentant; therefore, he does as the priest asks him to do by taking to the shrine of Ani the next day "one she-goat, one hen, a length of cloth and a hundred cowries "for a cleansing ritual. This is the first proof of his religious piety.

When Ogbuefi Ezeudu warns him to refrain from taking part in the killing of Ikemefuna, Okonkwo is headstrong and "bears a hand" in the killing of a boy who calls him father. When his friend, Obierika, confronts him with the inconsiderate killing, Okonkwo gives an explanation which amounts to a subterfuge:

> "You sound as if you question the authority and the decision of the Oracle, who said he should die" ... "But someone had to do it. If we were all afraid of blood, it would not be done. And what do you think the Oracle would do then?" ... "The Earth cannot punish me for obeying her messenger," Okonkwo said. "A child's fingers are not scalded by a piece of hot yam which its mother puts into its palm" (p. 60).

This explanation, which Okonkwo presents as evidence of his piety to Ani and the Oracle of the Hills and the Caves, fails to persuade Obierika; the omniscient reporter is apparently not deceived by it either since he had earlier reported, "Dazed with fear, Okonkwo drew his machete and cut him down. He was afraid of being thought weak" (p. 55). In essence, Okonkwo's explanation to Obierika is an example of how people can use religious practices as a pretext that enables them to pursue private and individual ambitions. We discover Okonkwo's hoax because Achebe's thematic and artistic techniques reveal it to us: from the beginning of the novel, the novelist lets us into Okonkwo's mind so we can know what motivates his particular actions. As Obierika rightly points it out to him, the Oracle did not specifically ask Okonkwo to be the one to kill his adopted son. Neither do the people. For the second time Okonkwo commits an "abominable" act which warrants the warning from Obierika: "What you have done will not please the Earth. It is the kind of action for which the goddess wipes out whole families" (pp.

60-61). Technically, however, the warning foreshadows the destruction and exile that follow Okonkwo's killing of Ezeudu's sixteen-year-old son.

From the novelist's point of view, Okonkwo has committed the highest offense: killing Ikemefuna, his adopted son. But unlike the first abomination of desecrating the Week of Peace, he fails to atone for his sin with a sacrifice. His two-day fast is a sign of sorrow but that is not a deliberate and adequate act of atonement, since he does not offer a matching sacrifice. Blood has been spilt and it should be redeemed with blood—the blood of animals if the sacrifice is voluntarily offered or human blood when the gods demand it. By intuition Okonkwo is tempted to do more than just fast, but again for fear of being thought weak he suppresses the feeling with the following monologue:

> "When did you become a shivering old woman." Okonkwo asked himself, "you, who are known in all the nine villages for your valor in war? How can a man who has killed five men in a battle fall to pieces because he has added a boy to their number? Okonkwo, you have become a woman indeed" (p. 59).

This passage underlines the conflict between what Okonkwo the pious and Okonkwo the ambitious does, and as it were, Okonkwo kills not because he is carrying out a ritual process, but because he wants to prove to his fellow elders and to himself that he is not a *woman* like his father Unoka, who could not stand the sight of blood. What follows later in the novel is as controversial as the killing of Ikemefuna:

> The drums and the dancing began again and reached fever heat. Darkness was around the corner, and the burial was near. Guns fired the last salute and the cannon rent the sky. And then from the center of the delirious fury came a cry of agony and shouts of horror. It was as if a spell had been cast. All was silent. In the center of the crowd a boy lay in a pool of blood. It was the dead man's sixteen-year-old son, who with his brothers and half-brothers had been dancing the traditional farewell to their father (p. 112).

Gods, Oracles and Divination | 41

Okonkwo has inadvertently committed a crime. It is a female crime because it has been inadvertent. He must flee from the clan because the crime is against the earth goddess, Ani. Thus one can say that he is punished for killing his adopted son; or, that he is merely fated by the gods to get involved in the accident.

The narrator uses the most sensitive imagery to describe Okonkwo's calamity: "He had been cast out of his clan like a fish onto the dry, sandy beach, panting." First, what the dry, sandy beach is to the fish (a foreign, unnatural and uninhabitable place, that is) is what Mbanta is to the exiled Okonkwo. Not only is Okonkwo not used to the customs of the people, he considers the men of Mbanta "effeminate." Second, the word "panting" reinforces the trauma and desperation concomitant with exile. In a "panting" situation, only a second person or party can save a victim. As we learn later on in the novel, it takes the combined efforts of Uchendu and Obierika to put Okonkwo back on track before he can run towards his goal of becoming one of the lords of his clan. Without the material and moral help of both men, it would have been impossible for Okonkwo to cope with the forlornness and despair that have begun to dominate his life; they come through in Okonkwo's thought, "Clearly his personal god or *chi* was not made for great things" (p. 119).

When we pit the narrator's comment with what was said earlier on in the novel, when things were working well for Okonkwo (that is, "Okonkwo was clearly cut out for great things"), there seems to be a contradiction. But it appears so only because a few people realize that Okonkwo kills a kinsfolk when he murders his adopted son, Ikemefuna. In addition, Okonkwo thinks to himself that no one knows his real motive when he deals the killing blow of his machete on the sacrificial lad. Ani who probes secret thoughts rewards Okonkwo openly by involving him in an accident in which he kills Ezeudu's son—an incident that unsettles him for life:

> The only course open to Okonkwo was to flee from the clan. . . . That night he collected his most valuable belongings into headloads. His wives wept bitterly and their children wept with them without knowing why . . . .

As soon as the day broke, a large crowd of men from Ezeudu's quarter stormed Okonkwo's compound, dressed in garbs of war. They set fire to his houses, demolished his red walls, killed his animals and destroyed his barns. It was the justice of the earth goddess, and they were her messengers. They had no hatred in their hearts against Okonkwo. His greatest friend, Obierika, was among them. They were merely cleansing the land which Okonkwo has polluted with the blood of a clansman (p. 113).

This way, the prophetic warnings from Ezeani and Obierika are fulfilled. Nearly all that makes Okonkwo an achiever is wiped out. He is to make a new start of life in exile.

Although Okonkwo's killing of Ezeudu's son is inadvertent, it is no accident that Achebe makes the victim the son of Ezeudu, the very old man who goes to warn Okonkwo against taking part in the killing of Ikemefuna. He says to Okonkwo:

"Yes, Umuofia has decided to kill him. The Oracle of the Hills and the Caves has pronounced it. They will take him outside Umuofia as is the custom, and kill him there. But I want you to have nothing to do with it. He calls you his father" (p. 52).

On the surface, we might regard Ezeudu's warning as helpful since it is intended to save Okonkwo from committing the murder of his adopted son, an act which we believe earns Okonkwo the wrath of Ani. But a closer look at the episode reveals, however, that the warning has dangerous consequences for both Ezeudu who gives it and Okonkwo who flouts it. Considering the ruling passion of Okonkwo's life, to tell Okonkwo that Umuofia had decided to kill Ikemefuna following the pronouncement of their oracle is to excite the warrior into action. You don't tempt a dog with a bone. Even though Okonkwo can see reason in the warning, he fears what other elders might say if he fails to show up for the ritual killing. In addition, the prior information removes the element of surprise capable of disarming him if he learns of the people's decision without warning.

Ezeudu's action towards Okonkwo makes him a tempter who

tempts an unguarded victim with what he loves most; he provides Okonkwo with the opportunity to prove his manliness through the ritual killing which takes him a step further towards achieving his goal of becoming the lord of the clan. To the people, but not to the goddess Ani, Ezeudu is an unknown traitor because he goes one day ahead of the commissioned lords to divulge the secret of the people and their oracle. However well Ezeudu means, his meeting with Okonkwo is treacherous to the people. We can fully appreciate the gravity of the offense if we imagine what could happen if the warning is given to a less pious and less power-hungry person than Okonkwo; such a person could panic and so reveal the secret to Ikemefuna who could run away. To the humanist the lad's escape is desired, but we are talking about the religious well-being of the people which is at stake. Although it is painful to think of an innocent child being killed for ritual purposes, yet the killing of Ikemefuna is believed to bring stability to the society and spiritual well-being to the people. Hence, in the traditional Igbo religious beliefs Ikemefuna becomes a sacrificial ram, therefore a savior.

It is in this context that Ezeudu, whose warning would have prevented the sacrifice, if heeded by Okonkwo, merits the condemnation of Umuofia had they known of his secret mission. In fact, if Okonkwo was not there to deal with the killing blow of the machete, Ikemefuna would have been wounded but not killed (p. 55); thus the ritual process would not have been complete. On his own part, Okonkwo merits some condemnation for killing his own adopted son especially as he does so for personal aggrandizement; but he also needs our sympathy for having been driven by fate so to do. Ezeudu and Okonkwo are both punished by the goddess, Ani, simultaneously through the single accident that claims the son of one and destroys the life-long ambition of the other. But however grave their punishments are, both men are not completely destroyed: Ezeudu dies before his son is killed. So he is spared the agony of burying a young son; he also has other sons and daughters who could keep his lineage alive. Okonkwo is exiled for seven years after which period he is free to return. He is also blessed with a friend in Umuofia and an uncle in Mbanta who help him to endure the traumas of exile. Finally, when he returns from exile Okonkwo takes his own life because he never learns to control his inordinate ambition of becoming the lord of his clan.

Furthermore, until the coming of the white man, Umuofia community appears to be a stable society with adequate legal and moral codes which provide answers to their social and religious problems, namely: killing of one's clansman, thievery, battering of women, and land disputes. The laws also have provisions for dealing with external aggression like the murdering of a clanswoman by an outsider. Strong men like Okonkwo and the local judiciary of "masked spirits" known as *egwugwu,* who represent the founding fathers of the nine villages of Umuofia, are responsible for maintaining law and order in the clan. Their authority is never impugned, but if anyone dares to challenge it, he is fought by warriors like Okonkwo. This is how Umuofia came to be known as *Umuofia obodo dike.*

With the settlement of the missionaries in Umuofia comes the first true test of its stability. In spite of the clan's internal weaknesses, many Umuofia citizens consider the missionaries' settlement as the beginning of the crumbling of their ill-fated society. The real challenge comes when Okonkwo is away in exile. When his friend Obierika tells him about the new religion, he inwardly believes that the missionaries are able to settle because his people "have lost the power to fight" now that he is not present to give them leadership. Through his answer to Obierika's question—"Have you not heard how the white man wiped out Abame?"—Okonkwo portrays himself as a general who would have provided the military leadership necessary to forestall the victory of the British force:

> "I have heard," said Okonkwo. "But I have also heard that Abame people were weak and foolish. Why did they not fight back? Had they no guns and machetes? We would be cowards to compare ourselves with the men of Abame. Their fathers had never dared to stand before our ancestors. We must fight these men and drive them from the land" (p. 159).

As soon as he returns from exile, he attempts to fight the missionaries the way he says he would; he heads the *egwugwu* that destroy Mr. Smith's church building. Because he succeeds in persuading his people in the market place "to do something substantial" even though "they had not agreed to kill the missionary or drive away the Christians," Okonkwo once more feels like his old self:

> For the first time in many years Okonkwo had a feeling that was akin to happiness. The times which had altered so unaccountably during his exile seemed to be coming round again. The clan which had turned false on him appeared to be making amends ... Okonkwo was almost happy again (p. 173).

Almost *happy* indeed! For both his leadership and happiness are short-lived: when his violent challenge of the missionary and the native Christian converts is tested by the British Commissioner whose forces destroyed Abame, and who now is involved in the present conflict, Okonkwo (with the other elders) becomes as weak and foolish as Abame people whom he earlier on condemned, despite his military preparedness of wearing the machete and being on the alert always. The court messengers arrest him and other elders on the orders of the British Commissioner, and humiliate them in the Commissioner's absence. Okonkwo chokes with hate. He blames others for failing to approve his plan of killing the white man before their arrest. He carries the hate home with him after their release. This is the first time that a man born of a woman has both challenged and humiliated him. So when he kills the head messenger, he does so with hate and as a personal revenge, not for a ritual purpose as he makes people believe when he kills Ikemefuna.

However, it is also true that some of Okonkwo's mistakes are made while he pursues some noble causes—fighting enemies of the clan. Most elders know that the advent of the white man in Umuofia made "things fall apart" for their community. So they cry out for the removal of the shame. An example of this outcry is borne in the speech of one of the oldest members of Uchendu's *Umunna*:

> "As for me, I have only a short while to live, and so have Uchendu and Unachukwu and Emefo. But I fear for you young people

because you do not know what it is to speak with one voice. And what is the result? An abominable religion has settled among you. A man can now leave his father and his brothers. He can curse the gods of his fathers and his ancestors, like a hunter's dog that suddenly goes mad and turns on his master. I fear for you; I fear for the clan ..." (p. 152).

That fear for the younger generation and for the fate of the clan is echoed later on in Umuofia by another old man:

"All our gods are weeping. Idemili is weeping, Ogwugwu is weeping, Agbala is weeping, and all the others. Our dead fathers are weeping because of the shameful sacrilege they are suffering and the abomination we have all seen with our own eyes." ... "No clan can boast of greater numbers or greater valor. But are we all here? ... Are all sons of Umuofia with us here? ... "They are not.... They have broken the clan and gone their several ways. We who are here this morning have remained true to our fathers, but our brothers have deserted us and joined a stranger to soil their fatherland.... We must root out this evil (pp. 182-3).

Okonkwo seizes the call to arms as a welcome opportunity to demonstrate once more his patriotism and valor without discretion. He understands how to "root out this evil" without regard to the danger, "We shall hit our brothers and perhaps shed the blood of a clansman." He runs that risk because the head messenger whom he kills is both a black man and a fellow Igbo man from another clan. In other words, he kills a kinsfolk for the third time. As before, his act merits condemnation by both men and gods. "He knew that Umuofia would not go to war. He knew because they had let the other messengers escape" (p. 184). But what finally kills his spirit and hastens his decision to take his own life is the voices of people asking, "Why did he do it?" This time his act is condemned not just by a few people and in private as in two previous occasions; it is condemned by the entire assembly of Umuofia men of valor and in a market place, sacred to the people.

Okonkwo's death may have marked the passage of a great era in

Umuofia, but his suicide is not a sacrifice to his great society. For neither the gods nor the people would consider suicide a form of sacrifice since suicide is an abomination in Igbo society. Okonkwo's death comes because he realizes that he has failed both the people and their goddess, Ani. Though he has the spirit to endure misfortunes such as the loss of his yams during the drought that hit Umuofia, the traumas of exile, and the humiliation of imprisonment, he does so with others. That is, in all three cases, the people are behind him. It is not the fear of what "the white man whose power you know too well" might do that makes him commit suicide. Rather it is the recognition of the truth of the statement, "It is more difficult and more bitter when a man fails *alone*" (p. 23)—words of wisdom his father, who is considered an *agbala*, left with him before dying.

The Downfall of Ezeulu

In discussing Ezeulu's downfall, it is important to bear in mind that the Chief Priest is the hero of a novel of traditional Igbo life, and custodian of his village traditions. As such, reasons for his destruction must be sought from the traditions of his people. This is why we should not treat lightly the people's rationalization of the hero's downfall at the end of the novel, or regard it as simplistic resolution of a complex dilemma.

When the novel opens, Ezeulu has already committed an offense that alienates him from the people: we are told in retrospect that he won a judgement against his clan in favor of Okperi. This incident, which is considered a crime by his people, is what ironically won for him the admiration of the enemy of the people, the white District Commissioner, Captain T.K. Winterbottom, who reduced the military might of the people by breaking their guns:

> The white man, not satisfied that he had stopped the war, had gathered all the guns in Umuaro and asked the soldiers to break them in the face of all, except three or four which he carried away. Afterwards, he sat in judgement over Umuaro and Okperi and gave the disputed land to *Okperi* (*AOG*, pp. 28-9).

In other words, the people are no longer capable of fighting their enemies; neither can they determine their own political and military affairs since the British Administration at Okperi has taken over such matters from them. Having thus lost control over their own governance, the people find it difficult to forget the crime of a Chief Priest who sold them out to an alien authority.

Ezeulu is very much aware of the people's feelings, but because he pursues absolute truth, he fails to apologize for telling the truth that ultimately hurts his people; instead he is angry with them:

> Every time he prayed for Umuaro bitterness rose into his mouth, a great smoldering anger for the division which had come to the six villages and which his enemies sought to lay on his head. And for what reason? Because he had spoken the truth before the white man. But how could a man who held the holy staff of Ulu know that a thing was a lie and speak it? How could he fail to tell the story as he had heard it from his own father? Even the white man, Wintabota, understood, though he came from a land no one knew. He had called Ezeulu the only witness of truth (pp. 6-7).

Ezeulu's interior monologue, which the narrator records here for us, poses a number of rhetorical questions which intensify the moral predicament of the Chief Priest. Any attempt to answer the questions could evoke some emotional responses from readers, which are capable of obscuring the important point at issue. For instance, Ernest Emenyonu calls the conflict in *Arrow of God* "one of those moral imponderables that cannot be reduced to cut and dried solution."[16] The people's reaction to the issue is that Ezeulu acted stupidly by agreeing to testify at all before a "white man whose father or mother no one knew" (*AOG* p. 7). They suspect that he did so for personal gains. In short, he sold their national secret to a stranger. Whether by design or mere coincidence, the later nomination of Ezeulu as Warrant Chief of his people by the District Com-

---

[16] Ernest Emenyonu, "Ezeulu: The Night Mask Caught Abroad by Day," *Pan- African Journal*, IV, 3 (1971), p. 408.

missioner vindicates the people's suspicion. The people's point is, if the Chief Priest is able at that moment of the novel to turn down the offer of the appointment saying, "Tell the white man that Ezeulu will not be anybody's chief except Ulu," he should have exercised the same good judgement earlier on by refusing to testify. Little did they realize that a person summoned to a court of law to render testimony has no other option than to do so. They argue that by agreeing to testify before the white man, he concedes his authority to the white man's administration which he later makes belated effort to reclaim. The truth he tells makes him an honest man before the white man but condemns the entire people as a bunch of liars. They would prefer being called liars without one exception (in order to keep their national secret) to having one honest man become "a tree that makes a forest."

As a polytheist Ezeulu's belief in Ulu, Idemili, Ani, etc. leaves him room for any new Gods who are shown to be potent, including Yahweh and Jesus Christ. He does not think it is difficult to manage: "while he remains a devout Chief Priest of Ulu and personally rejects the new religion of the Christians, he sends his son 'to be my eye' among them."[17] This is a serious error of judgement on the part of Ezeulu for there is no way Oduche, a Christian, can live with non-Christians without his Christianity contaminating the priesthood of his father. Ezeulu becomes aware of this contamination when it is already too late to avoid:

> But now Ezeulu was becoming afraid that the new religion was like a leper. Allow him a handshake and he wants to embrace. Ezeulu had already spoken strongly to his son who was becoming more strange every day. Perhaps the time had come to bring him out again (p. 42).

Regrettably, the damage has already been done; the Igbo culture is invaded by the alien religion:

---

[17] *Ibid.*, p. 408.

The bell continued ringing in its sad monotone. Nwafo came back to the *Obi* and asked his father whether he knew what the bell was saying. Ezeulu shook his head. 'It is saying: Leave your yam, leave your cocoyam and come to church. That is what Oduche says.' (*Ibid*)

The appeal that the Christian religion makes to the Igbo to forsake their traditional religion spells extermination as Ezeulu correctly interprets its. It foreshadows the defection of the people from their religion to the Christian church which we notice happening at the end of the novel.

Ezeulu's unconscionable quest for power is not only destructive to his family, it brings disorder to the community. Although Ulu and the high office of a Chief Priest are the creations of the people, Ezeulu acts as though he and Ulu cannot be chastised when they fail to meet the popular demands of the people. He knows that the powers of both god and priest are ascribed and, therefore, subordinate to the will of the people. Yet he chooses to bring his strong personality into his constitutional office, while imposing his will as that of Ulu on the people. This is why one cannot trust Ezeulu's telling of the oracle, Ulu. In fact, one suspects that the distrust of Ezeulu's role as a diviner of Ulu's will may have been the reason why Umuaro disobeyed him and went to war with Okperi. Nwaka, one of those suspicious of Ezeulu's sincerity, is always prepared to impute motives into Ezeulu's speeches:

> The long uproar that followed was largely of approbation. Nwaka had totally destroyed Ezeulu's speech. The last glancing blow which killed it was the hint that the Chief Priest's mother had been a daughter of Okperi (p. 17).

The point is, if Nwaka is right, Ezeulu uses the oracle he tells to prevent Umuaro from fighting his motherland, Okperi. Since Nwaka is as devoted to the gods of his clan as any other man of Umuaro, he knows the extent to which he can go in discrediting the Chief Priest and Ulu. However, this does not mean that Nwaka is right in every instance of his suspicion; rather, it means that considering the intelligence of the orator and his ability to analyze situations, he can easily detect Ezeulu's misinterpretation of Ulu's will for self-interest.

The office of the Chief Priest of Ulu is a ceremonial one; and the person who occupies it is no more than master of a sacred ceremony. Such an officer derives his powers from the people. The narrator carefully outlines this fact for us when he describes Ezeulu's re-enactment of the First Coming of Ulu:

> At that time, when lizards were still in ones and twos, the whole people assembled and chose me to carry their new deity. I said to them: "Who am I to carry this fire on my bare head? A man who knows that his anus is small does not swallow an *udala* seed."
> They said to me:
> "Fear not. The man who sends a child to catch a shrew will also give him water to wash his hand." I said: "*So be it.*" [my emphasis] ... From behind the heavy tread of all the people gave me the strength (pp. 70-71).

Ezeulu is a servant rather than the master of the people. He leads in the performance of rituals and ceremonies and divines the will of Ulu whenever the people have a need for consulting the oracle. As long as he confines his duties to the religious activities of the community he will continue to enjoy the respect of all. But when he attempts to wield undue political power, he meets stiff opposition from tough political leaders like Nwaka. This frustrates Ezeulu and prompts him to examine the nature and reality of his power:

> Whenever Ezeulu considered the immensity of his power over the year and the crops and, therefore, over the people he wondered if it was real. It was true he named the day for the feast of the Pumpkin Leaves and for the New Yam feast; but he did not choose it. He was merely a watchman. His power was no more than the power of a child over a goat that was said to be his. As long as the goat was alive it could be his; he would find it food and take care of it. But the day it was slaughtered he would know soon enough who the real owner was (p. 3).

He is not satisfied with this unflattering evaluation of his role and authority because he considers them secondary to those of the people; hence he vehemently rejects the hierarchical order of things in his society:

> No! the Chief Priest of Ulu was more than that, must be more than that. If he should refuse to name the day there would be no festival—no planting and no reaping. But could he refuse? No Chief Priest had ever refused. So it could not be done. He would not dare (p. 3).

Ezeulu is receiving good and saving signals from his own inner thoughts, but he is headstrong; so he angrily suppresses "the first voice [which] gets to Chukwu, or God's House"[18] in stronger terms:

> 'Take away that word *dare*,' he replied to his enemy. 'Yes; I say take it away. No man in all Umuaro can stand up and say that I dare not. The woman who will bear the man who will say it has not been born yet' (p. 3).

Of course, this enemy he chides is the better and more sensible part of himself; the part that wants to control his inordinate ambition of seeking both sacred and secular powers and eventually save him from destruction is rejected because "When death wants to take a little dog it prevents it from smelling even excrement." (p. 226)

The result is that he seeks the indirect alliance of the white man by sending Oduche to the white man's school. And after he returns from Okperi, he has a stronger need for power—to fight both his people and the white administration:

> The thought [to fight] became too intense for Ezeulu and he put it aside to cool. He called his son, Oduche.... He reminded Oduche of the importance of knowing what the white man knew.... 'When I was in Okperi I saw a young white man who was able to write his

---

[18] *Things Fall Apart* p. 59.

book with the left hand. From his actions I could see that he had very little sense. But he had power; he could shout in my face; he could do what he liked. Why? Because he could write with his left hand ... I want you to learn and master this man's knowledge so much that if you are suddenly woken up from sleep and asked what it is you will reply ...' (p. 189).

As Oduche is being trained to fight the foreigners, Ezeulu plans to punish his people, who allowed him to suffer at the hands of the white men, by refusing to name the day of the New Yam harvest. However, he is reminded by the authority of a *god* who is superior to Ulu, namely: the will of the elders:

'Yes, we are Umuaro. Therefore listen to what I am going to say. Umuaro is now asking you to go and eat those remaining yams today and name the day of the next harvest. Do you hear me well? I said go and eat those yams today, not tomorrow and if Ulu says we have committed an abomination let it be on the heads of the ten of us here. You will be free because we have set you to do it, and the person who sets a child to catch a shrew should also find him water to wash the odor from his hand. We shall find you the water' (p. 208).

And what does Ezeulu do? He treats their words with contempt even as he denies doing so, adding: "It could not be my wish to make the smallest man in Umuaro suffer. But this is not my doing. The gods sometimes use us as a whip" (p. 208). So in the face of the promise of an atonement sacrifice from the elders, Ezeulu is still defiant of all appeals. He thinks he is too smart for elders to understand his motives. But before the elders leave, Ofoka gives him a final injunction which serves as a warning against the penalties of his defiance and a foreshadowing of Ezeulu's son's death:

Let us ask Ezeulu to go back and tell the deity that we have heard his grievance and we are prepared to make amends. Every offence has its sacrifice, from a few cowries to a cow or a human being. Let us wait for an answer (pp. 208-9)

Although he goes to Ulu's shrine, the final but negative answer he gives purported to have come from Ulu is his own. He makes himself a god rather than an "arrow of god." He does not name the day. And so, "almost overnight Ezeulu had become something of a public enemy in the eyes of all and, as was to be expected, his entire family shared in his guilt" (p. 211).

His refusal to name the day of the new yam feast "disorders" the lives of the people and offends the Igbo trinity of the dead, the living, and the unborn. For instance, Amalu, a deceased Umuaro man could not be accorded a second burial: "Amalu's kinsmen would waste their substance in buying yams from neighboring clans when their own crop lay locked in the soil" (p. 218). His second burial is wrecked. The people believe that because Amalu is thus denied a second burial, his resurrection from *ala mmo* in the form of reincarnation affects the life of the unborn; it also displeases the living-dead ancestors. In the human world, there is a lot of misery and starvation and Ani, the goddess to whom the new yam feast is dedicated annually, is starved of sacrifices, as it were. Thus we find that what started out as a personal revenge on Ezeulu's enemies ends up becoming a fight against Umuaro ancestors, the unborn children, the people and their goddess, Ani. It is an abomination that requires cleansing with blood.

First of all, Ezeulu and his family are ostracized; figuratively, they are as marooned in their compound as the python his Christian son, Oduche, imprisoned in a box. They all know that something more ominous is going to happen. For example, after Matefi attends a wedding, she thinks about "the hostility that was visibly encircling them all in Ezeulu's compound. Something told her that someone was going to pay a big price for it and she was afraid" (pp. 211-12). Ezeulu has the same premonitions in a dream vision but his pride does not permit him to seek the forgiveness of his people and gods. But his son, Obika, although suffering from a fever, is willing to do something which might help improve his father's blurred image before the people; he carries the *ogbazulobodo* because, "'If I say no,' Obika told himself, 'they will say that Ezeulu and his family have revealed a second time their determination to wreck the burial of their village man [Aneto] who did no harm to them'" (p. 224). The action Obika takes results in his sudden death as he barely completes the ritual race of *ogbazulobodo* round the village. His death marks the fulfillment of Matefi's premonitions and Ezeulu's dreams. To the people, especially Ezeulu's religious rival, Ezidemili, the death becomes a sacrifice that the Chief Priest involuntarily offers to appease their gods: the spirits of the living-dead ancestors and the unborn, the living elders of Umuaro, and their goddess Ani, all of whom Ezeulu defiantly offended. His enemies claim victory in the battle that Ezeulu earlier expected to win because he had Ulu and superior intelligence as extra protection.

As in the case of Okonkwo, "It was not simply the blow of Obika's death, great though it was," but the humiliation which accompanies it that dements the Chief Priest (229). And like Okonkwo, he suffers *alone* because both Ulu whom he has always relied upon for spiritual protection and the people who hitherto gave him moral courage have all deserted him. The narrator heightens the impact of the moral and spiritual drain on the morale of the fighting priest when he says:

> Think of a man who, unlike lesser men, always goes to battle without a shield because he knows that bullets and machete strokes will glance off his medicine-boiled skin; think of him discovering in the thick of battle that the power has suddenly, with warning, deserted him. What next time can there be? Will he say to the guns and the arrows and the machetes: *Hold! I want to return quickly to my medicine-hut and stir the pot and find out what has gone wrong; perhaps someone in my household—a child, maybe—has unwittingly violated my medicine's taboo?* No (p. 228).

The narrator, in this passage, is emphasizing the nature of Ezeulu's perplexity. The power is not natural to him; it is ascribed to him by the god and the people whom he has unwittingly offended. Now that they (the god and the people) have stripped him of it, he finally recognizes the danger of violating the people's authority when it is already too late for him to appease them in the form of offering a voluntary sacrifice. The recognition of his helpless situation dements him. Ezeulu is finally destroyed.

Ulu's Role in Ezeulu's Destruction

Commentators such as G. D. Killam and David Carroll have expressed the opinion that Ulu in fact encouraged Ezeulu to wreak his revenge on Umuaro. Killam, for example, says: "But thoughts of reconciliation are blunted by his god who visits him" and "At the injunction of his god he exacts his revenge on his people."[19] Each of these two statements is followed by a long passage quoted from the novel to support his position. Carroll maintains a similar position when he comments:

> He [Ezeulu] is not allowed to enjoy his new found sense of community for long. As he is sitting in his compound, beginning "to probe with the sensitiveness of a snail's horns the possibility of reconciliation, or, if that was too much, of narrowing down the area of conflict," Ulu himself makes his one direct intervention in the novel and speaks to his priest.[20]

He also quotes the very passages Killam quotes to prove his point. Such opinions, reasonable though they sound (especially when expressed as an interpretation of isolated passages), are indicative of the commentators' misconception of the ways of Igbo gods to men. In addition, the commentators seem to miss Achebe's general intention in the novel which is to prove "that no man however great was greater than his people: that no one ever won judgement against his clan,"[21] in a traditional Igbo society. Put differently, Achebe uses his characterization of Ezeulu to prove that power belongs to the people and that individual citizens, however powerful, are subservient to the common weal.

The reported encouragement that Ulu gives to Ezeulu as he

---

[19] G. D. Killam, *The Novels of Chinua Achebe* (London: Heinemann Educational Books Ltd., 1971), pp. 75-76.

[20] David Carroll, *Chinua Achebe* (New York: Twayne Publishers, Inc., 1970), p. 112.

[21] *Arrow of God*, p. 230.

Gods, Oracles and Divination | 57

vacillates over wreaking his revenge on his people stems from this passage of the novel:

> But whatever it was, Ezeulu was not to be allowed to remain in two minds much longer. 'Ta! Nwanu!' barked Ulu in his ear, as a spirit would in the ear of an impertinent human child. 'Who told you that this was your own fight to arrange the way it suits you? You want to save your friends who brought you wine he-he-he-he-he!' Only the insane could sometimes approach the menace and mockery in the laughter of deities—a dry, skeletal laugh. 'Beware you do not come between me and my victim or you may receive blows not meant for you. Do you not know what happens when two elephants fight? Go home and sleep and leave me to settle my quarrel with Idemili, whose envy seeks to destroy me that his python may again come to power. Now you tell me how it concerns you. I say go home and sleep. As for me and Idemili we shall fight to the finish; and whoever throws the other down will strip him of his anklet!' (pp. 191-2)

There are several reasons for doubting whether these lines came from Ulu of Umuaro. First, Ulu's ways to Umuaro. Ulu is not a village god. He is a clan god created by Umuaro to protect all her citizens. Although Ezeulu gains more respect for being his priest, Ulu cannot use him as an arrow to punish the very people that the god was created to protect. Even if anyone did anything that warrants the punishment of the gods, that person would have to be punished by Ani, the goddess in charge of morality. And this is why the people jubilate over Ezeulu's tragedy because Ulu cannot protect his priest when Ani punishes him for his offenses. In other words, neither Ezeulu nor Ezidemili is right in claiming that their personal conflicts are the fights of their respective gods, Ulu and Idemili.

Secondly, the statements, "Or perhaps the thought of reconciliation were from a true source" and "This thought intoxicated Ezeulu like palm wine," which come before and after the passage tend to suggest that the Ulu whom the narrator includes in the passage is not Umuaro's god but Ezeulu's brainchild or obsession which his split personality personifies into Ulu.[22] For ever since he returned from his detention in Okperi, Ezeulu has been brooding over his revenge. Because it takes him so long to make his decision, the debate which takes place in his mind literally tears him into two selves: his more humane self wants him to show mercy, but his intransigent, therefore more forceful, self orders him to fight—an option which is more agreeable to his nature, which is always to be a winner.

Furthermore, Ulu is one half of Ezeulu in the guise of a god: "One half of him was man and the other half *mmo*—the half that was painted over with white chalk at important religious moments" (p. 192). But in his godlike form, Ezeulu is still Ezeulu with human tendencies even though he would love to be *mmo* for the sake of power. According to Emile Chartier, alias Alain, "Ulysses, wrapped up and sleeping under the leaves, like a shepherd's fire, is Ulysses none the less."[23] Explaining the statement Alain's translator, Richard Pevear, says:

> Alain is talking about the Homeric idea of gods wandering the world in human disguises, of which Ulysses, since he is not a god, is a metaphor: just as Ulysses is hidden under a beggar's rags, so it might be a god; the reserved fire of his nature is godlike, an image of the god-in-disguise. (*Ibid.* p. 1)

We may analogize Pevear's explanation by saying that the Ulu, who barked "Ta! Nwanu!" into Ezeulu's ear (p. 191), is Ezeulu possessed of divergent thoughts of revenge; but since he is not a god, he is a metaphor. In fact, what his Ulu tells him is no more than a reproduction of his inner desires: to destroy Idemili and his priest Ezidemili who seem to have more political power than the clan god, Ulu, and Ezeulu his priest. Ulu also makes a reference to an anklet which symbolizes wealth, for it is worn by high-titled men

---

[22] *Ibid.*, pp. 191-192.
[23] Richard Pevear, trans., *Alain/The Gods* (New York: New Directions Publishing Corporation, 1974), p. 1.

like Nwaka from Ezidemili's village; Ezeulu, who is not as wealthy desires to take it over from his wealthy enemies after defeating them. In addition, the laughter of the deity, "he-he-he-he-he," is actually Ezeulu's laughter when he is seized with the madness of his revenge; it is a masculine version of "Ha ha ha ha ha ...," the demented laughter of Ezeulu's mother (p. 222).

Finally, two *gods* go by the name of Ulu: one is Umuaro's god of security and the other Ezeulu's personified obsession for revenge. Ezeulu serves the former as his Chief Priest, but uses the latter as a prop for carrying out his revenge. So when the narrator says at the end of the novel:

> If this was so then Ulu had chosen a dangerous time to uphold that truth for in destroying his priest he had also brought disaster on himself, like the lizard in the fable who ruined his mother's funeral by his own hand. For a deity who chose a moment such as this to chastise his priest or abandon him before his enemies was inciting people to take liberties; and Umuaro was just ripe to do so (p. 230),

he refers specifically to the second Ulu, a metaphor for Ezeulu's fiery desire for power which not only destroys itself but also Ezeulu, its creator. It is this god, not Ulu of Umuaro, that Ezeulu reproaches in a lament rich in proverbial sayings and images (p. 226).

Ezeulu's destruction is as ironic as his being. Even when the people are tempted to rejoice over the tragedy of their enemy, their joy is subdued by the knowledge of who the victim is—the Chief Priest of the clan god, Ulu. Umuaro may be tempted to take liberties like harvesting their yam in the name of the son who becomes a Christian. However, since they do not do so in the name of the father, it is suspected that Umuaro are afraid of being chastised like Ezeulu by their god whom they are deserting for the new religion. If so, the thought of Ezeulu's destruction may yet bring Umuaro back to their traditional religion.

Achebe's Attitude Towards Igbo Traditional Religion

From our discussion thus far, we are tempted to make some observations on Achebe's attitude towards Igbo cosmology and traditional religion: He recognizes that the Igbo are a deeply religious people and that their religious beliefs influence everything they do in all walks of life. In addition, because of the Igbo spirit of competitiveness, even among their gods, their traditional societies are highly stratified and masculine in temperament. Hence, in exploiting the people's religious beliefs and ritual practices in his novels, Achebe distinguishes between nature gods and man-made gods, between clan gods and village gods, and between a pan-Igbo nature god and a village nature god.

The result of such distinctions is that Ulu, a clan but man-made god, is regarded by Ezeulu's detractors as inferior to Idemili, a village but nature god. Thus Ulu appears to exist as just a means of giving a hallowed underpinning to the public weal that created the god in the first place. But when it is the case of a pan-Igbo nature goddess, Ani, there is a genuine religious dimension in *Arrow of God* and *Things Fall Apart*. That is why Ani is regarded by the people as superior to Ulu and Idemili. So, although the gods may live in an egalitarian republic, they may not share equality of authority and sacrifice. In this regard, Ani, the direct daughter of Chukwu becomes the source of *nso ani*, crime against (goddess of the) earth, and/or crime against (laws of the) land.

4 | Names and Naming

> If you want to know how life has treated an Igbo man, a good place to look is the names his children bear.
> —Achebe in *Morning Yet on Creation Day*

Africans, especially the Igbo, know the indispensable part names play in their cultures and societies; and Chinua Achebe makes a good use of names and naming to express "ideas, aspirations, sorrows or philosophical comments"[1] on the lives of the people of his novels. For this reason, names and naming are discussed here to enhance appreciation of the meanings and functions of names in Achebe's novels, while increasing understanding of traditional Igbo culture and the novelist's general thematic concerns. My endeavors here should not be regarded as a literary onomastic study of the names,[2] but rather as a critical analysis

---

[1] Ruth Finnegan, *Oral Literature in Africa* (Nairobi: Oxford University Press, 1976), p. 471.

[2] Leonard R. N. Ashley recommends the study of literary onomastics. See his "Names Into Words and Other Examples of the Possibilities of Extending The Boundaries of Literary Onomastics," in *Literary Onomastics Studies*, Vol. VII, ed. Grace Alvarez-Altman and Frederick Burelback (Brockport, New York:State University, 1980), pp.1-24.

based on my critical training and native knowledge of Igbo culture.

Basically, four categories of names can be traced in Achebe's novels,[3] using cultural and religious derivations of the names as criteria. To the first group belong names of traditional characters found principally in *Things Fall Apart* and *Arrow of God,* novels which treat of traditional Igbo life just before and immediately after the advent of the white men in Igboland. The names are purely indigenous including, among others, Okonkwo, Obierika, Ezeulu, Nwaka and Ogbuefi Ezeudu.

The second category, also found in the two novels mentioned above, comprises Biblical and foreign names given to missionaries from outside the Igbo clans—Rev. James Smith and Mr. Goodcountry—and those given to Igbo Christian converts who now adopt such names as a mark of their conversion while retaining their family names: Okonkwo's son, Nwoye, becomes Isaac Okonkwo, and Ezeulu's son, Oduche will be called Peter when the time comes for his baptism.[4]

To the third category belong names which are found in modern societies of *No Longer At Ease* and *A Man of the People;* they are names which depict their bearers as either established Christians or "educated" or both. Hence we find Nwoye in *Things Fall Apart* being addressed as Mr. Isaac Okonkwo, Catechist of the Church Missionary Society in *No Longer at Ease* (p. 8), and Chief the Honorable M. A. Nanga, M. P., in *A Man of the People* (p. 1) not only regarding himself as highly educated, but also thinking he is honorable for being a member of parliament. The satire on his name will be discussed later.

Finally, to the last group of names belong the names of colonial administrators and officers which are Anglo-Saxon in character because Nigeria, the setting of all four novels, was ruled by Britain.

---

[3] These categories follow the ones outlined by Elizabeth M. Rajec in her "Franz Kafka and Phillip Roth: their use of Literary Onomastics (Based on *The Professor of Desire*)", in *Literary Onomastics Studies,* Vol. VII, pp. 69-70.

[4] Chinua Achebe, *Arrow of God* (London: Heinemann Educational Books Ltd., 1977), p. 49.

The names include the D. C., George Allen, Mr. Green, Captain Winterbottom and Mr. Clarke.

Achebe, in his novels, rewrites the colonial history of Nigeria (especially as it affects traditional Igbo communities) with special reference to the transformation that took place in the religious, educational, economic and socio-political culture of the people. To do so realistically, he creates characters who serve as parties to the tragic Igbo encounter with Europe, giving them names which seem to suggest, "By their names you shall know them." In other words, Achebe uses naming as a means of making historical comments on the establishment and development of Christianity, Western Education and British Administration in Nigeria; and the names contain subtle memories of the agents of such establishments and developments. Classifying the names as we have so far done helps to identify the characters as traditional or modern, indigenous or foreign, Christian or heathen, and educated or uneducated, depending on what meaning and importance one attaches to such colonial terminology, all too familiar in books which discuss African affairs. But it is an exercise in socio-anthropological identification of names which does not say very much about the novels as literary works.

Therefore, another way of classifying the names is to group them according to their literary function; that entails analyzing and evaluating how the names serve Achebe's fictional purposes. Approached this way, we find that the "names contribute to the literary flavor of formal and informal conversation, adding a depth or a succinctness through their meanings, overtones, or metaphors. They can also play a directly literary role."[5] Using then their literary role as a criterion, the names in Achebe's novels could be classified into five groups that overlap: dedicatory names; philosophical names; praise names; metaphoric names; and allusive names. The groups overlap because one name could belong to more than one of the groups, and the names, regardless of their individual groups, have a basic function—they identify and describe the characters who bear them.

---

[5] Finnegan, *op. cit.*, p. 472.

Dedicatory Names

Some of the traditional Igbo characters in Achebe's novels bear dedicatory names just as they do in actual Igbo societies. Such names include Nwankwo, Nweke, Nwoye and Nwafo; Okonkwo, Okeke, Okoye and Okafo given to males, or Mgbokwo, Mgbeke, Mgborie and Mgbafo given to females. They are names which refer to either the four days (Nkwo, Eke, Oye, Afo) on which their bearers were born, or to the deities in charge of the market days which make up the Igbo market week. Also, as in other societies, names in Igbo societies can distinguish the sexes of their bearers. Furthermore, in general Igbo grammar, the prefix, *oke* indicates male and *nne* female; but when describing the sex of a child, *oko* (short form of *okorobia* or boy) for the male and *mgbo* (from *agboghobia* or girl) for the female, are used instead of *oke* and *nne* which tend to suggest adulthood. The name, Okonkwo, which is a combination of Oko and Nkwo, means a male child born on Nkwo market day, just as the combination Mgbo and Afo which becomes [Mgb(o) afo] Mgbafo means a female child born on Afo market day. If, however, parents do not want to emphasize the sex of the child, they simply give him the name Nwafo, from [Nw(a) afo] nwa (child) born on afo (market day). But some of these names (Nwafo, Nwankwo, Nweke, and Nwoye) are usually given to males, although as a general principle, they do not emphasize the sex of their bearers.

Nkwo, regarded by some Igbo clans as the first of the four Igbo weekdays, has a very symbolic meaning to men like Okonkwo who are born on it; but modern Igbo calendars record Afo as the first weekday for all Igbo. However, any of the four days could be first and symbolic to the Igbo clan that holds its market on it. For Umuofia, the first day of the week is Nkwo.

By naming the hero of *Things Fall Apart* Okonkwo, Achebe creates an ideal masculine character, one who becomes an embodiment of masculinity and of all the qualities a man should possess in a warlike society such as Umuofia; he is an achiever, wrestler, titled man and warrior. Okonkwo is all these and more. He wants to be the first among his equals, just as his birthday, Nkwo, is the first among Igbo weekdays:

Okonkwo on his bamboo bed tried to figure out the nature of the emergency—war with a neighboring clan? That seemed the most likely reason, and he was not afraid of war. He was a man of action, a man of war. Unlike his father he could stand the look of blood. In Umuofia's latest war he was the first to bring home a human head. That was his fifth head; and he was not an old man yet. On great occasions such as the funeral of a village celebrity he drank his palm-wine from his first human head (p.10).

Because the hero's character matches his name, Okonkwo becomes one of those Igbo literary characternyms such as Omenuko, Dimkpa, Dimgba, and Agu—names assumed by some Igbo readers today who are in search of heroes. In order to prove to his people that he is worthy of his name, Okonkwo at times does cruel things like beating his wife and killing his adopted son and a court messenger, deeds that earn him the displeasure of both his people and the white men. In other words, those manly qualities which make him a celebrity are also responsible for his downfall; they are the germ of his hubris.

As a contrast of Okonkwo's masculinity, Achebe names the effeminate son of the hero Nwoye. His name suggests a child born on Oye but he is not manly enough to bear the name Okoye. To Okonkwo, Nwoye's only claim to being male is that he "wears" a male genitalia:

> He, Okonkwo, was called a flaming fire. How could he have begotten a woman for a son? At Nwoye's age Okonkwo had already become famous throughout Umuofia for his wrestling and his fearlessness.
>
> He sighed heavily, and as if in sympathy the smoldering log also sighed. And immediately Okonkwo's eyes were opened and he saw the whole matter clearly. Living fire begets cold, impotent ash. He sighed again, deeply (p.140).

Nwoye may not be as manly as his father, but he is more humane than Okonkwo who does things blindly in order to win fame. He understands the poetry of human suffering; therefore, he joins the

Christians, the words of whose hymn "were like the drops of frozen rain melting on the dry palate of the panting earth" (p.134). Thus we find that while the name of Okonkwo may connote violence and destruction, Nwoye's suggests gentleness and life. And while the father dies in his act of violence, the son outlives him to become Isaac, a catechist who helps to persuade his "flock" to stop killing twins and ostracizing their mothers.

Philosophical Names

Most of the Igbo names fall within this category. They are short compendious names formed from full-length philosophical statements that express how life has treated the parents of their bearers. They range from expressions of gratitude for good fortunes to hopes for a better tomorrow; from despair to outright defiance. Achebe comments on this kind of naming in *Things Fall Apart*:

> Ekwefi had suffered a good deal in her life. She had born ten children and nine of them died in infancy, usually before the age of three. As she buried one child after another her sorrow gave way to despair and then to grim resignation. The birth of her children, which should be a woman's crowning glory, became for Ekwefi mere physical agony devoid of promise. The naming ceremony after seven market weeks became an empty ritual. Her deepening despair found expression in the names she gave her children. One of them was a pathetic cry, Onwumbiko—"Death, I implore you." But death took no notice; Onwumbiko died in his fifteenth month. The next child was a girl, Ozoemena—"May it not happen again." She died in her eleventh month, and two others after her. Ekwefi then became defiant and called her next child Onwuma—"Death may please himself." And he did (pp. 69-70).

Had the children lived, their names would have been living memories of the sorrows and joys of Ekwefi's motherhood. With this background, Achebe introduces his readers to the reasons why Ezinma—"True Beauty"—is the favorite child of her parents, Okonkwo and Ekwefi. In this society where people are so fond of children, a woman without a child is not regarded as a useful person. Children count for more than wealth, which is why some patents name their child Ginikanwa—"What counts for more than a child?" Ekwefi herself was called "Crystal of Beauty" in her youth (p.156), but that beauty is presently eclipsed by the recurrent deaths of her infants. The name Ezinma, therefore, symbolizes life, the enduring beauty which counts for more than the physical beauty of the child. Her personal good behavior and love of her patents make her name very suitable. And being such valuable "wealth", Ezinma must be raised up with maximum care. But in her bid to do so, Ekwefi becomes an indulgent mother:

> Ezinma was an only child and at the center of her mother's world. Ekwefi even gave her such delicacies as eggs, which children were rarely allowed to eat because such food tempted them to steal. One day as Ezinma was eating an egg Okonkwo had come in unexpectedly from his hut. He was greatly shocked and swore to beat Ekwefi if she ever dared to give the child eggs again. But it was impossible to refuse Ezinma anything (p.69).

Uchendu—"Thought of Life"—is another of the philosophical names Achebe uses to develop his themes. He is Okonkwo's mother's kinsman who receives him in exile in Mbanta. After Okonkwo narrates his accidental killing if a clansman in Umuofia. Uchendu says with some relief; "It is a female ochu," and arranges the requisite rites and sacrifices (p. 199). Uchendu notices that Okonkwo is yielding to despair for having failed to become "one of the lords of his clan," so he gives Okonkwo some advice, which befits Uchendu's name:

> Be careful or you may displease the dead. Your duty is to comfort your wives and children and take them back to your fatherland after seven years. But if you allow sorrow to weigh you down and kill you, they will all die in exile (p. 122).

The advice revives Okonkwo. As a result, he decides to live like a man in Mbanta, receiving help from Uchendu and Obierika.

Uchendu's name and role are carefully chosen to contrast with those of the main character; even though Okonkwo is wealthy and warlike, he has a very poor and selfish attitude towards life. It appears he is incapable of any serious thinking, hence he allows others to do his thinking for him. Although he would like to regard himself as independent, he depends on others for survival: Nwakibie for seed-yams (p. 20); Ezeudu for advice before he realizes that killing his adopted son Ikemefuna is an abomination (p. 51); Obierika for share-cropping of his yams in Umuofia while he is in exile in Mbanta (p. 128); and Uchendu for counsel and rehabilitation in exile (p. 122). Once he is taught by Uchendu to have a better attitude towards life, Okonkwo remembers how important his deceased mother and her living kinsmen are. So he names one of his daughters Nneka—"Mother is Supreme" (p. 148), and another child Nwofia—"Begotten in the Wilderness" of his exile. (p. 148)

Other philosophical names found in *Things Fall Apart* include: Obierika—"The heart is great/unfathomable," explaining why the man is both a great friend and one capable of serious thinking; Chukwuka—"Chukwu is Supreme," so people worship Him; Akueke—"Gift of Creation" and therefore durable; and, Obiageli— "She who comes (by reincarnation) to enjoy wealth." These philosophical names express both individual and group views of life that characterize Igbo religious and cosmological beliefs.

Praise Names

This is a convenient term used to cover many honorific appellations and flattering epithets.[6] Achebe's novels, which discuss the traditional life of the Igbo, are full of praise names because in their society, where age is respected but achievement is revered,[7] such names are in popular demand. They are what gives significance to both the achievers (even after they are long dead) and their achieve-

---

[6] *Ibid.*, p. 475

[7] Chinua Achebe, *Things Fall Apart* (London: Heinemann Educational Books Ltd., 1977), p. 472.

ments in people's memories. Unlike dedicatory names which could be given to any child at all by his parents, praise names are achieved, not ascribed; hence they are elitist in character. However, the children of achievers may share the fame of their fathers, just as they do the infamy of the "womanly" fathers who are known by the Igbo as *agbala*.

The first group of people who are called praise names are *ozo*-titled men. An initiate of *ozo* society is called the name Ogbuefi which means "Killer of Cows." He is so called because the *ozo* initiation ceremony requires one to kill a cow to entertain older members of his society. The more titles one takes in the society the more cows or other costly animals he kills. Only the rich and wealthy can afford to join the societies and cults. Usually, one joins them at old age, when he has married many wives and produced many children who help to work the farms that produce the yams and cows for the title-taking ceremonies. But a young achiever like Okonkwo could join the societies because "as the elders said, if a child washed his hands he could eat with kings" (p. 8). Some of these praise names are Ogbuefi Udo, Ogbuefi Ezeudu, Ogbuefi Ndulue from *Things Fall Apart*; and Ogbuefi Nwaka, Ogbuefi Akuebue, Ogbuefi Anichebe Udeozo from *Arrow of God*.

Those who go by these names wield the highest political power in the clan:

> The news of Ezeulu's refusal to call the New Yam Feast spread through Umuaro as rapidly as if it had been beaten out on the *ikolo*. At first people were completely stunned by it; they only began to grasp its full meaning slowly because its like had never happened before.
>
> Two days later ten men of high title came to see him. None of the ten had taken fewer than three titles, and one of them— Ezekwesili Ezukanma—had taken the fourth and highest.
>
> "Yes, we are Umuaro. Therefore listen to what I am going to say. Umuaro is now asking you to go and eat those remaining yams today and name the day of the next harvest. Do you hear me well? I said go and eat those yams today, not tomorrow; and if Ulu says we have committed an abomination let it be on the heads of ten of

us here...." (pp.205 & 208)

Their orders to Ezeulu are not expected to be flouted without some serious political consequences. Ezeulu tries to flout them but he pays dearly for it. Although the titled elders have such powers and authority, they always try to use them for the common good of the people because they represent the founding ancestors of their villages. They give this kind of severe command only when the lives of the citizens are in danger; in this case, the clan is threatened by famine and starvation.

Next to the *ndichie*—ruling titled elders—are the spiritual leaders—the priests and priestesses—who are called praise names which describe their roles as chief ritual and ceremonial officers of their respective gods and goddesses. The names include Ezeani, Ezeulu, Ezidemili. It is their high offices that set them apart from other citizens. They are regarded as people who do difficult duties for men and gods; therefore, they merit the praise of those they serve. Powerful medicine men are also given praise names in recognition of their services to the community. For example, Aghadike is given the praise name, Anyanafummo—"Eyes that see spirits"—because he is a good diviner (*AOG*, p.112).

In some cases characters are given either derogatory or paradoxical "praise" names. In *Things Fall Apart*, the priestess of Agbala calls her god the praise name *Chi negbu madu ubosi ndu ya nato ya uto*— "God who kills a man when his life is sweetest"; that is, at the prime of his life (p. 97). The paradox of this name, of course, is that Agbala as protective god does not kill; only one's offenses do. Such offenses as fornication, battering women, and killing of one's clansman are committed at the prime of one's life. The paradoxical "praise" name, therefore, is intended to cow recalcitrant citizens into obedience. It intimidates even the strongman, Okonkwo and his wife, Ekwefi:

> The priestess suddenly screamed. 'Beware, Okonkwo!' she warned. 'Beware of exchanging words with Agbala. Does a man speak when a god speaks? Beware!
> I will come with you, too,' Ekwefi said firmly. 'Tufia-a!' the

priestess cursed, her voice cracking like the angry bark of thunder in the dry season. 'How dare you, woman to go before the mighty Agbala of your own accord? Beware women, lest he strike you in his anger. Bring me my daughter'(pp. 91-92).

The most satirical of the derogatory "praise" names is that given to the hero of *A Man of the People*, Chief the Honorable M.A. Nanga, M.P. The name is loaded with Achebe's oblique puns and subtle comments on the phony patriotism, pseudo-intellectualism, arrant philistinism and political bravado which characterized the activities of the Nigerian intelligentsia and politicians of the early sixties. Immediately after independence, Nigeria established a few local universities which admitted students for bachelors degree programs. Any graduate who happened to earn a masters from an overseas university became first among his equals; and an honorary doctorate was a one-of-a-kind achievement. The higher the degree one added to his name, the more praise he earned from admirers. The educated men paraded their degrees to the envy of the less-educated politicians. For example, the narrator stresses that "The Minister of Finance at the time was a first-rate economist with a Ph.D in public finance. He presented to the Cabinet a complete plan for dealing with the situation. [But] The Prime Minister said 'No' to the plan" (p. 3). The envy comes through in the commentary carried by *The Daily Chronicle*, an official organ of the P.O.P.:

> Let us now and for all time extract from our body-politic as a dentist extracts a stinking tooth all those decadent stooges versed in text-book economics and aping the white man's mannerisms and way of speaking. We are proud to be Africans. Our true leaders are not those intoxicated with their Oxford, Cambridge or Harvard degrees but those who speak the language of the people. Away with the damnable and expensive university education which only alienates an African from his rich and ancient culture and puts him above his people.... (p. 4)

We recognize the hypocrisy in the call for things African when it is realized that even as they condemn the acquisition of foreign degrees, the politicians, especially Mr. Nanga, secretly yearn for them in order to put themselves above their people. Nanga did no go to college but he abbreviates his first two names to give him a "natural" degree, M.A. in addition to being "Chief and Honorable." The addition of M.P. (which means Member of Parliament) has the sonority of Master of Politics. Having thus "crowned" himself a masters degree holder, he aspires to receive the highest degree, Honorary Doctorate (D.Lit.), from an American University, which is as "honorable" as the Honorable Member of Parliament himself:

> In spite of this inauspicious beginning Mr. Jalio went ahead and said many flattering things about Chief Nanga, albeit with a clouded face. He said it was a fitting and appropriate tribute to his concern for African Culture—a concern which was known all over the world— that a university in far away America was soon to honor him with a doctorate degree (p. 63).

The people like Nanga and that is why he is "A Man of the People"; and that suggests that they are as phony as the character they admire.

A few white officers are given derogatory/paradoxical "praise" names. For example, apart from his world-war title of Captain, Winterbottom bears with pride a "praise" name—for, he disarmed the local warriors through cunning and distrust—which the natives gave to him for his wanton destruction of their guns:

> You will be going there frequently on tour. If you hear anyone talking about Otiji-Egbe, you know they are talking about me. Otiji-Egbe means Breaker of Guns. I am even told that all children born in that year belong to a new age-grade of the Breaking of Guns (p. 37).

Winterbottom, serving the British Administration in Nigeria as District Officer, is a civilian officer but he prefers to be addressed as Captain Winterbottom, a title which serves as a reminder of his military achievements overseas during the Second World War. At one point, the Captain recounts what transpired between him and the natives to a junior officer, Mr. Clarke the Education Officer, in order to reassert his militarism; he tells the story not only to win respect from Clarke but also to solicit indirectly his submission to the Captain's authority.

The natives also gave a derogatory "praise" name, similar to that given to Captain Winterbottom, to a notorious and drunken road overseer in *Arrow of God*:

> There was at the time a big program of road and drainage construction following a smallpox epidemic. Chief James Ikedi teamed up with a notorious and drunken road overseer who had earned the title of Destroyer of Compounds from the natives. The plans for the roads and drains had long been completed and approved by Captain Winterbottom himself and as far as possible did not interfere with people's homesteads. But this overseer went around intimidating the villagers and telling them that unless they gave him money the new road would pass through their compound (p. 57).

This corrupt practice of a white man's agent which appears to have attracted a native, James Ikedi, that he teamed up with the road overseer, was reported to the District Officer, Captain Winterbottom, but instead of being condemned, it was encouraged:

> There was no doubt whatever in the mind of Captain Winterbottom that Chief Ikedi was still corrupt and highhanded only cleverer than ever before. The latest thing he did was to get his people to make him an *obi* or king, so that he was now called His Highness Ikedi the First, Obi of Okperi. This among a people who abominated kings! This was what British Administration was doing among the Ibos, making a dozen mushroom kings grow where there was none before (p. 58).

Apart from underlining the contemptible origin of Chief Ikedi's name, the passage bemoans the crudities of British Administrative methods in Igboland which promoted the corruption of the Africans and engendered enmity between them. The resultant corruption and enmity created opportunities for foreign intervention.

Metaphoric Names

In talking about metaphoric names one bears in mind how the names function as metaphors for some subjects. However, we do not intend here a usage of metaphor which introduces the term "tenor" for the subject to which the metaphoric name is applied and the term "vehicle" for the metaphoric name itself; rather, we treat the names as metaphors whose tenors are not stated but are implied in their verbal contexts.[8] For example, when the narrator states: "As a young man of eighteen he Okonkwo had brought honour to his village by throwing Amalinze the Cat,"[9] the subject to which the metaphoric word Cat is applied (that is the agility of the wrestler) is the tenor while the metaphoric word itself is the vehicle. But in the following passage,

> The bride's name was Okuata. In tallness she took after her father who came of a race of giants. Her face was finely cut and some people already called her Oyilidie, because she resembled her husband in comeliness. Her full breasts had a very slight upward curve which would save them from falling and sagging too soon (*AOG*, p. 116),

we find the metaphoric name, Oyilidie, which means "One who resembles her husband in comeliness." The name as metaphor has an unstated but implicit tenor which is comeliness. Oyilidie is a nickname which also gives a further qualification to the woman's actual name, Okuata. Okuata means literally "Fire cannot destroy." Hence when both the proper name and the nickname are combined and given to one bride, we find in her a piece of comeliness which is as indestructible as a piece of metal forged in fire. What a name to have! It is no wonder then that on her wedding night other girls express their joy and admiration in a befitting epithalamic song:

---

[8] M.H. Abrams, *A Glossary of Literary Terms*, 3rd Edition (New York: Holt, Rinehart and Winston, Inc., 1971), p. 61.

[9] *Things Fall Apart*, p. 3.

The girls sang a song called *Ifeoma*. Goodly Thing had come, they said, so let everyone who had good things bring them before her as offering. They made a circle round her as she danced to their song. As she danced her husband-to-be and other members of Ezeulu's family broke through the circle one by one or two at a time and stuck money on her forehead. She smiled and let the present fall at her feet from where one of the girls picked it up and put it in a bowl (*Ibid*).

Achebe uses metaphoric names more than any other kind of name as a literary technique. Although such names may sound like other common Igbo names, their contextual appearances in the novels help to reduce the ambiguities that foreign readers often encounter. Robert M. Wren, for example, alleges:

> Often names are somewhat ambiguous. There are several sources of ambiguity. Igbo is a tonal language in which vowels may have rising, falling, or neutral tone. Each tone is capable of altering the meaning of the word entirely. Achebe has not cluttered his text with tonal marks, nor with marks indicative of closed and open vowels (there are exceptions in *Arrow of God* XVI, 186,191), so pronunciation of the names may be uncertain, even for native Igbo speakers. Finally, meaning is often dependent upon context; the same word may have several different meanings.[10]

I agree with Wren that "often names are somewhat ambiguous", but only if such names are read in isolation (that is without any consideration for their contextual appearance) or when Achebe deliberately intends them to be ambiguous for special effects. Let us examine some of the examples that Wren uses in the same section of his book. First, the meaning of Obika. He says, "Ezeulu's son Obika has a name that clearly combines *obi* with the suffix *-ka*, which indicates

---

[10] Robert M. Wren, *Achebe's World: The Historical and Cultural Context of the Novels of Chinua Achebe* (Washington D.C.: Three Continents Press, 1980), pp. 173-174.

superiority. Now *obi* is the hut of the head of the family and, by extension, it means one's home or origin.... 'There's no place like home' is a possible translation of Obika."

Yes, *obi* as a word could mean hut and the suffix *-ka* can indicate superiority; but when we consider the role Obika plays in the entire novel, the translation does not fit well. Wren translates the suffix *-ka* as indicating superiority but Achebe intends *-ka* to mean "supreme" whenever it is used (as in Nneka and Chukwuka from *TFA*, pp. 123, 165). Therefore, if we translate *obi* as heart and *-ka* as supreme, we get "the heart is supreme" as a translation of Obika. In context, of course, Obika's role is connected with the heart. He has the heart to love, and his marriage with Okuata is used as an illustration of Igbo marriage custom in *Arrow of God* (p. 115 ff); he alone has the heart to run the ritual race of *ogbazulu obodo* despite his fever, in order to stop the ostracism of his family; we are told "A fire began to rage inside his chest" which suggests a possible heart problem (p. 226); and his death also causes his father's heart to break. Besides, Obika is abbreviated from Obierika of *Things Fall Apart* whose role also is connected with heart, just as Nwaka is abbreviated from Nwakibie, both of whose roles are connected with titles, wealth and nobility. So Wren's statement, "Ezeulu's antagonist is Nwaka, a name that translates literally 'superior child'," is sociological information which is irrelevant to the literary function of the name. One is happy that Wren acknowledges that, "That is an absurd name for a titled, rich, and powerful man" (p. 174).

Second, the contradiction Wren finds in his own translation of the name Okagbue Uyanwa, "great-one-who-kills-suffering-child," is due to his heavy dependence on either an Igbo dictionary for meanings of isolated words, or Igbo informants who do not "know" the language. Okagbue Uyanwa means literally "one who uses the spoken word to kill illness of a child." Put in context, the medicine man uses the spoken word to exorcise the evil spirits believed to attack the *ogbanje*. Even when he uses medicines and amulets, he makes them potent by saying incantations, prayers and invocations which are living words that can produce definitive curative effects on the illness.

As a guide to appreciating the literary functions of the metaphoric names, one should always consider the context in which the names are used. Secondly, although the names may be common European or Igbo names, they should be regarded as Achebe's creative inventions whose functions are mainly relevant to the particular context in which they are used. An illustration of this reminder could be found in the name Dr. Savage. Ordinarily, Europeans bear the name without any qualms about its meaning. But to the Igbo (and Achebe who writes about them) who attach importance to meanings of names, such a name must have a significance. The meaning and significance of the name are described thus:

> Winterbottom's delirium lasted three days and in all that time Dr. Savage rarely left his bedside. She even postponed the operations which she performed every Wednesday for which that day was known throughout the village as *Day of the Cutting Open of Bowels*. It was always a sad day and the little daily market which had sprung up outside the gates of the hospital to supply the needs of patients from distant clans attracted fewer market women on Wednesdays than on any other day of the week. It was also noticed that even the sky knew that day of death and mourned in gloom. (*AOG*, p. 150)

Dr. Savage is a surgeon; she performs surgical operations on people in order to save their lives. Ironically, the natives mistake her work of mercy for savagery because surgery causes pain and may even result in loss of the lives it is intended to save. Thus the people regard the doctor as the agent of pain and death, and her name as a metaphor for savagery. Achebe implies the irony of the surgeon's work in her full name, Dr. Mary Savage, which is an oxymoronic selection.

Allusive Names

The names of some of the characters are allusions to extratextual contexts, not names properly speaking. Such names add color and allusiveness to the character description of those who bear them. For instance, when Okonkwo beats up his wife during the Week of Peace, he offends Ani and the people:

They called him the little bird *nza*, who so far forgot himself after a heavy meal that he challenged his *chi* .... This year they talked of nothing else but the *nso-ani* which Okonkwo had committed. It was the first time for many years that a man had broken the sacred peace. (*TFA*, p. 28)

Among the Igbo, the folktale about the proverbial bird *nza* is both popular and funny. The bird is so small and fragile that one is amused to imagine him posing like a wrestler before a crowd of people challenging either his creator or spirit-double to a wrestling match. To do so means signing his own death warrant as well as bringing about disorder in nature. In addition, *nza* has a false sense of his strength. Once the heavy meal is digested and excreted, he comes back to his senses driven by hunger. In other words, *nza* is unaware of the limitation of his momentary contentment with life. When applied to the hero, the name *nza* reminds the people of Okonkwo's poor parentage and momentary affluence in the society. His father was an *agbala* before he died. As the son of such a poor man, Okonkwo had no class until rich people like Nwakibie helped him to make a good start in life which his father could not provide for him. The people believe that their gods, particularly Ani, blessed him, therefore it becomes the height of ingratitude and insult for Okonkwo to break the peace of the land during the sacred week—an act which they regard as an abomination to the goddess of provision, Ani. Okonkwo is too infinitesimal to challenge the earth goddess. Readers of the novel know that "Inwardly, he was repentant. But he was not the man to go about telling his neighbors that he was in error" (p. 28). However, apart from his failure to show regret openly for his offense, his neighbors have a generally poor opinion of him because "Okonkwo knew how to kill a man's spirit," usually by dealing brusquely with less successful men and forgetting that his father was one of such men; his achievements have gone to his head, as it were.

An allusive name similar to *nza* is given to Akukalia and Umuaro in *Arrow of God*; but instead of just being given an animal name, Akukalia is described in a folktale as "a great wrestler whose back had never known the ground" (p. 26). From the folktale, one notices that Akukalia is pushed by the encouragement of unwary elders to challenge everybody, including men and gods. The result of such fame-driven and mad adventure is suicide: "So they sent him his personal god, a little wiry spirit who seized him with one hand and smashed him on the stony earth" (pp. 26-27). We also notice that those whom Achebe gives the allusive names have always had a false sense of their strength and achievements. Just as Akukalia fights an Okperi man because Umuaro elders unwittingly encourage him to do so, Umuaro in this scene is being encouraged by their orator, Nwaka, to fight "a war of blame" with Okperi. Ezeulu unsuccessfully advises against war:

> "Men of Umuaro, why do you think our fathers told us this story? They told it because they wanted to teach us that no matter how strong or great a man was he should never challenge his *chi*. This is what our kinsman did—he challenged his *chi*. We were his flute player, but we did not plead with him to come away from death. Where is he today? The fly that has no one to advise it follows the corpse into the grave. But let us leave Akukalia aside; he has gone the way his *chi* ordained.
>
> "But let the slave who sees another cast into a shallow grave know that he will be buried in the same way when his day comes. Umuaro is today challenging its *chi*.... Is there any man or woman in Umuaro who does not know Ulu, the deity that destroys a man when his life is sweetest to him? Some people are still talking of carrying war to Okperi. Do they think Ulu will fight in blame? Today the world is spoilt and there is no longer head or tail in anything that is done. But Ulu is not spoilt with it. If you go to war to avenge a man who passed shit on the head of his mother's father, Ulu will not follow you to be soiled in the corruption...." (p. 27)

From Ezeulu's speech we can obtain the allusive names, unwary "fly" and impudent "wrestler" given to Akukalia; and "flute player" of death or *ogbu opi onwu* given to Umuaro elders. The names give us a lot of insight into the character of Akukalia who dies because of his impudence and impatience—traits which also characterize the role of the elders when they fail to give good counsel to the young and impatient, who are rather driven to their graves:

> Umuaro killed four men and Okperi replied with three, one of the three being Akukalia's brother, Okoye. The next day, Afo, saw the war brought to a sudden close. The white man, Wintabota, brought soldiers to Umuaro and stopped it (p. 28).

Thus the revenge for the death of Akukalia is carried out by Umuaro in spite of Ezeulu's disapproval of it, but it costs them three extra lives; a cost which a little patience and caution would have prevented.

In *No Longer At Ease,* the allusive name *nza* is used again but this time as a reference to an aspiring but audacious politician who, hearing the news about popular politicians, "took it into his head to challenge the national hero:"

> "He is a foolish somebody," said one of the men in English. "He is like the bird *nza* who after a big meal so far forgot himself as to challenge his *chi* to a single combat," said another in Ibo (p. 148).

What the people are condemning is not the ambition of a young man becoming a political candidate; rather it is his effrontery in challenging their national hero, whom they think is beyond the opposition of a young, unfledged and inexperienced man. Such an adventure could result in the young man's destruction. The futility of a young man's challenge of his elder is conveyed in the statement that Edna's father makes to Odili in *A Man of the People*:

> "My in-law is like a bull," he said, "and your challenge is like the challenge of a tick to a bull. The tick fills its belly with blood from the back of the bull and the bull doesn't even know it's there. He carries it wherever he goes—to eat, drink or pass ordure. Then one day the cattle egret comes, perches on the bull's back and picks out the tick...." (p. 106)

While one regards "bull" and "tick" as allusions made to Chief M. A. Nanga and Odili Samalu respectively as they engage in campaign struggles, the politicians as a group are described in another context as vultures:

> "There were three vultures," said the ex-policeman after the applause had subsided. "The third and the youngest was called C. P. C." (p. 124-5)

What is common to all the examples of allusive names that we have so far cited is that they are descriptive names taken from folktales, especially etiological tales. They are names used to describe the behavior of young men who fail to show respect for age which the people value so much. But the names can also be given to people who commit other social offenses such as insincerity or unnecessary cunning. An example of this latter group of allusive names is found in a folktale about a tortoise who boycotted his mother's funeral; it is told by Nathaniel as an indirect condemnation of Obi Okonkwo for failing to attend his mother's funeral in Umuofia. Although it is a bad joke told in a bad time, Tortoise is nevertheless a fitting name for the man who cunningly shirks his filial duties.[11]

Strictly speaking, the allusive names belong to the metaphoric names group, but they are put here in a separate group because of their proverbial qualities. For instance, when Amalinze is called the Cat, our first response to the name is to think of what it connotes— the agility of the animal which helps it to avoid touching its back on the ground; and then the animal quality is transferred to the human being whose quickness is comparable to that of the cat. Cat is a metaphoric name. But when Obi Okonkwo is called a Tortoise, the connotation of the name goes beyond a casual reference to the physical movement of the animal. Hence Tortoise is an allusive name which recalls all the folktales which involve the behavior of Tortoise and each of such tales has some cunning in it. Allusive names contain elements of proverbs, folktales, metaphor and personification

---

[11] Chinua Achebe, *No Longer at Ease* (London: Heinemann Educational Books Ltd., 1977), pp. 148-149.

all of which are encapsuled in a single name used in identifying a character. In spite of the cryptic qualities of allusive names, folks understand them as easily as they do proper proverbs.

Other Names

So far the discussion of names has covered those names that Achebe gave to human beings and, in a few cases, to some gods. But since Achebe also makes a literary use of names of non-humans, such other names as those given to clans and villages, spirits, age groups, and places require our brief attention.

The clan and village names which the author uses most in his novels are those with the prefix, *umu*, as in Umuofia, Umuazu, Umuaro, Umuachala, Umunneora, Umuagu, Umuezeani, Umuogwugwu and Umuisiuzo. Umu means "children" of whoever or whatever follows the prefix. Hence Umunneora literally means "children of mother of crowd." The crowd is the Igbo community that traces its origin to one woman's sons. According to V. C. Uchendu,[12] Igbo society has a strong patrilineal emphasis. The whole society can be mapped into a number of agnatic groups (*umunna*). And rights over the use of land depend primarily on agnatic descent, and secondarily on local residence. Achebe, therefore, uses the village and clan names not only as a means of indicating the agnatic descent of the people about whose lives he is writing but also as a way of emphasizing the social security and comfort that are concomitant with the lineage of a founding father. The Igbo man's knowledge of his common descent with others in a village or clan is what has preserved the age long extended family system—a social institution which provides moral and social security to Igbo people. For example, in *Things Fall Apart*, Okonkwo can boldly ask Nwakibie for a grant of yams for share cropping without any security. Nwakibie is not a close relative, but he gives Okonkwo the yams because they have a common descent which makes Okonkwo

---

[12] Victor C. Uchendu. *The Igbo of Southeast Nigeria* (New York: Holt, Rinehart and Winston, 1965), p. 64.

address Nwakibie as *Nna ayi* ("our father").¹³ It is to Uchendu, one of the members of his extended family that Okonkwo goes in exile.¹⁴ The killing of a clansman is regarded as an abomination because of the same reason that all clansmen are *umunneora*. No man with an iota of conscience can kill his brother unless the killing is inadvertent. In a word, the place names Achebe uses generally indicate the kinship system of the Igbo.

In the actual Igbo world, the system provides the same moral and social security: to avoid incest, an Igbo man goes outside of his own agnatic group or village to marry, and in time of adversity, he runs to his "brothers" for protection. What happened to the Igbo during the recent Nigerian Civil War (1967-1970) is a perfect example of the moral and social security that the Igbo extended family system provides. Those driven out of various regions of Nigeria were rehabilitated by their kinsmen when they returned to Igbo country. And after the war, they did not wait for the government in Lagos to help them rebuild their broken lives; they depended on their rich agnates "to get up"¹⁵ and were given social security and comfort.

This seeming aside on clan and village names is useful in answering Ihechukwu Madubuike's thematic question, "What is in a name?"¹⁶ Village and clan names serve psychological and therapeutic purposes to citizens of such places. A citizen of Umuofia *obodo dike* (Land of the brave) does not fear outside invasion because the name of the clan alone is enough to scare unfriendly and *womanly* villages to a point of not planning any wars at all against Umuofia. Those who risk offending Umuofia, as did Mbaino—"four *(clan)* villages"—whom Ogbuefi Ezeugo contemptuously calls "Those sons of wild animals," are usually made to pay a heavy price for their insult; Mbaino gave Ikemefuna and a young girl to Umuofia to

---

¹³ *Things Fall Apart*, p. 18.
¹⁴ *Ibid.*, p. 117.
¹⁵ Uchendu, *op. cit.*, p. 64.
¹⁶ Ihechukwu Madubuike, *A handbook of African Names* (Washington, D.C.: Three Continents Press, 1976), p. 7.

replace Ogbuefi Udo's wife whom they murdered.[17] In *No Longer At Ease*, the same group effort is made by the Umuofia Progressive Union to give Obi Okonkwo some moral support as he faces bribery charges in a Lagos courtroom. They know he is guilty but he must be saved first before being reproached:

> The men of Umuofia were prepared to fight to the last. They had no illusions about Obi. He was, without doubt, a very foolish and self-willed young man. But this was not the time to go into that. The fox must be chased away first; after that the hen might be warned against wandering into the bush (*NLAE*, p. 5).

Place names describe obliquely the history and behavior of the villages or clans and their citizens. Let us examine a few of them:

Umuofia, "Children of land area" owned by a founding father. The citizens must unite and fight to protect the land and avoid shaming the living-dead ancestors of the clan.

Umuazu, "Late comers" into the clan; when the clan is distributing its property, Umuazu are the last to receive a share.

Umuaro, "Weighty community": because Ulu unites the villages that make up the clan and thus gives them strength to fight Abam head-hunters and arsonists.

Umuagu, "Descendants of Agu"; Agu means tiger which originally becomes a praise name given to a man who is as quick and aggressive as a tiger. The citizens of Umuagu are inspired by the name to develop a military prowess necessary for defending their clan and the reputation of their founding fathers.

Umuachala, The same as Umuofia except that the original land area was covered by *achala*, a type of bamboo.

Umuezeani, "Children of Ezeani"; it is a name which differentiates

---

[17] *Things Fall Apart*, pp. 10-12.

the original owners of the land from late comers to the clan such as Umuazu. From Umuezeani the priest of the earth goddess is appointed. His high priestly office names him Ezeani. Umuezeani is a "holy" village since the clan priests are chosen from there.

The symbolism of the names is taught to the citizens through initiation rites. Talking drums evoke emotional responses from villagers during festal and ritual occasions as they call the praise names of the villages. Village leaders elicit the same emotional response during clan meetings. Umuofia is *obodo dike* and Umuaro is *obodonesi!* The response of "Yaa!" which follows the salutation of "kwenu"[18] signifies strength, unity and agreement that the clan needs in order to "act like one" when pursuing a common enemy. If the response is not given by the people, then no action will be taken at all. "Unity is strength" is a popular Igbo saying.

The psychological significance of the names given to age groups and their masks can be illustrated with the following examples from *Arrow of God*. Obika's age group and their new mask are called Otakagu—a name which means literally "one who devours more than a tiger"; it is a good descriptive name for the tumultuousness and aggressiveness of the youths and the new Mask they are launching:

> The coming of a new Mask was always an important occasion especially when as now it was a Mask of high rank. In the last days there had been a lot of coming and going among members of the Otakagu age group. Those of them who had leading roles to play at the ceremony would naturally be targets of malevolence and envy and must therefore be 'hardboiled' in protective magic. But even the others had to have some defensive preparation rubbed into shallow cuts on the arm (*AOG*, p. 194).

Perhaps it is this kind of spiritual and occult preparation which

---

[18] *Things Fall Apart*, p. 12 and *Arrow of God*, p. 26.

the youths make that emboldens Obika to attack Otakekpeli, a man known throughout Umuaro as a wicked medicine man. But it seems that Achebe uses the occasion to tell us about the rash, aggressive and intransigent nature of Obika, the son of a headstrong Chief Priest, Ezeulu:

> Obika was now pointing at Otakekpeli and then pointing at his own chest. He was telling the man that if he wanted to do something useful with his life he should get up. The other man continued to laugh at him. Obika renewed his progress but not with the former speed. He prowled like a leopard, his machete in his right hand and leather band of amulets on his left arm. Ezeulu was biting his lips. It would be Obika, he thought, the rash, foolish Obika. Did not all the other young men see Otakekpeli and look away? But his son could never look away. Obika—
> Ezeulu stopped in midthought. With the flash of lightning Obika had dropped his machete, rushed forward and in one movement lifted Otakekpeli off the ground and thrown him in the nearby bush in a shower of sand... (p. 198).

Agaba is another age group Mask. The narrator remarks that "it stood for the power and aggressiveness of youth. It continued to progress and its song, such as it was. As it got near the center of the *ilo* it changed into the song called *Onye ebuna uzo cho ayi okwu*. It was an appeal to all and sundry not to be the first to provoke the ancestral Mask" (p. 199). One wishes Obika had heeded the advice. Agaba then becomes the opposite of Otakagu in temperament.

Commenting on how names become a part of characterization in West African novels, E. N. Obiechina observes that:

> Though in the traditional culture, the individual, apart from his physical characteristics, is also distinguishable by his proper name and praise name, title name and perhaps aliases as well, it must be observed that he is less an autonomous individual than in the Western sense.
> ... He is born into a clan already bearing an ancestral stamp, for he is supposed to be under the tutelary influence of one of his

ancestors whose name he bears. He will, if he lives long enough, beget children who will continue the life of the clan.... The individual has a real existence only in terms of the general social framework of the community.... Thus at birth he becomes a new member of his clan, at his naming ceremony he acquires a personal identity and a personality, at initiation he ceases to be a child and becomes a social adult, at marriage he begins his own nuclear family and acquires a higher responsibility for protecting his descendants and guarding the mores and traditions of the clan.[19]

The types of names—proper names, praise names, title names, and some aliases—as well as functions of names and naming that Obiechina's commentary touches upon are all covered in Achebe's novels. We have used our own arbitrary terminology and classification as a convenient means of giving the names a literary evaluation.

In summary, the onomastic strategies Achebe employs in his novels are characteristic of his realistic writing—a quality that makes his works faithful to actual Igbo folkways. Although the use of specific names may vary from novel to novel, generally names identify character types, reflect the philosophical and moral positions which the characters represent, establish metaphorical connections among characters, and provide clues to the meaning of a novel's action. Onomastics for Achebe is thus not merely an ornamental device, but is one of the most vital aspects of his art.[20]

---

[19] Emmanuel Obiechina, *Culture, Tradition and Society in The West African Novel* (Cambridge: Cambridge University Press, 1975), p. 83.

[20] The conclusion is a paraphrase of Paul F. Furguson's concluding paragraph of his essay, "By Their Names You Shall Know Them: Flannery O'Connor's Onomastic Strategies," in *Literary Onomastics Studies* Vol. VII, pp. 87-105.

5 | Rituals and Ceremonies: The Dramatic Elements

> The festivals thus brought gods and men together in one crowd. It was the only assembly in Umuaro in which a man might look to his right and find his neighbor and look to his left and see a god standing there ...
> —Achebe's narrator in *Arrow of God*

Rituals and ceremonies are among the more important folkways which Achebe exploits in his novels. Because they are associated with men and gods in a religious assembly, their religious significance tends to overshadow their dramatic substance. Yet when the novels are critically examined, one cannot resist the temptation of regarding the Igbo rituals and ceremonies in them as embodying folk drama and entertainment.

There is a general agreement among scholars the world over that the important thing about drama is that it is an "imitation of action." Ola Rotimi, for instance, declares that "the standard acceptance of the term Drama within a cultural setting, at any rate, implies 'an imitation of an action ... or of a person or persons in action,' the ultimate object of which is to edify or to entertain. Sometimes, to do both."[1] He, however, warns that "some African ritual ceremonies reveal instances of 'imitation' either of an experience in life, or of the behavior patterns of some powers. Others merely represent certain powers without the mimetic impulse to recreate the ways and details of those powers. What could be, and has frequently been, mistaken for Drama in most African traditional displays, appears when this latter type of non-imitative ceremonial effervesces with movement, rhythm, and spectacle, beyond the ordinary."[2]

Although Rotimi's formulations of what really is drama, and what is not, are understood and well taken, it is important to point out, in the interest of the argument of this chapter, that we are not here dealing with ritual drama *per se*. Rather, our business is to describe and discuss the dramatic elements contained in the rituals and ceremonies that one reads about in Achebe's novels. The reason for dealing with the subject matter that way is that the traditional Igbo society (which the novel's society represents) does not distinguish the edifying object of drama from the entertainment one. Both objects are always rolled into one. In other words, what is not considered purely as *drama* could have some *dramatic* elements that are worthy of being talked about intellectually.

As we attempt, therefore, to outline the dramatic elements, it is important to observe that folk drama and entertainment, in their many manifestations, including their ritual manifestation, are very specifically communal in character. More than any of the other arts, they require a group audience at all stages of enactment; quite often, in fact, they demand the participation of the audience in the action or song. For this reason, some theorists have argued, quite convincingly (as Echeruo reminds us), that drama flourishes most in a society that has developed a strong consciousness of itself *as a community*. We should, however, add that drama flourishes best in a community which has satisfactorily transformed ritual into celebra-

---

[1] Ola Rotimi, "The Drama in African Ritual Drama", ed. Yemi Ogunbiyi, *Drama and Theatre in Nigeria: A Critical Source Book* (Lagos, Nigeria: *Nigeria Magazine*, 1981), p. 77.
[2] *Ibid*, p. 77.

tion and converted the mythic structure of action from the religious and priestly to the secular plane.[3]

In fact, the Igbo clans and villages in Achebe's novels do not qualify as communities that "have satisfactorily transformed ritual into celebration and converted the mythic structure of action from the religious and priestly into the secular plan."[4] Take, for instance, the appearance of Ezeulu in *Arrow of God* (pp. 66-73) to reenact the First Coming of his God and consecration of the first Chief Priest. He has to explain who he is and he goes back to history and myth. That whole episode is festival, celebration, mythology, and religion, all rolled into one act which we could call folk drama, but not in the sense that it could be shown just as public entertainment. Thus, we find that as the Igbo know it, dramatic ritual ceremonies, although lacking clear-cut definition as drama, can have their own forms without necessarily having to conform to classical formulations of drama. But even in its *undefinable* forms, Igbo drama, embodied in rituals and ceremonies, can be reinterpreted and recreated in formal and modern Nigerian drama—an experiment which Kalu Uka has conducted with Achebe's *Arrow of God*, transforming it into a play titled *A Harvest for Ants: A Dramatized Re-creation of Chinua Achebe's Arrow of God*.[5]

With this background in mind, we can then discuss Igbo rituals and ceremonies as folk drama and entertainment by examining such

---

[3] The paragraph is a paraphrase of M.J.C. Echeruo's thoughts on the relationship between drama and society. See his "The Dramatic Limits of Igbo rituals," *Critical Perspectives on Nigeria Literatures* ed. Bernth Lindfors (Washington, D.C.: Three Continents Press, 1976), p. 76.

[4] Echeruo expresses the opinion that Igbo communities have not yet satisfactorily transformed ritual into celebration and converted the mythic structure of action from the religious and priestly into the secular plan. However, Ezeulu's reenactment of the First Coming of Ulu could be regarded as folk drama that is staged once a year, provided that its religious significance is de-emphasized.

[5] The title is listed in the 1979-1980 Three Continents Press Catalogue, Washington D.C.

elements as community and audience; stage, costuming and spectacle; representation, mime and dance; plot and music. These elements are here discussed individually only to assist our analysis; they are not usually separated in actual Igbo performances.

Stage, Costuming, and Spectacle

The village *ilo* and market square could be regarded as equivalents of what is known as stage in modern drama, but only in the sense of their serving as regular meeting places of religious occasions, political discussion, and for the staging of more stable seasonal and annual celebrations—e.g., new yam festivals and wrestling matches. However, such Igbo stages do not have restrictive demarcations and conveniences like walls, roofs, and fixed seats as one finds in stages of other lands. Thus, the rigid spatial boundaries of modern theaters are avoided, allowing the audience to participate in the dramatic action: anybody can jump from the audience into the center of the "stage" to perform one or two steps of the dance, clap hands to the rhythm and fury of the *ekwe* (drum), and do some miming to evoke the laughter of the spectators. Members of the audience may sing a familiar song with the actors without running the risk of being hushed by other spectators, as they would be in theaters in Western societies. In a word, the open stage, by offering spectators a standing invitation to participate in the dramatic action, enables them to establish a sense of community with the lead actors. However, some stages, especially those belonging to esoteric and occult groups, or individuals, such as the *ozo* society or very powerful medicine men, are more restrictive in nature and their spectators always observe the dramatic enactments from a distance.

Another advantage in having an open stage is that no one is excluded from the celebration because he cannot pay his way into the theater. As a matter of fact, the audience is not expected to contribute towards the funding of any folk entertainment, but individual spectators can come out of the audience into the ring to donate money:

> The girls sang a song called *Ifeoma*. Goodly Thing had come, they

said, so let everyone who had good things bring them before her as offering. They made a circle round her and she danced to their song. As she danced her husband-to-be and other members of Ezeulu's family broke through the circle one or two at a time and stuck money on her forehead. She smiled and let the present fall at her feet from where one of the girls picked it up and put it in a bowl (*AOG*, p. 116).

Although the wedding dance and offering may appear spontaneous to the audience, the entire wedding ceremony is a re-enactment of previous weddings of past seasons; it undergoes a series of private rehearsals before it becomes a public celebration. In this sense, therefore, a wedding ceremony is a folk drama, folk entertainment, or folk opera—terms explained in Rotimi's article.[6]

The Igbo people's love and appreciation of art and beauty is apparent in the way they carve their masks and gods, and in the way they dress for ceremonial occasions. In the area of folk drama, their love of beauty is expressed in the form of costuming and body make-up:

> The festival was now only three days away. Okonkwo's wives had scrubbed the walls and huts with red earth until they reflected light. They had then drawn patterns on them in white, yellow and dark green. They then set about painting themselves with cam wood and drawing black patterns on their stomachs and on their backs. The children were also decorated, especially their hair, which was shaved in beautiful patterns. The three women talked excitedly about the relations who had been invited, and the children revelled in the thought of being spoiled by these visitors from the motherland. Ikemefuna was equally excited. The New Yam Festival seemed to him to be a much bigger event here than in his own village, a place which was already becoming remote and vague in his imagination

---

[6] See Ola Rotimi, "Traditional Nigerian Drama," ed. Bruce King, *Introduction to Nigerian Literature* (Lagos, Nigeria: University of lagos and Evans Brothers Ltd., 1971), p. 36.

(*TFA*, pp. 34-35).

The passage exemplifies how the Igbo have expanded what began as a ritual ceremony into secular entertainment. The renovation of walls and huts and the decoration of bodies are an annual ritual which is performed to end the old year and usher in the new. The "visitors from the motherland" include men and spirits, gods and deities in a religious and festal celebration. Hence the physical and psychological renewal which is inspired by religious beliefs and celebration consummates in a secular performance at the village *ilo* or marketplace.

In other words, both ritual and secular observances are carried out by the same celebrants, although the master of ceremonies for both aspects of the celebration, the Chief Priest, is a religious appointee. The situation, then, is that the dramatic limits we find in Igbo rituals are there because of the nature of individual rituals— whether the ritual is private or public, individual or communal, meditative or celebrative—but not because the ritual has been expanded into life as such nor because that life has been given a secular base. And, of course, given the religious practices and cosmological beliefs of the traditional Igbo, it is almost irrelevant to distinguish the secular from the sacred.

Furthermore, costuming in Igbo ceremonies, as in conventional drama, not only pleases the eye, but also expresses the characters or roles the actors are playing. For instance, the narrator reports that Nwaka, the rich orator from Umunneora and archenemy of Ezeulu, "had a great Mask which he assumed on this and other important occasions. The Mask was Ogalanya or Man of Riches, and at every Idemili festival crowds of people from all the villages and their neighbors came to the *ilo* of Umunneora to see this great Mask bedecked with mirrors and rich cloths of many colors" (*AOG* p. 39). The passage does two things: it qualifies Nwaka as a rich man, who also is a peacock; and it shows that Nwaka's ostentatious display of his wealth at important occasions generally steals the show from Ezeulu, the Chief Priest. Nwaka's attitude generates some hatred in Ezeulu which eventuates in the bitter conflict between the priest and his clansmen, Umuaro—a conflict which enables the foreign mis-

94 | Rituals and Ceremonies

sionary, Mr. Goodcountry, and his Christian religion to gain a foothold in the clan.

The face, name, decoration, and sex of the masks can also reveal the aggressiveness, celerity, and temperament of the masqueraders. For instance, when Enoch unmasks an *egwugwu* in public, Achebe uses very descriptive and emotional language to portray the physical and psychological disposition of the other "bereaved" ancestral spirits in order to convey to his readers the full impact of the confusion into which Umuofia was thrown by Enoch's over-zealousness:

> That night the Mother of the Spirits walked the length and breadth of the clan, weeping for her murdered son. It was a terrible night. Not even the oldest man in Umuofia had ever heard such a strange and fearful sound, and it was never to be heard again. It seemed as if the very soul of the tribe wept for a great evil that was coming— its own death.
>
> On the next day all the masked *egwugwu* of Umuofia assembled in the market place. They came from all the quarters of the clan and even from the neighboring villages. The dreaded Otakagu came from Imo, and Ekwensu (Devil), dangling a white cock, arrived from Uli. It was a terrible gathering. The eerie voices of countless spirits, the bells that clattered behind some of them, and the clash of machetes as they ran forwards and backwards and saluted one another, sent tremors of fear into every heart. For the first time in living memory the sacred bullroarer was heard in broad daylight.
>
> From the market place the furious band made for Enoch's compound. Some of the elders of the clan went with them, wearing heavy protections of charms and amulets. These were men whose arms were strong in *ogwu*, or medicine. As for the ordinary men and women, they listened from the safety of their huts (*TFA*, pp. 168-169).

This passage, although describing the violation of a mask, is an enactment of action taken to deal with similar incidents in the past. Hence we find such dramatic elements as conflict, plot, action, movement, suspense, sound, lighting (night and day), mood, setting, and, tone of description which matches the dramatic moment. In addition, we have the sacred audience who watch and listen "from the safety of their huts." When the *egwugwu* finally arrive at the Christian hut, they find Mr. Smith standing his ground protected by the color of his skin. Tension mounts higher. But actors and spectators are afraid of what may happen next. Finally, the resolution comes:

> Mr. Smith stood his ground. But he could not save his church. When the *egwugwu* went away the red earth church which Mr. Brown had built was a pile of earth ashes. And for the moment the spirit of the clan was pacified (p. 172).

We can visualize both parties to the conflict heaving a sigh of relief, for the situation could have been worse, had there been any bloodshed. Also, there is purification of the guilt attached to Enoch's rash action and the *egwugwu's* reaction to it, both of which created confusion and tension in Umuofia. The purification of the guilt is represented in the sentence, "And for the moment the spirit of the clan was pacified."

The Igbo, as a general way of life, like things colorful: their ceremonies, clothes, body decorations, masks and speeches are all very colorful. In their folk drama too, one expects the Igbo to make a colorful spectacle. Since most of their dramatic performances are carried out in the open air, the physical environment—the sunny or cloudy sky, the colors of the rainbow, and the lush green vegetation—provides a background scenery surrounding and blending with a crowd of gaudily dressed suppliants and celebrants in a religious or secular assembly. We have already seen the effect of Nwaka's particolored Mask, Ogalanya, on the audience. Ezeulu is himself painted in black and white; one half of him is man and other half spirit. And his family, representative of other Umuaro families, has their own decorations to make:

> Ezeulu's younger wife examined her hair in a mirror held between her thighs. She could not help feeling that she did a better job on Akueke's hair than Akueke did on hers. But she was very pleased with the black patterns of *uli* and faint yellow lines of *ogalu* on her

body. In previous years she would have been among the first to arrive at the marketplace; she would have been carefree and joyful. But this year her feet seemed to drag because of the load on her mind. She was going to pray for the cleansing of her hut which Oduche had defiled.... The weight of this feeling all but crushed the long awaited pleasure of wearing her new ivory bracelets which had earned her so much envy and hostility from her husband's other wife, Matefi (AOG, pp. 66-67).

The ceremonies are occasions when rich people, e.g., Nwaka, exhibit their riches to the envy and hostility of less successful clansmen:

> They were just in time to see the arrival of the five wives of Nwaka and the big stir they caused. Each of them wore not anklets but two enormous rollers of ivory reaching from the ankle almost to the knee. Their walk was perforce slow and deliberated like the walk of an Ijele Mask lifting and lowering each foot with weighty ceremony. On top of all this the women were clad in many colored velvets. Ivory and velvets were not new in Umuaro but never before had they been seen in such profusion from the house of one man (p. 68).

Achebe juxtaposes this description of Nwaka's family display of opulence with that of Ezeulu's not-too-rich family as an indirect way of pointing out that even when Igbo society appears to be egalitarian, there is still noticeable social difference in it—between the rich and the poor and within the elite class itself. In fact, in several passages of Achebe's novels, strangers actually condemn some Igbo for their inordinate exhibitionism. For instance, the head messenger in *Things Fall Apart*, whom Okonkwo finally kills, asks in jest:

> "Who is the chief among you? We see that every pauper wears the anklet of title in Umuofia. Does it cost as much as ten cowries?" (p. 175)

And about Igbo speeches, one knows, from reading Achebe's novels, that an Igbo can never make a full speech without coloring it with one or two proverbs or proverbial sayings. We will evaluate the importance of this verbal art in the next chapter.

Community and Audience

Although we touched upon community and audience in the discussion of stage, costuming and spectacle, it must be mentioned that community and audience in Igbo rituals and ceremonies include the Igbo trinity of the living, the living-dead ancestors, and the unborn. The ancestors are represented during festivals by masked spirits or what Achebe calls *egwugwu*. Their appearance is regarded by the living as the active link between the world of man and the world of spirits. It is also believed by the Igbo that the rituals and ceremonies attract the presence of the spirits of those yet to be born. Hence, women in search of babies make themselves as attractive and as "pure" as possible so as to attract the reincarnation of such spirits from the spirit world.[7]

One of such festivals is the Festival of the Pumpkin Leaves. It is also believed by the Igbo that the rituals and ceremonies of purification and unity, an annual ceremony in which the great *ikolo* (talking drum) calls the six villages of Umuaro one by one in their ancient order is an indirect way of reminding them of the necessity of peace and unity—in other words, a re-enactment of the founding of the clan. It is a dramatic occasion when Ezeulu re-enacts the First Coming of Ulu and how each of the four days put obstacles in his way. At the beginning, Ezeulu and his six assistants do not appear. They remain in seclusion to observe the Umuaro community play their own part of the drama. When they do appear, the people in turn become the audience. But since women are more involved in the ceremony than men, they begin and end the ceremony (*AOG*, pp. 66-73).

The point about Igbo audience is that in all public ceremonies, everybody is a part of the cast; that is, each is both spectator and actor to varying degrees. You may have a few lead actors such as

---

[7] Opinion expressed by my informant, Chief Ogbonnaya Eke.

masked spirits, singers, drummers and ushers, when the ceremony starts; but when the drumming and dancing reach fever pitch, you find people jumping into the circle to take active part in the celebration. It is this spontaneous response to the mystic message of the talking drum and the feeling of being openly invited to share in the celebration that create the sense of community in the Igbo audience.

One other distinguishing feature of the Igbo audience is its dynamic character. As has been mentioned earlier in this chapter, the lack of restrictive gadgets such as fixed seats, walls and demarcations makes it easier for the audience to move from one part of the "stage" to another, following the movement of the performers. Ezeulu, though in a different context, describes aptly this special quality of the Igbo audience when he says, "The world is like a Mask dancing. If you want to see it well you do not stand in one place" (*AOG*, p.46). But the free movement of the audience could get out of hand and bring disaster; e.g., Okonkwo inadvertently kills Ogbuefi Ezeudu's sixteen-year-old son because of the chaotic movements of the audience and performers.

Anyway, not all ceremonies attract unruly audiences. Wrestling, for example, may be as exciting as any other Igbo public celebration, yet since it often involves inter-village or clan competitions, its audience tends to be more nervous and orderly than that of a ceremony such as the Festival of the Pumpkin Leaves in which the celebrants have no reputation at stake. The organization of the "stage" for wrestling matches is quite formal; only when a competitor is thrown do people go wild and disturb the arrangement:

> The whole village turned out on the *ilo*, men, women and children. They stood round in a huge circle leaving the center of the playground free. The elders and grandees of the village sat on their own stools brought there by their young sons or slaves .... The wrestlers were not there yet and the drummers held the field. They too sat just in front of the huge circle of spectators, facing the elders. Behind them was the big and ancient silk-cotton tree which was sacred. Spirits of good children lived in that tree waiting to be born. ... The drummers took up their sticks and the air shivered and grew tense like a tightened bow.

The two teams were ranged facing each other across the clear space. A young man from one team danced across the center to the other side and pointed at whomever he wanted to fight. They danced back to the center together and then closed in.... But the really exciting moments were when a man was thrown. The high voice of the crowd then rose to the sky and in every direction (TFA, pp. 42 & 45).

We notice from this passage that as in conventional theaters certain corners of the *ilo* are designated for the elders and titled men, drummers, singers, spectators, and the lead actors—the wrestlers—so as to avoid the chaos that would ensue if everybody, actors and audience, was to occupy anywhere they pleased. In addition, there are scouts who usher in the actors when the "stage" is ready, and beat back over-enthusiastic spectators into the crowd. There is rowdiness but it is checked from time to time.

Representation, Mime and Dance

The ceremonies which embody Igbo dramatic forms have their roots in ritual and religious practices. Ironically, the first to write about Igbo life and its formal dramatic elements were Igbo expatriates; among them Olaudah Equiano (or Gustavus Vassa the African).[8] Olaudah Equiano's description of a village dance in his book, *Equiano's Travels*, would seem to support the above observation. In that description, one can detect some dramatic elements such as representation of events (e.g., battle), music and dance, as well as columns of actors drawn from every segment of Igbo community—men and women, boys and girls—all of which are also found in Achebe's descriptions of Igbo ritual and ceremonies.[9]

---

[8] See *The Conch* III, 2 (September, 1971), p. 11 and Ernest Emenyonu, *The Rise of the Igbo Novel* (Ibadan: Oxford University Press, 1978), p. xii.

[9] See Adrian A. Roscoe, *Mother is Gold: A Study in West African Literature* (Cambridge: Cambridge University Press, 1971), p. 77. The paragraph reads:

We may look at the judicial system of the people and find a representational element which could turn a pure court scene into a dramatic episode because, according to Obiechina, "there is hardly any important area of human experience which is not linked to the supernatural and the people's sense of religion and religious piety. Achebe shows how these things are part and parcel of the ideological interpretation of experience in the traditional social context."[10] With this in mind, let us examine one of the two great court scenes in Achebe's novels—the Uzowulu versus Mgbafo case in *Things Fall Apart*.

Although in modern novels set in earlier socio-political times dramatic elements can still be discerned from courtroom proceedings, as in the second great court scene in Achebe's novels, "The Trial of Obi Okonkwo" in *No Longer at Ease*, yet, what qualifies the Uzowulu-Mgbafo case as drama is that it has so much plot, music, dance, mime, audience and celebration that a foreign spectator could regard the trial as one of those "tribal" ceremonies for which the African is famous. Uzowulu is the plaintiff. But as the hearing progresses, he is accused of constantly battering his wife, Mgbafo, in the past, but this time his in-laws go to beat him as a revenge for

---

Thus every great event such as a triumphant return from battle or other cause of public rejoicing is celebrated in public dances, which are accompanied with songs and music and suited to the occasion. The assembly is separated into four divisions, which dance either apart or in succession, and each with a character peculiar to itself. The first division contains the married men, who in their dances frequently exhibit feats of arms and the representation of battle. To these succeed the married women, who dance in the second division. The young men occupy the third and the maidens the fourth. Each represents some interesting scene of real life such as a great achievement, domestic employment, a pathetic story, or some rural sport, and as the subject is generally founded on some recent event, it is therefore ever new (pp. 3-4).

[10] Emmanuel Obiechina, *Culture, Tradition and Society in the West African Novel* (Cambridge: Cambridge University Press, 1975), p. 208.

the punishment their sister suffers in his hands. So, Uzowulu presses charges against his wife and in-laws. The jury is made up of nine masked spirits called *egwugwu*, who represent the nine founding fathers of the clan.

The case is described by Achebe as a ceremony. However, our analysis of it yields the following dramatic elements:

Time: "After the midday meal," as soon as the edge has worn off the sun's heat and it was no longer painful on the body. That is about 4:00 P.M.
Place: The village *ilo*—open but sacred theater, where all great village ceremonies and meetings are held.
Cause: Uzowulu versus Mgbafo, *et al.*; plaintiff—Uzowulu, and defendants—Mgbafo and her brothers.
Jury: Senior Ancestral Spirits or *Egwugwu*.
Spectators: Large crowds of Umuofia, especially titled men and elders.
Deposition: Uzowulu steps forward and presents his case. He accuses his in-laws of beating him up in his house and taking away his wife and children without returning his bride-price, an offense he claims is against the law of the land. Odukwe, representing the defendants, admits the truth of the charges but defends their action by pointing out how Uzowulu has beaten up their sister every day of the nine years they have been married. They are prepared to release both mother and children to Uzowulu if he "should recover from his madness and come in the proper way to beg his wife to return."
Verdict: Handed down to the court by Evil Forest (and we quote him in full):

Evil Forest rose to his feet and order was immediately restored. A steady cloud of smoke rose from his head. He sat down again and called two witnesses. They were both Uzowulu's neighbors, and they agreed about the beating. Evil Forest then stood up, pulled out his staff and thrust it into the earth again. He ran a few steps in the direction of the women: they all fled in terror, only to return to their places almost immediately. The nine *egwugwu* then went away to consult together in their house. They were silent for a long time. Then the metal gong sounded and the flute was blown. The *egwugwu* had emerged once again from their underground home. They saluted one another and then reappeared on the *ilo*.

"Umuofia Kwenu!" roared Evil Forest, facing the elders and grandees of the clan.

"Yaa!" replied the thunderous crowd; then silence descended from the sky and swallowed the noise. Evil Forest began to speak and all the while he spoke everyone was silent. The eight other *egwugwu* were as still as statues. "We have heard both sides of the case," said Evil Forest. "Our duty is not to blame this man or to praise that, but to settle the dispute." He turned to Uzowulu's group and allowed a short pause. "Uzowulu's body, I salute you," he said.

"Our father, my hand has touched the ground," replied Uzowulu, touching the earth.

"Uzowulu's body, do you know me?"

"How can I know you, father? You are beyond our knowledge," Uzowulu replied. "I am Evil Forest. I kill a man on the day that his life is sweetest to him."

"That is true," replied Uzowulu.

"Go to your in-laws with a pot of wine and beg your wife to return to you. It is not bravery when a man fights with a woman." He turned to Odukwe, and allowed a brief pause. "Odukwe's body, I greet you," he said. "My hand is on the ground," replied Odukwe. "Do you know me?"

"No man can know you," replied Odukwe.

"I am Evil Forest, I am Dry-meat-that-fills-the-mouth, I am Fire-that-burns-without-faggots. If your in-law brings wine to you, let your sister go with him. I salute you." He pulled his staff from the hard earth and thrust it back. "Umuofia kwenu!" he roared and the crowd answered. "I don't know why such a trifle should come before the *egwugwu*," said one elder to another.

"Don't you know what kind of man Uzowulu is? He will not listen to any other decision," replied the other.

As they spoke two other groups of people had replaced the first before the *egwugwu* and a great land case began (*TFA*, pp. 84-85).

The passage is a perfect play script: it contains dialogue between Evil Forest and the two parties; there are stage directions like "He turned to Uzowulu's group and allowed a short pause," which a director could give to an actor—"Turn to the left, face Uzowulu's group and allow a short pause before you read your next line." Meticulously Achebe describes the voice, movement and tone of each of the characters. He allows us to know the kind of person the plaintiff is—irascible, defiant and a liar. His demeanor in court reveals his repulsive nature at home.

What begins as a serious case of battering of a woman and a counter assault on the plaintiff ends as a comedy because of the few jokes contained in the deposition of the case and the entertainment that the representational movement of the *egwugwu* provides. There is music as the iron gong is sounded and the flute is blown to usher in the sacred jury. As the *egwugwu* approach the *ilo*, "the drum sounded again and the flute blew. The *egwugwu* house was now a pandemonium of quavering voices: *Aru oyi de de dei!* filled the air as the spirits of the ancestors, just emerged from the earth, greeted themselves in their esoteric language" (p. 84). The spectacle is terrifying because, this day, the nine greatest masked spirits in the clan are abroad. The few steps they dance to the rhythm and mystic message of the talking drums could be regarded as mime. And when Evil Forest walks towards the crowd his unspoken message is understood by the scuttling women and children: "Run or I kill you on the day that your life is sweetest to you."

Achebe's description of this court scene fulfills the twin purposes of literature: namely, to entertain and instruct. Apart from being entertained with the public display of the masked spirits and the humor of the testimony of the litigants, Achebe's readers are taught some customs of the Igbo: the kinship groups provide moral and material support for their members. Mgbafo could have died if she had no relatives to save her from the battering of her husband. And when they take her away, they provide food and shelter for her and her children. The jury of *egwugwu* are representatives of the nine villages of Umuofia—an indication of the democratic character of the

Igbo judicial system.

The verdict itself needs our comments. Evil Forest says "Our duty is not to blame this man or to praise that, but to settle the dispute." The emphasis is on settlement. The wisdom of the elders in this is that in a family dispute there are neither victors nor vanquished. If one party is given a severe punishment, the unpunished party will still feel the effect of the other's punishment because, as a family, they are one. To the outsider, the penalty for Uzowulu's crime is too light; but to the Igbo the public reprimand, "It is not bravery when a man fights a woman" which Evil Forest hands down, is severe enough. It reduces Uzowulu to the level of a woman in a manly society such as Umuofia. And, of course, this reprimand is a second humiliation, the first being his having been beaten by his in-laws, who prove in word and deed that they are responsible people. Because of their apparent weakness, some women are taken advantage of by men, but there are always other men who are ready to fight such social crimes as battering of women.

Plot and Music

Some rituals and ceremonies have definable plots which, along with other dramatic elements, can constitute fully realized drama. The Uzowulu-Mgbafo case is one example, and Ezeulu's re-enactment of the First Coming of Ulu is another. Both of these ceremonies have ritual aspects; that is to say, they begin as ritual re-enactments but as their ritual action progresses and becomes a public celebration, ritual is absorbed in dramatic action and *mythos* becomes plot. That plot is narrated by a flutist, a minstrel and the talking drum. In *Arrow of God*, for example, Ezeulu acts as a minstrel as he approaches the center of the market place to re-enact the First Coming of Ulu and how each of the four Days—Igbo weekdays of Eke, Oye, Afo, and Nkwo—put obstacles in his way. What follows below is a narration of the plot of the ritual action that later becomes a public celebration and drama:

> At that time, when lizards were still in ones and twos, the whole people assembled and chose me to carry their new deity. I said to

them:

"Who am I to carry this fire on my bare head? A man who knows that his anus is small does not swallow an udala seed."

They said to me:

"Fear not. The man who sends a child to catch a shrew will also give him water to wash his hand.

I said: "So be it."

And we set to work. That day was Eke: we worked into Oye and then into Afo. As day broke on Nkwo and the sun carried its sacrifice I carried my Alusi and, with all the people behind me, set out on that journey. A man sang with the flute on my right and another replied on my left. From behind heavy tread of all the people gave me strength. And then all of a sudden something spread itself across my face. On one side it. was raining, on the other side it was dry. I looked again and saw that it was Eke.

I said to him: "Is it you Eke?"

He replied: "It is I, Eke, the One that makes a strong man bite the earth with his teeth."

I took a hen's egg and gave him. He took it and ate and gave way to me. We went on, past streams and forests. Then a smoking thicket crossed my path, and two men were wrestling on their heads. My followers looked once and took to their heels. I looked again and saw that it was Oye.

I said to him: "Is it you Oye across my path?"

He said: "It is I, Oye, the One that began cooking before Another and has more broken pots."

I took a white cock and gave him. He took it and made way for me. I went on past farmlands and wilds and then I saw that my head was too heavy for me. I looked steadily and saw that it was Afo.

I said: "Is it you Afo?"

He said: "It is I, Afo, the great river that cannot be salted."

I replied: "I am Ezeulu, the hunchback more terrible than a leper." Afo shrugged and said: "Pass, your own is worse than mine."

I passed and the sun came down and beat me and the rain came down and drenched me. Then I met Nkwo. I looked on his left and saw an old woman, tired, dancing strange steps on the hill. I looked to the right and saw a horse and a ram. I slew the horse and with the ram I cleaned my machete, and so removed that evil. (*AOG*, pp. 70-71)

Continuing, the narrator comments on the accompanying music:

> By now Ezeulu was in the center of the marketplace. He struck the metal staff into the earth and left it quivering while he danced a few more steps to the *Ikolo* which had not paused for breath since the priest emerged.... All the women set up a long, excited ululation and there was renewed jostling for the front line.... The *Ikolo* drum worked itself into frenzy during the Chief Priest's flight especially its final stages when he, having completed the full circle of the market place, ran on with increasing speed into the sanctuary of his shrine, his messengers at his heels. As soon as they disappeared the *Ikolo* broke off its beating abruptly with one last KOME (*AOG*, p. 72).

Ezeulu's narration, the esoteric drum message, the women's ululation and clapping of hands form the Igbo dramatic elements of plot and music.

Folk Entertainment

Being very fond of entertainment, the Igbo regard their public rituals and ceremonies primarily as folk entertainment. Entertainment goes on in every area of their lives. For example, after each day's heavy work in the farms, fathers and their sons gather in the *obi* to entertain themselves with the retelling of legendary history as they await the evening meals the womenfolk are preparing. The women and their daughters have their own womanish stories to tell, as they wait for the yams and cocoyams to cook:

> At such times, in each of the countless huts of Umuofia, children sat around their mother's cooking fire telling stories or with their father in his *obi* warming themselves from a log fire, roasting and eating maize. It was a brief resting period between the exacting and arduous planting season and equally exciting but lighthearted month of harvests (*TFA*, p. 31).

It is during storytelling sessions like this that the lore of the clan is handed down from fathers to their sons; the lore includes heroic stories of the clan which eventually become the plot of the dramatic displays of the masquerade:

> So Okonkwo encouraged the boys to sit with him in his *obi*, and he told them stories of the land—masculine stories of violence and bloodshed. Nwoye knew that it was right to be masculine and to be violent, but somehow he still preferred the stories that his mother used to tell, and which she no doubt still told her younger children—stories of the tortoise and his wily ways, and of the bird *eneke-nti-oba* who challenged the whole world to a wrestling contest and was finally thrown by the cat (*TFA*, p. 48).

Nwoye's quiet rejection of violence which we notice here crystallizes when he openly joins the Christians and his violent father places a curse on him.

Entertainment goes on when people are working hard: readers may recall how in *Arrow of God* "a native gang of laborers" engaged to work on a new road entertained themselves on the first day by singing a song that told how much they were paid a day:

> As soon as they were signed on the first day and told how much they would be paid they devised a work song. Their leader sang: '*Lebula toro toro*' and all the others replied: 'A day,' at the same time swinging their machetes or wielding their hoes. It was a most effective work song and they sang it for many days:
>
> > *Lebula toro toro*
> > *A day*
> > *Lebula toro toro*
> > *A day*
>
> And they sang it in English too! (p. 76)

The workers devise the work song to keep their sanity, otherwise they either protest to the colonial *"masters"* and risk losing their jobs to workers from other clans, or receive a few wallops of the master's whips for being disobedient *"boys."* The workers' attitude expresses the Igbo man's survival mechanism or work ethic, *Ma ahughi ka emere, emee ka ahuru*—"If the desirable is not available then the available is made desirable." One notices Achebe's oblique comment on what the workers are doing to the English language in the line, "And they sang it in English too!"—namely: they corrupt the language (*Lebula* for laborer; *toro* for three pence) to suit their poetic purpose. (Achebe does the same thing in his novels—using his form of English to protest to the *"masters"* what he feels is wrongly done to his people and their culture. Some critics call it "the Caliban motif"[11] in African literature).

When death strikes, everybody is unhappy; but to defy the pang of death, the people turn their sorrow into joy by performing first and second funeral rites with pomp and pageantry. Funerals are one of those Igbo rituals and ceremonies that contain dramatic elements. There is poetry in the rhythmic weeping and wailing from mourners, and sporadic but synchronizing lamenting and sighing from the aged and infirm. The rituals which precede the actual interment of the body have their own spectacle and fascination. Achebe describes one of the pre-interment rites thus:

> Di-go-go-di-go-di-di-go floated in the message laden night air. The faint and distant wailing of women settled like a sediment of sorrow on the earth. Now and again a full chested lamentation rose above the wailing whenever a man came into the place of death. He raised his voice once or twice in manly sorrow and then sat down with the other men listening to the endless wailing of the women and the esoteric language of the *ekwe*. Now and again the cannon boomed. The wailing of the women would not be heard beyond the village, but the *ekwe* carried the news to all the nine villages and even beyond. It began by naming the clan: *Umuofia obodo dike*, "the land of

---

[11] Lloyd Brown explains the term in his essay, "Cultural Norms and Modes of Perception in Achebe's Fiction," *Critical Perspectives on Nigerian Literatures*, ed. Bernth Lindfors (Washington, D.C.: Three Continents Press, 1976), pp. 131-145.

the brave."

Umuofia obodo dike! Umuofia obodo dike! It said this over and over again, and as it dwelt on it, anxiety mounted in every heart that heaved on a bamboo bed at night. Then it went nearer and named the village: *Iguedo of the yellow grinding stone!* It was Okonkwo's village. Again and again *Iguedo* was called and waited breathlessly in all the nine villages. At last the man was named and people sighed "E-u-u, Ezeudu is dead" (*TFA*, pp. 109-110).

We notice here the sense of ritual in Achebe's reporting of the news of Ezeudu's death and the events on the night of that death. He methodically records for us every bit of sound, movement, feeling, mood, and the instruments used for the ritual. He not only attempts to evoke our emotional response to the death of the old man by creating a synchronous picture, but he also persuasively attempts forcing us to recognize the dignity of that aspect of Igbo culture which deals with death as a human phenomenon.

A Final Word on Igbo Rituals and Ceremonies

So far, we have looked at the dramatic and entertainment qualities of Igbo rituals and ceremonies in Achebe's novels, and found that the masquerades—dances of masked figures of various kinds—seem to include almost all the elements of Igbo folk drama. Maybe because the masquerades are cultic in nature and their dramatic acts unwritten, some critics tend to think that "there seems to be little or no linguistic content, though there is sometimes a rudimentary plot"[12] in them. Such critics may be right; but only in the sense that they regard only the story line of events being enacted as plot. Had they considered the plot to be a combination of the story told by the singer, the esoteric message of the talking drum, the anecdotes of the flutist, and the sign language of the dancers, they would have been overwhelmed by the richness and complexity of the plots

---

[12] Ruth Finnegan, *Oral Literature in Africa* (Nairobi Kenya: Oxford University Press, 1976), p. 509.

of some of these ceremonies.

The Igbo performers in the novel do not dance mainly to the beat of the songs and drumming; as they dance, they are actually responding to a combination of esoteric messages transmitted to them by the singers and talking drums. It is a re-living of the original event, say inter-tribal war, which necessitated the dramatic performance in the first place; that is the mythos of the ceremony.

The plot of the ceremony evokes spontaneous emotions felt by the performers and expressed in the forms of shouting, wailing, stamping, gyrating, trembling and gamboling. Warlike men like Okonkwo usually have much stronger responses to the drumming and music for they speak the language of action which the warriors understand:

> Okonkwo cleared his throat and moved his feet to the beat of the drums. It filled him with fire as it had always done from his youth. He trembled with the desire to conquer and subdue. It was like the desire for women (*TFA*, p. 43).

To conclude, most of the Igbo rituals and ceremonies Achebe includes in his novels embody dramatic elements which qualify them as folk drama, folk opera, or simply folk entertainment. The limitation one has in appreciating fully the entertainment that the ceremonies, as folk drama, offer is, therefore, one of definition: on the one hand, there is the insistence on the use of classical criterion which does not totally suit African dramatic displays, and on the other, the inability of the African to coin a term in a European language which represents what he feels and knows to be the true dramatic forms of his people. For example, one is thinking of *Egwu na Amu* (transliterated "Play and Entertainment") as the Igbo translation of folk play and folk entertainment. *Egwu na Amu* is a functional term for, like most other Igbo names, it describes the thing or idea it stands for according to its function. Some of the Igbo rituals and ceremonies, despite their religious origins and import, provide entertainment to the people all the year round, since they may be weekly, monthly or yearly rituals and ceremonies.

6 | Proverbs

> Among the Igbo the art of conversation is regarded very highly, and proverbs are the palm oil with which words are eaten.
> —Achebe's narrator in *Things Fall Apart*.

Proverbs are among the easily distinguishable folkways in Achebe's novels. The author uses proverbs, as a verbal art, to comment on the behavior and activities of the principal characters, to intrude upon the narrative flow of the novels in order to draw his readers' attention to a particular point that the narrator is making, and to reveal succinctly Igbo moral and ethical codes based on the cosmological and religious beliefs of the people about whom he is writing. Because of the importance of proverbs to Achebe's artistry and to the people's verbal art, a proper study of the proverbs found in Achebe's novels ought to begin with a full appreciation of the narrator's assertion that "Among the Igbo the art of conversation is regarded very highly, and proverbs are the palm oil with which words are eaten."[1]

From the assertion, we recognize the point that, as a highly regarded art, Igbo conversation has to have its formalities; it requires

---

[1] Chinua Achebe, *Things Fall Apart*, (London: Heinemann Educational Books Ltd., 1966), p. 6.

some responsibilities on the part of the conversationalist such as knowing what to say, when and how to say it, to whom it should be said, as well as the ability to communicate without being nasty, offensive or misunderstood. In other words, these are rhetorical demands that Igbo conversation makes on the people who practice it; they constitute a rhetorical stance which can elevate a speaker's conversation to the level of oratory. A good conversation, therefore, is the beginning of Igbo oral performance or oral literature; and proverbs are an invaluable mnemonic device for keeping the literature alive.

As a rhetorical aid and stylized verbal form, the Igbo proverb is termed by the narrator "the palm oil with which words are eaten." The metaphor is very significant because there is hardly any Igbo menu or recipe that does not include palm oil, just as there is hardly any good Igbo speech without the speaker interlacing it with some proverbs. That means proverbs are very important and current in Igbo language and literature, for they express the life and civilization of the people. And that is why they are found in folktales, folk songs, drum language, dirges, and in common prayers and incantations. Some of them could be esoteric in the sense that they are used by a group of elders and titled men and are hard to interpret because sometimes they are oracular. Their images are drawn from all walks of human and animal life—from farming, eating, sex, hunting, wrestling, angling, ritual sacrifices, etc.

Furthermore, the proverbs are both old and current in the linguistic habits of the people; they are old in the sense that they are usually the prerogative of the elders who use them to teach the younger generations the wisdom and lore of the people; and they are current in that any observant person can create his own proverbs as long as he observes the conventions of presenting them in a way that is acceptable to the people, because proverbs are a highly stylized form of verbal art. The easiest way to present new proverbs is to introduce them with either "As our elders said ... " or "As the saying goes ... " And some people would even name their fathers as the source of their proverbs. This is a way of making proverbs "the wit of one, and the wisdom of many."[2] Achebe is aware of these formal requirements for creating proverbs and he incorporates them in his novels.

He recreates traditional Igbo proverbs and creates new ones which sound like the old, because he has the eye and sensitivity of a hawk; like his hero, Ezeulu, he sees where others do not. As one of the first Igbo writers, Achebe is qualified to create proverbs without the use of "As the elders said;" after all, he is a literary elder to many an Igbo writer. At times Achebe combines the traditional and the newfangled sententious expressions into one speech in a novel such as *A Man of the People*, which happens to treat city life but has some of its incidents and episodes happening in the villages. We find this in Samalu's speech in which he scolds his son, Odili, for contemptuously challenging Chief Nanga, "a man of the people," to a political game:

> "A mad man may sometimes speak a true word," said my father, "but, you watch him, he will soon add something to it that will tell you his mind is still spoilt. My son, you have again shown your true self. When you came home with a car I thought to myself: good, sense is entering his belly at last. . . .
>
> "But, I should have known. So you really want to fight Chief Nanga! My son, why don't you fall where your pieces could be gathered?
>
> "If the money he was offering was too small why did you not say so? Why did you not ask for three or four hundred? But then your name would not be Odili if you did that. No, you have to insult the man who came to you as a friend and—let me ask you something: Do you think he will return tomorrow to beg you again with two-fifty pounds? No, no son. You have lost the sky and you have lost the ground. . ." (p. 120).

---

[2] Austin J. Shelton, "The 'Palm Oil' of Language: Proverbs in Chinua Achebe's Novels," *Modern Language Quarterly*, 30 (1969), p. 89.

"You have lost the sky and you have lost the ground" could have been introduced with "As our elders said . . . " to make it sound like an old proverb. Yet Achebe left it as it is to make it sound like a new one.

As a way of life in Igbo societies, one does not insult a person who comes to him as a friend; Odili is expected to speak his mind if he is not satisfied with something rather than insult him in silence; no enemy should be underestimated, and one must anticipate failure and its impact before challenging a formidable enemy. Also, the passage touches upon the importance of a man having good relationships with his people. For example, that Odili loses the sky and the ground means he has no tactical base at all from where to fight Nanga. That is, he has insulted his father (the earth), his home base and Nanga (the sky), his opponent who now knows without any shadow of doubt that he is an enemy, a situation of alienation and isolation for Odili. The father's scolding is prudential advice which is intended to make Odili more cautious as he works for a successful electioneering. However, whether or not Odili takes the advice is another matter.

Analysis of the Proverbs

1 *Things Fall Apart*
Achebe's use of Igbo proverbs, follows the thematic contents of the novels. For instance, on the basis of the aspirations, activities and fears of the principal character of the novel, one can generalize by saying that *Things Fall Apart* is the story of Okonkwo who, for fear of being thought weak like his unmanly father, Unoka, worked hard to bring honor to himself and to his clan, Umuofia, and in the process committed criminal offenses and moral crimes (perhaps under the influence of the gods) which eventually resulted in his own downfall. Hence, the proverbs and other sententious expressions which the author uses to comment on the events of the novel and to express the people's opinion of Okonkwo could be reduced to two main types: commendatory and admonitory proverbs. The former type is used to praise Okonkwo when he does commendable things, and the latter to admonish him for his abominable acts.

However, in between these two main types are proverbs which the author employs to comment generally on the moral and ethical lives of Umuofia clansmen.

One of the first proverbs in *Things Fall Apart* is used by Unoka (meaning "home is supreme," and suggesting the dignity of the Igbo family system) to disarm Okoye to whom he owes fewer cowries than he owes his other creditors. Unoka says: "Our elders say that the sun will shine on those who stand before it shines on those who kneel under them" (p. 7). In this context, he implies that he will pay his heavy debts first; however, the novelist uses the proverb to set the scene of the argument of the entire novel. The sun, which is a metaphor for achievement, is the center of attraction for every Umuofia man. Those who make an effort—that is, work hard enough—will get recognition before the lazy ones. The proverb, spoken by Unoka himself, foreshadows the answer he receives as he consults the oracle, Agbala:

> You have offended neither the gods nor your fathers. And when a man is at peace with his gods and his ancestors, his harvest will be good or bad according to the strength of his arm. You, Unoka, are known in all the clan for the weakness of your matchet and your hoe. When your neighbors go out with their axe to cut down virgin forests, you sow your yams on exhausted farms that take no labor to clear. They cross seven rivers to make their farms; you stay at home and offer sacrifices to a reluctant soil. Go home and work like a man (p. 16).

Unoka kneels and waits for the sun to shine on him, but of course, it does not, and so Unoka receives infamy rather than reputation. Okonkwo is aware of his father's failure. He is ashamed of it and therefore decides to aim for the sun. "Fortunately, among these people a man was judged according to his worth and not according to the worth of his father. Okonkwo was clearly cut out for great things" (p. 7).

Through personal struggle and hard work, Okonkwo becomes an achiever. He is the greatest wrestler in Umuofia, a husband of three wives, father of eight children, a great warrior who has five human heads to prove his military might, and owner of "two barns full of yams" and two titles. The narrator, speaking for the elders of Umuofia, commends Okonkwo's efforts in the words of the proverb, "As the elders said, if a child washed his hands he could eat with kings. Okonkwo had clearly washed his hands and so he ate with kings and elders" (p. 8). This proverb is preceded by the Igbo maxim, "Age was respected among his people, but achievement was revered." And it explains why Okonkwo is allowed to eat with kings and elders. That is, his maturity in the form of personal achievements breaks the hierarchical barrier between the child and the elders who themselves are also achievers.

As the story of Okonkwo's achievements unfolds, the narrator introduces the maxim, "As our people say, *a man who pays his respect to the great paves the way for his own greatness,*" which reveals Igbo youths' respect for age and reverence for achievement. The elders and achievers do not only expect the young to pay them the respect they deserve, but also custom actually demands it of the young. That is why Achebe's novels are full of praise names such as "Ogbuefi ..." and "Eze ..." as well as the respectful addressing of the elders as *"Nna ayi."* Okonkwo's use of the maxim is a reaffirmation of what the society holds to be true and adopts as a philosophy of life.

The phrase, "I have brought you this little kola," is an expression which portrays Okonkwo as humbling himself in order to become worthy of the presence of the great man. Kola is an item of tribute, actually a small nut, which signifies friendship and neighborly disposition. But as a metaphor, it underscores the smallness of Okonkwo's tribute vis-à-vis the great wealth of Nwakibie out of which Okonkwo will be given something to start life with. Okonkwo says, "A man who pays respect to the great paves the way for his own greatness" as a means of singing the praise of his benefactor and at the same time assuring Nwakibie that he, Okonkwo, is ambitious of greatness; therefore, he will work hard to take good care of Nwakibie's seed yams. The result is that having been so flattered, Nwakibie pays back compliments of greatness to Okonkwo and then grants him his request:

It pleases me to see a young man like you these days when our youth has gone so soft.... Eneke the bird says that since men have learned to shoot without missing, he has learned to fly without perching. I have learned to be stingy with my yams. But I can trust you. I know it as I look at you. As our fathers said, you can tell a ripe corn by its look. I shall give you twice four hundred yams. Go ahead and prepare your farm (p. 20).

We may add that in an actual situation, be it in Igboland or an industrial society, a borrower of yams or money must first of all create a friendly atmosphere between him and his benefactor, before asking for a loan. One way of doing so is for the borrower to sing the praise of his benefactor. Secondly, the borrower must present an impressive credit record or collateral before the loan is made. These two conditions are met by Okonkwo and that is why Nwakibie not only grants him the loan of 400 seed yams but also doubles the number.

The next commendatory proverb, "The lizard that jumped from the high iroko tree to the ground said he would praise himself if no one else did" (p. 20), is self-praise that Okonkwo utters to Nwakibie in order to make himself more attractive and thus mitigate the impact of his father's lack of reputation on his own life. It is not unlike the Igbo to utter such self-praise, if only to feel good about themselves, while seeking the admiration of their listeners. That is why Ezeulu, in a different situation though, tells his friend Akuebue:

> I can see things where other men are blind. That is why I am known and at the same time I am Unknowable. You are my friend and you know whether I am a thief or a murderer or an honest man. But you cannot know the Thing which beats the drum to which Ezeulu dances. I can see tomorrow; that is why I can tell Umuaro: *come out from this because there is death there or do this because there is profit in it*. If they listen to me, o-o; if they refuse to listen, o-o, I have passed the stage of dancing to receive presents (*AOG*, p. 132).

Okonkwo's self-praise is part of his saying "yes, for when a man says yes, his *chi* says yes also" (*TFA*, p. 25). In other words, "As a man danced so were the drums beaten for him" (*AOG*, p. 70).

Achebe portrays the elders of Okonkwo's society as fairminded because, in spite of the fame Okonkwo's successes and achievements bring to them, they are not afraid to admonish Okonkwo with proverbs when he makes a mistake. For example, at a kindred meeting, Okonkwo unwittingly calls an untitled man a woman and

> Everybody at the kindred meeting took sides with Osugo when Okonkwo called him a woman. The oldest man present said sternly that *those whose palm kernels were cracked for them by a benevolent spirit should not forget to be humble.* Okonkwo said he was sorry for what he had said, and the meeting continued (p. 24).

The proverb in this passage is an indirect means that the old man uses to remind Okonkwo of his poor parentage without openly calling him the son of an *agbala*, adding that Okonkwo would not be an achiever without the help of a "benevolent spirit." The narrator's comment which follows the incident appears to contradict the truth of the proverb:

> But it was not really true that Okonkwo's palm kernels had been cracked for him by a benevolent spirit. He had cracked them for himself. Anyone who knew his grim struggle against poverty and misfortune could not say he had been lucky. If ever a man deserved his success, that man was Okonkwo. At an early age he had achieved fame as the greatest wrestler in the land. That was not luck. At the most one could say that his *chi* or personal god was good. But the Igbo people have a proverb that when a man says yes his *chi* says yes also. Okonkwo said yes very strongly; so his *chi* agreed. And not only his *chi* but his clan too, because it judged a man by the work of his hands (p. 24-25).

Indeed, Okonkwo is everything the narrator says he is, but when we trace the origin of Okonkwo's success as a wealthy farmer and owner of two yam barns, husband of three wives and taker of two titles, we then realize the truth, even the wisdom, of the proverb. At the literal level of the proverb, benevolent spirit refers to his personal god or *chi*, but deeply considered, Nwakibie is the personal god or "benevolent spirit" who cracked Okonkwo's "palm kernel." If Nwakibie had refused to grant him a loan of seed yams, Okonkwo would not have "paved the way for his own greatness" (p. 18). The narrator's comment is made only as a reflection of what may have motivated Okonkwo to call Osugo a woman. From his even-handed treatment of the themes of the novel, it seems that the apparent contradiction between the truth of the old man's proverb and the narrator's comment is a stylistic device which Achebe uses to show the two sides to Okonkwo's success and achievement; his hard work and struggle on the one hand, and the endowment of a benevolent clansman on the other.

Both of these elements are the key to his success. He cannot maintain one and neglect the other and still be a successful man. In addition to both elements, there is the need for a man to be humble among his fellow clansmen and not offend their gods. All these requirements are contained in a passage we have briefly looked at earlier on—that is, the passage where Chika, the priestess of Agbala, tells Unoka that "when a man is at peace with his gods and his ancestors, his harvest will be good or bad according to the strength of his arm" (p. 16). From it, we can begin to see that in spite of his achievements, Okonkwo is not better than his father in terms of deficiencies. Unoka apparently had crops to sow but he did not work hard enough to reap good harvests, and so he dies a poor man. On a more positive note, Unoka does not disobey the gods and men; he got along very well with people as he played music—the food of love and life—to them. But because his people used a different parameter to measure success, he was adjudged an *agbala*.

Okonkwo, on the other hand, is aggressive, energetic and hardworking. He brings honor to his clan and to himself as the greatest wrestler in Umuofia. His military might is impressive enough to earn him the honor of serving as emissary of war to Mbaino. On the negative side, however, he bullies and fights his family; and most seriously, he offends his elders and gods: the former he disobeys and the latter he commits abominations against, such as killing a clansman inadvertently and an adopted son willfully. And so when he desecrates the Week of Peace by beating one of his wives in a fit of rage, he is admonished with a proverb which expresses the people's disapproval, even though he has offered the appropriate purification sacrifice:

> People said he had no respect for the gods of the clan. His enemies said his good fortune had gone to his head. They called him the little bird *nza* who so far forgot himself after a heavy meal that he challenged his *chi* (p. 28).

This is the second public denunciation of Okonkwo's inordinate acts through the use of a proverb. When he kills Ikemefuna and the head messenger, he is reproved by Obierika and the people respectively without mincing their words. But it is Okonkwo who tries to proverbialize, probably to confuse his hearer. He attempts to justify his brutal killing of Ikemefuna before his friend, Obierika, by saying: "The Earth cannot punish me for obeying her messenger," adding the proverb, "... A child's fingers are not scalded by a piece of hot yam which its mother puts into its palm" (p. 61). But Obierika who always exercises good judgement makes it clear to him that his act was not authorized by Ani, therefore, merits her punishment.

The proverb, "A child's fingers are not scalded by a piece of hot yam which its mother puts into its palm," stresses the importance of obedience and responsibility in traditional Igboland. The child, representing any Igbo citizen, must submit to the authority of Ani (who is referred to in the proverb as mother because the role of Ani, the Earth-goddess, is the subject-matter). For her part, the goddess is responsible for ensuring the safety of the child that she is sending on an errand. In an actual (social) situation, a mother picks out a piece of yam from a boiling pot with tongs, blows cool air on the yam before handing it out to the child. The child has no way of knowing how cool the yam is before receiving it from its mother, but it relies on the knowledge that its mother would never allow its palms to be scalded. If indeed its palms are scalded, the mother is to blame for not carrying out her parental duties properly. We will come to this notion of obedience and responsibility when we discuss Ezeulu and Ulu; but considering Okonkwo's case, we see a man who is doing a dangerous and brutal job which no one asked him to do;

therefore, he cannot look for Ani's parental protection when the consequences of his acts catch up with him.

2 No Longer at Ease

We witness the beginning of the disintegration of traditional Igbo society in *Things Fall Apart* as a result of the coming of the white men into Umuofia (with their religion, trade and government) which helps to weaken further a society that already has some social weaknesses such as killing of twins and ostracizing their mothers, dedicating some innocent citizens to gods and making them outcasts or *osu*, brutally killing fellow Igbo people of other clans at the least provocation, and rigidly stratifying society into "haves" and "have nots," the free and the unfree. The white men offer the downtrodden of the society a new hope and a seemingly better quality of life in the form of Western education, Christian religion, new business opportunities and new jobs. For instance, one could become a cleric, a civil servant, or find other jobs which take people away from Igboland to other parts of Nigeria and even beyond.

Achebe's *No Longer at Ease* dramatizes the unease of a new man, Obi Okonkwo, torn between two worlds of his new society—the traditional struggling to survive and the new not yet weaned. In this novel, therefore, we find the dominant proverbs of corruption and protectiveness being used by both the narrator and the people themselves to comment on the new social conditions and the new man.

No Longer at Ease begins with the end of its dramatic action; the hero of the novel and Okonkwo's grandson, Obi Okonkwo, has already committed a social crime—taking of bribes—for which he is being tried in a Lagos Law Court, as well as a religious sin—accepting an *osu* as a fiancée. His people, members of Umuofia Progressive Union in Lagos, are summoned to save him from the shame of imprisonment and summary dismissal from his public service position. To save him would also mean saving themselves from clan disgrace since "if one finger brings oil it soils the others" (p. 68). But some members are not happy about helping Obi any further because they have already done so much for him:

> 'We paid eight hundred pounds to train him in England,' said one

of them. 'But instead of being grateful he insults us because of a useless girl. And now we are being called together again to find more money for him. What does he do with his big salary? My own opinion is that we have already done too much for him' (p. 4).

This opinion, though popular, is not taken very seriously because Obi must first be saved before being chastised:

> For, as the President pointed out, a kinsman in trouble had to be saved, not blamed; anger against a brother was felt in the flesh, not in the bone. And so the Union decided to pay for the services of a lawyer from their funds (p. 4).

The maxim in this passage, "A kinsman in trouble had to be saved, not blamed; anger against a brother was felt in the flesh, not in the bone," does two things: first, it points up the urgency of group salvation of Obi by Umuofia, a salvation which could be hindered by people wasting precious time blaming Obi; second, it also indicates the protectiveness of Umuofia clansmen, a characteristic expressed in another proverb, "An only palm fruit does not get lost in the fire" (p. 6).

According to Gareth Griffiths,

> The central theme of *No Longer at Ease* is the distance between what is said to be and what is. For example, the morality of public office offered by Mr. Green, the white civil servant, is a facade, like the accountant's clean collar in Conrad's *Heart of Darkness*. It asserts an ideal, but one irrelevant to the problems of the time and place; and it is bitterly exposed in Mr. Green's tired and cliché-ridden sermons on the effects of the climate on the 'African character.' But equally unacceptable is the UPS [sic] President's suggestion that Obi's crime is not that he has accepted a bribe, but that he has not taken 'time to look around first and know what is what.' The proverbial morality of the tribe is no clear guide in this new world, as the language of the UPS members clearly shows.

And he quotes the narrator:

The President said it was a thing of shame for a man in the senior service to go to prison for twenty pounds. He repeated twenty pounds, spitting it out. 'I am against people reaping where they have not sown. But we have a saying that if you want to eat a toad you should look for a fat and juicy one.'[3]

Logical and persuasive as his argument may sound here, it is unfortunate that Griffiths wrongly interprets what he calls "the proverbial morality of the tribe," apparently because he mixes up two speakers in the passage and more so because he fails to apprehend the mood of the meeting and the cultural reference of the President's proverb.

The President does *not* suggest "that Obi's crime is not that he has accepted a bribe but that he has not taken 'time to look around first and know what is what'," as Griffiths inaccurately alleges. Everybody, including the President, is angry because of the series of disappointments they have had with Obi, who fails to find jobs for his fellow clansmen, proposes to marry an *osu* against all advice, and who, at the moment, brings a "national" disgrace to the entire clan. In fact, one of those talking excitedly about the latest scandal summarizes the people's disappointment and frustration when he says:

> 'I know it was a bad case.... We are just throwing money away. What do our people say? He that fights for a ne'er-do-well has nothing to show for it except a head covered in earth and grime' (p. 5).

It is against this background and mood that the President's, as well as other men's, utterances should be evaluated and interpreted. Surely, the President recognizes Obi's crime of accepting a bribe. "I am against people reaping where they have not sown," is his first reaction and a condemnation of the crime. He adds, "But we have

---

[3] Gareth Griffiths, "Language and Action in the Novels of Chinua Achebe," *African Literature Today*, 5 (1971), p. 92.

a saying that if you want to eat a toad you should look for a fat and juicy one"—the meaning of which Griffiths misses; it is a saying which expresses a traditional Igbo work ethic, "Whatever you want to be, be the best in it," and not a particular moral principle.

In the first place, a toad is not a pleasant animal to eat, just as taking bribes is not a pleasant thing for a decent man to do. But should Obi be tempted, as he was, to eat a toad, he should have had an impressive thing to show for it; the toad should be temptingly fat and juicy, so that anyone seeing its size can understand why he was overcome by the temptation. Secondly, eating a toad is like performing a stunt; one has to go for a super performance that is worth the risk once one decides to do it at all. Thus, when the President says it was a thing of shame for a man in the senior service to go to prison for twenty pounds, he is condemning the extravagance of their prodigal son, Obi; an extravagance which created, in the first place, the need for him to look for more money from illegal sources. And Umuofia clansmen, especially Obi's grandfather, are known for aiming higher. For instance, when Okonkwo seeks revenge in *Things Fall Apart*, he goes for the head messenger. Had Obi accepted a huge amount of money as bribes, the President would have condemned the crime, for he is against anyone reaping where he has not sown; but he would have admired Obi's ambition. It is in this sense that one agrees with Lindfors who says that "Obi is an unheroic figure and his kinsmen who attend his trial cannot understand why he took such risks for so little profit."[4] It is the combination of the pettiness of the crime and the smallness of the amount of the bribe that disgusts the President and causes him to spit out Obi's activity, which is not worth the scandal it has caused among his kinsmen. Indeed, Obi's low ambition makes him "a bird that flies off the earth and lands on an anthill. It is still on the ground" (p. 146).

Obi is further denounced for being tactless in carrying out his criminal offense of accepting a bribe:

---

[4] Bernth Lindfors, *Folklore in Nigerian Literatures* (New York: Africana Publishing Company, 1973), p. 81.

'It is all lack of experience,' said another man. 'He should not have accepted the money himself. What *others do* [my emphasis] is tell you to go and hand it to their houseboy. Obi tried to do what everyone does without finding out how it was done' (p. 5).

This is another statement that Griffiths regards as part of "the proverbial morality of the tribe." The clansman, who makes the statement, is not condoning bribery as a criminal offense; rather he is criticizing the failure of a fellow clansman. He says "others do" tactfully accept bribes, and he tells how. Those others may or may not be Umuofia Civil Servants alone who occupy positions of influence. They may have accepted bribes from the Umuofia man in the manner described. So, Achebe uses the bribery case of Obi as a moral theme, to condemn the proverbial culture of the Igbo who regarded cheating government, an alien institution, as lying outside the proper boundaries of morality.

Commenting on the morality of *Things Fall Apart* and *No Longer at Ease*. Lindfors argues that:

> Okonkwo erred by daring to attempt something he did not have the power to achieve; this makes him a tragic hero. Obi erred by stooping to take bribes; this makes him a crook. To put it in proverbial terms: Okonkwo wrestles his *chi*, Obi swallows a toad. It is not only the stupidity but the contemptibility of Obi's ways that many of the proverbs in the novel [*NLAE*] help to underscore.[5]

And Griffiths responds to it by saying:

> But the process seems to me to be more complex, and the role of the proverbial commentary more ambiguous. It is not only a reduction in the hero we observe, but also a reduction in the scale of the moral universe he moves into. In the proverbial commentary we are aware not only of Obi's inadequacy, but also of the inadequacy of the proverbial culture itself. It no longer provides a valid morality

---

[5] *Ibid.*, p. 82.

from which Obi's 'crookedness' excludes him. In fact, it is one source of the pressure which makes Obi capitulate to the practice of his time and take bribes. It is this proverbial wisdom on which the UPS draws to justify its demands that Obi acts on behalf of the tribal community. Indeed, it would seem that one of the major functions of his residual tribal organization is to effect bribes and to obtain posts under false pretenses.[6]

While agreeing with Griffiths to an extent that Obi's situation and the moral universe he moves into are more complex than Lindfors apparently represents them in his proverbial analogy, we find that there is no doubt that to the people most of the proverbs in the novel help to underscore the stupidity and contemptibility of Obi's ways. Of course, we have already explained above why the people feel that way about Obi. Also, we agree with Griffiths that the role of the proverbial commentary is more ambiguous (than it was in *Things Fall Apart*) because the people's proverbial culture is dual in nature: ethnic and national. And that is a situation which perhaps makes the culture inadequate. The obvious implication is that for Obi to survive, he has to take prudential measures as he acts in the two worlds of the novel. For there are two moral worlds: the macrocosmic world of Lagos (Nigeria) and the microcosmic world of Umuofia kinsmen. In fact, the President who knows how to survive in both worlds does not lose his temper (as some of his clansmen somehow justifiably have done) to the point of abandoning Obi; he knows that it is his responsibility to ensure that "An only palm fruit does not get lost in the fire." In fact, we find more proverbs of protectiveness in the novel:

The fox must be chased away first, after that the hen might be warned against wandering into the bush (p. 5).

If all snakes live together in one place, who would approach them? [a proverb about unity which results in the protection of individu-

---

[6] Griffiths, *op. cit.*, p. 93.

als] (p. 8).

The kinsman in trouble had to be saved, not blamed; anger against a brother was felt in the flesh, not in the bone (p. 5).

The emphasis on kinship and unity is also expressed in the people's aphoristic song:

> He that has a brother must hold him to his heart,
> For a kinsman cannot be bought in the market.
> Neither is a brother bought with money. (p. 129)

These are examples of sayings which express the maxims and life philosophy of Umuofia clansmen abroad, and which also reflect the proverbial culture of the clan at home. Umuofia Progressive Union has a duty to perform to Obi, and in turn Obi has to perform his to them as well. Unfortunately for Obi, their demands include helping his clansmen "to get up"[7] by finding them jobs. The moral dilemma the situation poses for Obi is overwhelming, but had he been closer to his people and listened to some of their advice, he may have avoided some of the issues which led to his taking bribes—a social offense which earns him a term of imprisonment.

It may be argued persuasively that there is some ambiguity in the Umuofia maxim, "Ours is ours but mine is mine" (p. 29). Lindfors argues that:

> Obi accepts some of the values expressed in these proverbs, but his own individualistic attitude is probably best summed up in the saying "Ours is ours but mine is mine." Obi's problem lies in having to make choices between the old values and the new, between "ours" and "mine."[8]

---

[7] Victor Uchendu, *The Igbo of Southeast Nigeria* (New York: Holt, Rinehart and Winston, 1965), pp. 34-37.

[8] Lindfors, *op. cit.*, p. 104.

That may be true from Obi's point of view; but from Umuofia's point of view, as well as that of the narrator, Obi's problem lies in having to make choices between the cultural values of his native Igbo and the national aspirations of Nigeria. To them, the ethnic progress is more important than the national. This might sound unpatriotic of Umuofia Progressive Union, but that is the way it is; for the narrator reports:

> "Have they given you a job yet?" the chairman asked obi over the music. In Nigeria the government was 'they.' It had nothing to do with you or me. It was an alien institution and people's business was to get as much from it as they could without getting into trouble (NLAE, pp. 29-30).

Here is the people's concept of the Nigerian nation. It is one which questions the birth of the Nigerian nation as a creation of the British. Individual ethnic groups do not believe in it, and that is one reason why tribalism is a major social disease in Nigeria. We find this theme also in A Man of the People. To the people, *tribalism* is real. Obi attempts to deal with the corruption that *tribalism* breeds but fails because he does not possess the moral stature for the battle. Indeed, Achebe wants to confront it very seriously and more thoroughly in his writing, but he waits until his fourth novel. For the moment, however, he must go back to his *tribal* society, looking for answers; that way Achebe can tell Nigerians (and readers of Nigerian literature) "where the rain started to beat them."[9]

3 Arrow of God

Achebe's third novel, *Arrow of God*, especially its hero Ezeulu, has been looked at extensively in chapters III and IV of this study; therefore, what follows here is just a brief discussion of the proverbs contained in it.

The theme of the destruction of traditional Igbo ways, which

---

[9] Chinua Achebe, "The Role of a Writer in a New Nation," *Nigeria Magazine*, 81 (June 1964), p. 158.

Achebe explores in *Things Fall Apart*, is still his main preoccupation in *Arrow of God*. Hence, we find that the dominant proverbs and other aphoristic expressions are those of confrontation and destruction. There is confrontation between local priests, traditional and foreign religions, village and alien administrations, one village and another within Umuaro clan; and finally, men attempt to make their human quarrels divine wars, interpreting their personal wills as those of their gods. Achebe uses proverbs to make subtle comments on the human drama, letting us into the minds of the characters. The characters themselves employ proverbs as a means of lending authenticity to their points of view, so that in some cases the reader notices ambiguities and contradictions in the application of the proverbs. We hasten to remark that the proverbs do not change, only their situations and applications are subject to change.

The major characters, Ezeulu, Nwaka, Captain Winterbottom, Oduche, and the Umuaro elders, are all prepared to fight whomever they perceive as enemies, in spite of their limited vision of events. Each of them is troubled by a lack of accurate understanding of what others are doing. Oftentimes, they misjudge their enemies' intention and thus add more fuel to the general tension and confusion or conflicts that one finds in the novel. Only the omniscient reporter and the readers are in a privileged position to appraise the characters' individual roles and pass a moral judgement on their aspirations and failures.

The first controversial act which causes conflicts in the novel is Ezeulu's decision to send his son, Oduche, to the Christian church and school to "be [his] eye there." It draws criticism from his enemies, especially Nwaka. Furthermore, it is the constant reference to Oduche's role in the conflicts that makes his name an excellent example of how Achebe uses names to comment on issues in his novels. Oduche means "that which is on the mind." Indeed, Oduche's activities are the concern of everybody in the novel: his father sends him to the Christians as a secret agent; his mother thinks he is sacrificed to the alien religion; Ezidemili believes Ezeulu sent Oduche to kill his sacred python; and Mr. Goodcountry knows Oduche is the rock on which he will build his new church. That is, Oduche is on the mind of everybody. Let us see how Ezeulu uses him to advantage.

Ezeulu is aware of the change which is taking place in his society and is concerned about it. He, however, does not want to deal with it in a tactless manner as Okonkwo does in *Things Fall Apart*; so he sends his son to the Christians, and befriends the head of the British Administration, Captain Winterbottom. He attempts to justify his rueful decision by quoting two proverbs:

> I am like the bird Eneke-nti-oba. When his friends asked him why he was always on the wing he replied: "Men of today have learned to shoot without missing and so I have learned to fly without perching."
>
> "The world is like a Mask dancing. If you want to see it well you do not stand in one place" (pp. 45-46).

To explain the proverbs to Oduche he adds:

> "My spirit tells me that those who do not befriend the white man today will be saying *had we known* tomorrow" (p. 46).

That sounds good, but it is a move that can cause his abdication of power as the Chief Priest of Ulu. By comparing himself with Eneke-nti-oba, Ezeulu is praising himself for being naturally endowed with foresight. Eneke-nti-oba is a bird with ears (*nti*) shaped like a traditional dish made from a gourd (*oba*). One might regard it as a listening device (Frisbee-shaped) which enables him to know in advance when hunters approach. Thus he flies away from them before they even aim and shoot. Because he eludes the hunters, they think he is always on the wing. As Ezeulu uses it, the proverb emphasizes the precaution that one takes before it is too late to avoid danger. It is also a precaution that requires constant movement and adjustment, like the movement of a Mask dancing, which helps one to see all sides to a thing—the implied meaning of the second proverb.

Apart from the opposition which comes from Ezeulu's enemies, the Chief Priest has already begun to feel the heat of dividing his own household into Christian and non-Christian parties. Oduche is paying more allegiance to his new-found religion than to his old one. The school can now send him anywhere without first of all obtaining his father's permission. So Ezeulu says:

> Listen to what I shall say now. *When a handshake goes beyond the elbow we know it has turned to another thing.* It was I who sent you to join those people because of my friendship with the white man, Wintabota.... I did not send you so that you might leave your duty in my household (pp. 13-14).

The proverb refers to confrontation. During the "Hunting Age", two hunters used to shake hands as a way of showing that none of them was armed with stones or herbs to harm the other. But "when the handshake went beyond the elbow," the other knew that it had turned into another thing—challenge to a wrestling match, or even physical assault. Whatever form it took, the challenger had some advantage over the challenged because the latter was unprepared for what he saw. That is, what began as exchange of pleasantries ended in an unfair fight.

Applied to the proverbial situation in the novel, the school, as agent of Captain Winterbottom, is taking advantage of Ezeulu by exploiting his "friendship with the white man." The wrestling motif in this proverb foreshadows the disadvantage Ezeulu suffers in the end. He thinks the white administrators are very powerful, so he wants to beat them to their own game by sending Oduche to understudy them and come back to strengthen his own powers. He explains his reason for doing so to his friend, Akuebue, using proverbial imagery: "Shall I tell you why I sent my son? Then listen. A disease that has never been seen before cannot be cured with everyday herbs" (p. 133). In other words, he reveals a motive which shows he wants to bite the white man before he gets bitten. His friend warns against it because it is a dangerous and ambiguous adventure:

> If you send your son to join strangers in desecrating the land, you will be alone. You may go and mark it on that wall to remind you that I said so (p. 134).

Ezeulu ignores the warning and ends up alienating both his people and the white administrators.

The notion of desecration embodied in Akuebue's reply is an echo of Ezeulu's own word. They both are talking about the desecration of traditional Igbo religion and the eventual destruction of some of their traditional institutions. Ezeulu believes that the whites are doing this desecrating. Therefore, as a Chief Priest who "takes away" the sins of people once a year, during the Festival of the Pumpkin Leaves, Ezeulu apparently wants to offer a purification sacrifice:

> A disease that has never been seen before cannot be cured with everyday herbs. When we want to make a charm we look for the animal whose blood can match its power; if a chicken cannot do it we look for a goat or a ram; if that is not sufficient we send for a bull. But sometimes even a bull does not suffice, then we must look for a human (p. 133).

Lindfors observes that "Ezeulu's son is to be the human sacrifice which will enable the clan to make medicine of sufficient strength to hold the new disease in check. In other words, Ezeulu decided to sacrifice his son in order to gain power to cope with the changing times."[10] If this is so, why would it be a one man's decision and not that of the entire clan? However, Akuebue is talking about the desecration of the institution of Ezeulu's own office. The sacrifice Ezeulu offers for it is much more severe than the loss of Oduche; in addition, it requires the sudden death of Obika, which dements the Chief Priest at last.

Oduche creates a scene when he captures and imprisons a sacred python. His father, Ezeulu, and the rest of his household are drawn to Oduche's strange, moving school bus. As Ezeulu examines the box, he commands his family to keep their distance: "Every one of you go back to the house; 'The inquisitive monkey gets a bullet in the face.'" Shelton accurately explains how it applies to Ezeulu himself:

---

[10] Lindfors, *op. cit.*, p. 104.

Ironically, this applies to his own case, his own desire to learn from the Christians, for out of a desire to know, he caused this outrage. Although Oduche releases the python, his act was nonetheless abominable, and leads Anosi to comment: "I have already said that what this new religion will bring to Umuaro wears a hat on its head" (p. 55).

This is probably Achebe's figure of speech, but remarkably like an *ilu*, revealing that his metaphor making is fundamentally traditionalist. Similar is the figure of speech which Edogo, Ezeulu's son, overhears: "What that man Ezeulu will bring to Umuaro is pregnant and nursing a baby at the same time" (p. 63).[11]

The python episode, coupled with Captain Winterbottom's rather "unmannerly" summons of Ezeulu to the Government Hill within twenty hours, gives Ezeulu's enemies the chance to condemn publicly his unseemly ties with the white man, as they gather to consider what is becoming at the moment a clan emergency. Nwaka, Ezeulu's archenemy, replies in proverbs that Ezeulu should make a choice between doing something to end his friendship with the white man and suffering the consequences of the friendship *alone*:

> "Does Ezeulu think that their friendship should stop short of entering each other's house? Does he want the white man to be his friend only by word of mouth? Did not our elders tell us that as soon as we shake hands with a leper he will want an embrace?
> ... What I say is this ... a man who brings ant ridden faggots into his hut should expect the visit of lizards. But if Ezeulu is now telling us that he is tired of the white man's friendship our advice to him should be: *You tied the knot, you should also know how to undo it. You passed the shit that is smelling; you should carry it away.* Fortunately the evil charm brought in at the end of a pole is not too difficult to take outside again" (pp. 143-144).

---

[11] Shelton, *op. cit.*, p. 104.

From these proverbs we notice the images of disease, contamination, and unrest that the characters use to describe the white man's presence and activities in traditional Igbo societies of Umuofia in *Things Fall Apart* and Umuaro in *Arrow of God.* First, the white man has a "white skin," which is an Igbo metaphor for leprosy; a leper is totally isolated for fear of his contaminating others. So, if anyone wants to shake hands with a leper, they argue, he should be prepared to embrace the leper as well; for that is the easiest method a leper uses to "convert" others into the "brotherhood" of lepers. Second, the unrest referred to in the proverb about ant ridden faggots is not only a disharmony that Christianity brings between believers and non-believers wherever it is allowed to thrive, but also the noise that follows the proselytizing activities such as open air preaching, ringing of church bells at odd hours, and sing-song nights. The religious activities of the Christians are in direct opposition to traditional Igbo religious activities.

Nwaka remarks, finally, that "Fortunately the evil charm brought in at the end of a pole is not too difficult to take outside again," meaning that Ezeulu's friendship with Captain Winterbottom is easy to sever because the white man is an outsider. That is, Ezeulu can do without the relationship, if he wants to, without any loss at all.

On the matter of the white man's presence being a source of social unrest in Umuaro, Ezeulu and the leaders of Umuaro are agreed. This is why both parties continue to use the proverb about the ant ridden faggots. Lindfors says:

> It is worth noting that the proverb about bringing ant ridden faggots home is quoted twice by Ezeulu himself. He uses it to reproach himself when his mission educated son is found trying to kill a sacred python (p. 72).

Here, monetarily at least, Ezeulu seems willing to accept responsibility for the abomination. Ezeulu uses the proverb a second time when a friend accuses him of betraying his people by sending his son to the white man's school. Ezeulu counters by pointing out that he did not bring the white man to his people; rather, his people brought the white man upon themselves by failing to oppose him when he first arrived. If they wish to blame someone, they should blame themselves for meekly submitting to the white man's presence and power. "The man who brings ant ridden faggots into his hut should not grumble when lizards begin to pay him a visit" (p. 163). This is a key proverb in *Arrow of God* for it enunciates a major theme: that a man is responsible for his actions and must bear their consequences.[12]

It is also a major theme in *Things Fall Apart*. For, the accusation that Ezeulu levels against Umuaro should belong more properly to Umuofia, Okonkwo's society, where the opposition of the white man and his institutions is a one man struggle. Obierika laments his people's meek submission to the white man's presence and power as he tells Okonkwo:

> The white man is very clever. He came quietly and peaceably with his religion. We were amused at his foolishness and allowed him to stay. Now he has won our brothers, and our clan can no longer act like one. He has put a knife on the things that held us together and we have fallen apart (*TFA*, p. 160).

Just as Okonkwo uses a proverb to shift the responsibility of his murdering Ikemefuna to the Earth-goddess, saying that "A child's fingers are not scalded by a piece of hot yam which its mother puts into its palm" (p. 61), so does Ezeulu who uses the "ant ridden faggots" proverb to blame Umuaro leaders for waging a war of blame against Okperi, which brought the white man's armed forces to their clan. In addition, Ezeulu repeats among other proverbs, the very proverb Okonkwo uses on Ani to shift blame from himself to Ulu, chastising Ulu indirectly for not stretching out his parental arms to protect him during a crisis; but he forgets that his failure to obey his clan leaders and name the day for the New Yam Feast is an abomination: to men and to their gods which requires cleansing with human blood.

Obika is to be that sacrificial ram that his father involuntarily

---

[12] Lindfors, *op. cit.*, p. 86.

offers for appeasement. As Obika begins the ritual race of *ogbazulobodo* he recites proverbs which heighten the awe of the night spirit, foreshadow the destruction of Ezeulu (including Obika's sudden death), and describe Ezeulu's present dilemma in Umuaro. The poetic qualities of the proverbs help to heighten the emotional response of the readers (who understand the meanings of the proverbs) to the impending tragedy. Some of the proverbs are:

(a) *The fly that struts around on a mound of excrement wastes his time; the mound will always be greater than the fly.* The fly is Ezeulu trying to challenge his people, the proverbial mound of excrement. That is, the people will always be stronger than he, the individual.

(b) *It is ofo that gives rainwater power to cut dry earth.* This refers to the ascribed power of Ezeulu (from the people and their god, Ulu) that enables him to perform difficult spiritual duties; it also refers to the superior intelligence he boasts of having. That power is potent only when exercised judiciously.

(c) *When the air is fouled by a man on top of a palm tree the fly is confused.* The man on top of a palm tree is Ezeulu who plunges his people into spiritual confusion, instead of guiding them; so the people look for salvation in the Christian church.

(d) *Even while people are still talking about the man Rat bit to death Lizard takes money to have his teeth filed.* Even as Ezeulu and his family are worried over the public enemy they have become as a result of Ezeulu's failure to name the day of the New Yam Feast, they are thrust into further confusion and worry by the death of Obika.

(e) *He who will swallow udala seeds must consider the size of his anus.* Ezeulu ought to have considered the limits of his powers before engaging in a long drawn fight with his people.

(f) *The fly that has no one to advise him follows the corpse into the ground.* As Ezeulu rejects the advice of people such as Akuebue and his fellow elders because he enjoys using his spiritual powers against his people, he is consumed by the same absolute power that he wields.

(g) *The mighty tree falls and the little birds scatter.* Ezeulu's destruction instills fear into less powerful men of the clan.

(h) *When death wants to take a little dog it prevents it from smelling even excrement.* This applies to both Ezeulu and Obika; Ezeulu is warned about the consequences of the course of action he plans to take against his people, but he fails to heed any advice because he is fated to be destroyed. In the same manner, Obika fails to accept the warning his body gives him as he suffers from fever because he wants to save his family from further public scandal (p. 225-226). When Obika dies and Ezeulu is informed about the disaster, he feels betrayed by Ulu, the god he has served so well. So he meditates aloud in the form of proverbial commentary:

> But why, he asks himself again and again, why had Ulu chosen to deal thus with him to strike him down and then cover him with mud? What was his offense? Had he not divined the god's will and obeyed it? When was it ever heard that a child was scalded by the piece of yam its own mother put in its palm? What man would send his son with a potsherd to bring fire from a neighbor's hut and then unleash rain on him? Who ever sent his son up the palm to gather nuts and then took an axe and felled the tree? But today such a thing had happened before the eyes of all. What could it point to but the collapse and ruin of things? Then a god, finding himself powerless, might take flight and in one final, backward glance at his abandoned worshippers cry:
>
>> If the rat cannot flee fast enough
>> Let him make way for the tortoise! (p. 229).

The questions in this passage, like most other rhetorical questions, are not intended to be answered but to raise important issues. They can be reduced to a single question, "What kind of god is Ulu who so betrays his loyal priest at the time of crises?" But before attempting an answer, we need to ask another question—namely, "Who is asking these questions and under what circumstances?" To answer the last question first, Ezeulu is asking these questions; after losing a son, he is delirious and wants the sympathy of the very audience that he is attempting to deceive, by making emotional statements intended to shift the responsibility of the disaster he brings to his family and clan to an unspeaking god. For even if the opinion of Ulu is sought on the matter, Ezeulu is still the one to tell the oracle.

The answer to the first question is found in Chapter III of this study, where we argued that Ulu, who treats his Chief Priest the way we have seen, is Ezeulu's personified obsession for revenge. It is he who, finding himself powerless before another *god*—the power of the people—takes flight and in one final, backward glance at his worshipper, Ezeulu, cries, "You thought I could help you to win a fight against your own people?" It is that Ulu of whom Shelton says, "but Ulu is a trickster himself,"[13] and not the Ulu, Umuaro clan god of security. It is in this sense that we agree with Shelton that

> *Arrow of God* is a story centered upon Ezeulu's struggle to maintain or increase his own god's power and prestige, the story of a man in high position who behaves strangely by sending his son among the Christians, who is too stubbornly proud, whose extreme individualism is barely hidden (if at all) under quite superficial rationalism, who too narrowly and inflexibly interprets religious regulations and thereby sets himself and his god against his people, with the result that the people and even the Christians win, while he and his god lose.[14]

4 A Man of the People

In the fourth novel, *A Man of the People*, Achebe deals with the problem of political corruption in contemporary Nigeria. As is to be expected, most of the sententious expressions are no longer as traditional as they are in *Things Fall Apart* and *Arrow of God* because both the villagers and the people of the city found in *A Man of the People* have been affected by "modern" ways, including contemporary political, economic, religious and educational systems, all expressed in a language which is neither traditional nor modern. The proverbs that Achebe uses to reflect the people's thought, wisdom, morality

---

[13] Shelton, *op. cit.*, p. 106.
[14] *Ibid.*, p. 106.

and philosophy of life are as contemporary as the socio-economic and political systems of the society. Hence, the dominant proverbs and maxims are those of corruption and destruction.

The novel dramatizes the political and moral lives of two principal characters, M.A. Nanga, M.P. and Minister of Culture, and a young school teacher, Odili Samalu. Nanga is a corrupt politician who manages to use all subtle but immoral methods to persuade the electorate to regard him as "a man of the people." He makes it impossible for his young opponent, Odili, to convince the same electorate of the political corruption that goes on in their society. Since Odili's political motivation grows out of his revenge for Nanga's seduction of his mistress, it is hard for the reader to know whether Odili's political fervor is an expression of his inherent nationalism or mere revenge. Odili, in fact, tries to seduce Nanga's fiancee who is groomed to become Nanga's "parlor wife." In the end, Odili loses the political battle but wins the marital game as he at last marries Nanga's fiancee. Nanga, on the other hand, loses both struggles because a military coup occurs which makes him lose his job, and he is also locked up with "every member of the Government" (p. 65).

Earlier on, while claiming to be "a man of the people," and as a way of proving to Odili, in particular, and the people in general that he is good and educated, Nanga uses such pious platitudes as "Not what I have but what I do is my kingdom" (p. 3) and "Do the right and shame the Devil" (p. 12); but his ruthless drive for money and power is far from being pious. And when criticized, he accuses his critics of "character assassination" and answers that "no one is perfect except God" (p. 75). Furthermore, he frequently complains of the troubles and burdens that Government Ministers have to bear and readily agrees when someone remarks, "Uneasy lies the head that wears the crown" (p. 68). These are sententious expressions that characterize Nanga and his society. Nanga uses them to deceive the less "educated" and ignorant electorate who have been taught during the colonial era that everything Western was superior to anything traditional. Unfortunately, Nanga only says these maxims but he does not sincerely practice them. Thus, he becomes "one of the finest rogues in Nigerian fiction."[15]

Nanga's political opponent, Odili, has his own platitudes to express. As a more educated person than Nanga, he uses foreign literary cliches, Biblical metaphors, and proverbial expressions to "beautify" his conversations and speeches as a way of proving that he is not only more Westernized, but also that he is more scholarly than his opponent. Lindfors remarks that "His narrative is sprinkled with imported metaphors and proverbial expressions—e.g., 'kicked the bucket,' (p. 28) 'pass through the eye of a needle,' (p. 63) 'one stone to kill two birds with,' (p. 152) 'attack ... is the best defense,' (p. 162) 'a bird in the hand' (p. 165)—but he always uses them appropriately."[16]

The movement of the dramatic action of the novel begins from the city and goes to the countryside. Indirectly, Achebe is implying that the political corruption inherent in the modern political institutions and practices are foreign influences on the traditional systems.

Such immoral influence come in the forms of white man's money and business practices. The corrupting influence of the white man's money on Igbo community life is constantly decried by people who realize the great extent that some immoral men can go in obtaining it. For example, a villager tells Odili, "I have said that what the white man's money will bring about has not shown itself yet" (p. 84). This sounds like a quotation of a Biblical line which says that "the love of money is the root of all evils." But when applied to the situation at hand, we can see the reality of the danger in the social evil. Here, Josiah, a village shopkeeper, is stealing money from a village blind beggar, Azoge. It is a crime which makes one agree with the villager that "What money will do in this land wears a hat"[17] (p. 85). The narrator's condemnation of extreme love of

---

[15] The paragraph is a paraphrase of Lindfors's ideas in *Folklore in Nigeria Literature*, pp. 88-89.

[16] *Ibid.*, p. 89.

[17] Explaining the sententious statement, my informant, Chief Eke of Ihechiowa, said that wearing of hats was a form of disguise and that the wearer could hide something on his head. Hence, "What money will do in

money comes through in these lines:

> 'Yes, the blind beggar, Josiah is not touched by Azoge's illfortune and he is not satisfied with all the thieving he does here in the name of trade but must now make juju with Azoge's stick.' At this point he turned aside to greet another villager and they both shook their heads over the abomination (p. 84).

Later in the scene, another villager compares Josiah's greed with the insatiety of the earth. He says, "Some people's belly is like the earth. It is never so full that it will not take another corpse" (pp. 86-87). It is proverbial imagery that emphasizes the unending nature of the social evil; it has no cure just as nobody has found a cure for death.

This proverbial imagery elicits another proverbial response from another villager. The narrator says, "But the most ominous thing I heard was from Timothy, a middle-aged man, who was a kind of Christian and a carpenter." He then names the ominous thing:

> 'Josiah has taken away enough for the owner to notice,' he said again and again. 'If anyone ever sees my feet in this shop again let him cut them off. Josiah has now removed enough for the owner to see him' (p. 86).

It is the key to understanding the novel as a political satire and Odili's actions in it. Nanga has ben taking all kinds of women to bed, but the moment he takes Odili's mistress to bed, he removes enough for the owner to notice; and so Odili fights back. The "eating" politicians have been eating the nation to a point that young men have noticed; they form young political parties to oppose the old. But the real owners, represented by the military, stage a protest in the form of a military coup, to stop the practice.

Achebe's satire on the "eating" politicians begins with the acro-

---

this land wears a hat" is a witty way of expressing the ominous effect of the white man's money on the traditional Igbo village.

nyms he gives to the political parties: POP (People's Organization Party), a word which is used informally to refer to popular music, parties, and entertainment in which there is a lot of "wining" and "dining" and PAP (Progressive Alliance Party), a word for light breakfast made of cornstarch (*akamu*)—they both connote eating. However, the rate and amount of eating differ from party to party; and the novel is full of imagery and statements about eating. For instance, Nanga tells his people: "Our people must press for their fair share of the national cake" (p. 12). The opponents of the hungry politicians are described as "the hybrid class of Western-educated and snobbish intellectuals who will not hesitate to sell their mothers for a mess of pottage" (p. 6).

Other important proverbial expressions in the novel are:

(a) "It was like the man in the proverb who was carrying the carcass of an elephant on his head and searching with his toes for a grasshopper" (p. 71). Nanga has a wife and other mistresses in town. He would not be satisfied with them unless he ravishes Elsie, Odili's mistress.

(b) "As the saying goes it is only when you are close to a man that you can begin to smell his breath" (p. 83). This proverb applies to the relationship between Odili and Nanga. Until Odili visits Nanga in Lagos he never realizes how vulnerable Nanga is with women.

(c) "My brother, when those standing have not got their share you are talking about those kneeling. Have you ever heard of a woman going to America when she doesn't know ABC?" (p. 89). This is a modern version of the proverb Achebe uses in *Things Fall Apart* (p. 7) to comment on Okonkwo's endeavors towards achievement. Mrs. Nanga uses it to point out to Odili the hierarchical order of things. This is one of those examples of how the contexts of a proverb can result in different, often opposed, meanings. She cannot accompany Nanga to America because she is illiterate.

(d) "Our people say: if you fail to take away a strong man's sword when he is on the ground, will you do it when he gets up ...?" (p. 91). Edna's father is an "eating" in-law of Nanga. He wants to enjoy his in-law when he has not claimed his wife and gone away.

(e) "I believe that the hawk should perch and the eagle perch, whichever says to the other *don't*, may its own wing break" (p. 122). Ordinarily, this is a proverb which the Igbo adopt as a maxim stressing coexistence of people of divergent interests. In this context, the eagle and the hawk are the political parties, P.O.P. and P.A.P., which are now preying upon the chicken, the Nigerian nation—another eating leitmotif.

A Man of the People contains fewer number of traditional proverbs spoken by Igbo leaders and elders than those in *Things Fall Apart* and *Arrow of God* because the older societies have given way to the new in the latest novel, taking with them their verbal expressions which include the proverbs. In other words, the destruction of the homogeneous linguistic groups of the early novels makes it impossible for the proverbs to thrive in a new and alien society. However, "*A Man of the People,* although replete with figurative language, contains far fewer proverbs and customary sayings, in proportion to its length, than the other novels, but where the author does employ such sayings other than for realism in dialogue, they are as functional as in his other writing."[18]

In general, Achebe's dexterous use of Igbo proverbs to comment subtly on the activities of the characters and to express the moral and ethical principles of the various societies of his novels attests to his excellent artistry as an author; it also reveals the richness of the verbal arts of the culture about which the author realistically writes. And although Achebe creates the proverbs and maxims of his native Igbo, his major success is that "he did but clothe in happier form what others had already felt, or even already uttered; for a proverb has oftentimes been in this respect 'the wit of one, and the wisdom of many.'"[19]

---

[18] Shelton, *op. cit.*, p. 109.

[19] Richard C. Trench, *Proverbs and their Lessons* (London: Kegan Paul, Trench, Trubner, and Co. Ltd., 1905), p. 15.

7 Folk Stories

> In our folk stories a man gets to the land of spirits when he has passed seven rivers, seven forests and seven hills.
>
> —Achebe's narrator in *No Longer at Ease*

The way the Igbo "tell" it, a folk story would comprise many narrative types such as legends, fairy tales, animal tales, myths, and riddles; the umbrella term for these folk narratives in Igbo is *akuko* ("story") told by the fireside. This appears to be Achebe's attitude to folktales in his novels. For him, the term, "folk stories" that he actually uses in Chapter Five of *No Longer At Ease*, would embrace all the major tales in Igbo folklore.[1] Folk stories, as traditional materials, are used by Achebe to express in his novels the lore of traditional Igbo societies. To the children, folk stories are mainly evening entertainment, while the adults regard them essentially as a useful means of handing down their traditions to the younger generations. Achebe uses the folk stories as a literary technique to make subtle and indirect comments on the behavior of characters, to make authorial observations on particular events and

---

[1] Achebe's reductionist concept of the folktale is also reflected in William Bascom's definition of folklore. See William Bascom, "Folklore and Anthropology," *Journal of American Folklore*, Vol. 66 (1953), pp. 283-290.

episodes, and to create some comic relief after a tense moment. All three uses may foreshadow or recapitulate the events of one novel or a general theme of two or more novels. Because of such important functions of folk stories, we will identify, classify and comment on some of the very important folk stories included in the novels.

The kinds of folk stories which feature frequently in Achebe's novels include didactic animal tales or fables. In addition, there are three single-motif tales about human beings; a fairy tale; an endless tale; an anecdote; two jocular tales; and some references made to Igbo legends.[2] Although the tales and legends may be popular among the Igbo and most West African societies, what is particularly fascinating about the folk stories is Achebe's reconstruction and use of them in the service of his art. Such a use attests to the richness of Igbo verbal art and the dexterity of Achebe's use of various levels of language.

Didactic Animal Tales

Achebe either alludes briefly to Igbo didactic animal tales (or fables), or reconstructs in full familiar ones so as to comment subtly on a particular character, following the character's role in or response to particular event or episode. For instance, after Okonkwo has beaten one of his wives during the Week of Peace, he is made to offer a purification sacrifice. In addition to observing that Okonkwo is repentant, the narrator remarks, "They called him the little bird *nza*." By alluding to the tale in this episode, the narrator is succinctly saying that Okonkwo has a false sense of his momentary affluence; after all, Okonkwo has not yet escaped his poor parentage completely. However, the narrator is wary in making the second remark; that is, having said earlier that "he [Okonkwo] was repentant," it would be a contradiction in narration if he simply said that Okonkwo is the little bird *nza*, implying that Okonkwo is not repentant. So he allows the clansmen to discern between the observation of the omniscient

---

[2] See John W. Johnson's article, "Folklore in Achebe's Novels," *New Letters*, Vol. 40, 3 (1974), pp. 95-107.

reporter, which is internal and objective, and that of Okonkwo's fellow clansmen, which is external and limited. Thus the omniscient reporter represents Achebe reporting what he sees and hears as accurately as he possibly can, thereby making his narrative objective and trustworthy.

A similar allusion is made to another bird, this time to *"Eneke-nti-oba,* who challenged the whole world to a wrestling contest and was finally thrown by the cat." (*TFA,* p.48) *Eneke-nti-oba* has a false sense of his ability to elude hunters; because he can hear in advance hunters who approach stealthily even before they have time enough to aim and shoot at him, he thinks that his special power, which derives from the special listening device in his ears and which no other animal or human possesses, cannot be surmounted. But the cat, who can move without making any sound, outwits him. In other words, *Eneke's* power, like any other powers, is never absolute; therefore, one should not show off his special powers or talents. In context, the story about *Eneke-nti-oba* does more than the proverb. It assumes the status of an anecdote. First, Achebe juxtaposes it with "stories of the land—masculine stories of violence and bloodshed" which Okonkwo takes pride in telling to Nwoye and Ikemefuna to emphasize the difference between father and son and their preferences, as well as their individual temperaments. The juxtaposition produces some contrast. In addition, Okonkwo tells the boys the masculine stories with the intention of inducting his effeminate son, Nwoye, into the masculinity of Umuofia life. However, that intention is reversed because Nwoye still prefers the stories that his mother used to tell, and the reversal produces irony.

Also, the animals mentioned in the tales are associated with cunning which is the game the father and his son are playing with each other. *Eneke-nti-oba* is a fitting metaphor for Okonkwo who literally wrestles with everybody, including Amalinze the Cat, and throws them all (p. 3); and figuratively he challenges his *chi*. On the other hand, he is figuratively thrown by his own effeminate son Nwoye who, for doing so, becomes a Cat. Achebe explains the cunning trick Nwoye plays on his father before he finally defects to the Christian camp:

That was the kind of story (about vulture, Earth's emissary) that Nwoye loved. But he knew that they were foolish women and children, and he knew that his father wanted him to be a man. *And so he feigned that he no longer cared for women's stories* [my emphasis]. And when he did this he saw his father was pleased, and no longer rebuked him or beat him (pp 48-49).

Furthermore, that Nwoye can succeed in fooling his father without Okonkwo ever finding it out implies that Nwoye is more sensitive than his violent and blood-thirsty father. Later in the novel, we come across passages which reveal more and more the sensitive qualities of Nwoye: namely, after a group of elders visits Okonkwo and confers with him about Ikemefuna, Okonkwo calls Ikemefuna later in the day and tells him that he is to be taken home the next day. Nwoye overhears it and bursts into tears, whereupon his father beats him heavily (p. 52). One may say that Nwoye's action is a natural reaction to a little boy's loss of an adopted brother. He is quick in sympathetic and aesthetic response. This point of view is underscored with a point made in another passage:

> As soon as his father walked in, that night, Nwoye knew that Ikemefuna had been killed, and something seemed to give way inside him, like the snapping of a tightened bow. He did not cry. He just hung limp. He had the same kind of feeling not long ago, during the last harvest season (p. 55).

Here, the narrator fully describes Nwoye's eerie feeling about Ikemefuna's murder to emphasize the contrast between Nwoye's humane feeling for others and the cruelty of his society. The narrator adds:

> It was after such a day at the farm during the last harvest that Nwoye had felt for the first time a snapping inside him like the one he now felt. They were returning home with baskets of yams from a distant farm across the stream when they heard the voice of an infant crying in the thick forest. A sudden hush had fallen on the women, who had been talking, and they had heard that twins were

put in earthenware pots and thrown away in the forest, but he had never yet come across them. A vague chill had descended on him and his head had seemed to swell, like a solitary walker at night who passes an evil spirit on the way. Then something had given way inside him. It descended on him again, this feeling, when his father walked in, that night after killing Ikemefuna (pp. 55-56).

It is this feeling of compassion for suffering people that sets Nwoye apart from his society, driving him towards Christianity, and eventually qualifying him to answer to "the Lord's call" in *No Longer at Ease* as Mr. Isaac Okonkwo, catechist of the Church Missionary Society (p. 8).

In the same passage of *Things Fall Apart* that we have been considering, Achebe reconstructs the tale of "Vulture, Earth's emissary to the Sky" (pp. 48ff). In a journal article, "Symbolic Structure in *Things Fall Apart*,"[3] Donald Weinstock and Cathy Ramadan give a detailed and impressive critical appreciation of Achebe's employment of the tale to "foreshadow, recapitulate, interweave" and connect the major themes and events of the novel.[4] Achebe, they say, gives it as an example of "the kind of story that Nwoye loved":

> He remembered the story she often told of the quarrel between Earth and Sky long ago, and how Sky withheld rain for seven years, until crops withered and the dead could not be buried because the hoes broke on the stony Earth. At last Vulture was sent to plead with Sky, and to soften his heart with a song of the suffering of the sons of men. Whenever Nwoye's mother sang this song he felt carried away to the distant scene in the sky where Vulture, Earth's emissary, sang for mercy. At last Sky was moved to pity, and he gave to Vulture rain wrapped in leaves of cocoyam. But as he flew home his long talon pierced the leaves and the rain fell as it had never fallen before. And so heavily did it rain on Vulture that he did not return to deliver his message but flew to a distant land, from

---

[3] *Critique: Studies in Modern Fiction*, Vol. II, I (1969), pp.33-41.
[4] *Ibid.*, pp.35-36.

where he had espied a fire. And when he got there he found it was a man making a sacrifice. He warmed himself in the fire and ate the entrails (p. 48).

Even though Weinstock and Ramadan's explication of Achebe's structural use of the tale appears complete and total, there are a few points they have made which require closer examination. One of them is the point about the Vulture's talon piercing the bundle of rain. They ask a very thought-provoking question, "If Vulture represents a force for good, as has been claimed above, why does its claw release destruction?" But the answer they give is not persuasive at all:

> Similarly, the explanation may simply be that it is the creature's nature to act as it does. Vulture cannot help doing what his animal body and instincts dictate. Similarly, Nwoye cannot help becoming a Christian, for his temperament draws him instinctively to Christianity: "It was the poetry of the new religion, something felt in the marrow that captivated him" (p. 132). Inadvertent acts by both Nwoye and by Vulture bring temporary discomfort and harm.[5]

If one understands that "it is the creature's nature to act as it does" means Nwoye acts according to his nature, then the explanation may not simply be that Nwoye cannot help becoming Christian. Rather it means that resenting his father's, indeed his tribe's violent ways is natural to him since he is quite unlike his father. The narrator is careful to say "something felt in the marrow," and not "something in the marrow," which is to say that as a result of his natural tendency to hate everything that this father loved—because Nwoye is a "reincarnation" of Unoka (p. 60)—he deeply appreciates the message of the new religion if only to spite his father's own religion, whose practices involve violence; this is not to say that becoming a Christian was necessarily in his nature. It is this ambivalent disposition towards his father's religion which, like the talon of

---

[5] *Ibid.*, pp.37-38.

the vulture, punctures the Christian love his conversion is meant to bring to his people. Put simply, Christian love, like other kinds of love, is both gentle and dangerous depending on who handles it. The rain fell heavily on Nwoye, the metaphoric vulture, because he brought opposition to his land, a deed that alienated him from his family. In fact, it earned him the curse of his father and the admonition of Obierika.

Another objectionable explanation offered by Weinstock and Ramadan is that "Further, the fire which Vulture sees is obviously Okonkwo. As he sits gazing into a log fire and wondering how he could ever have fathered such a 'degenerate and effeminate' son, we are told—and thrice reminded—that he was popularly called the 'Roaring Flame'" (pp. 137-138). This piece of evidence does not apply to the context of the entire tale. The fire which the Vulture espied is the religious zeal of the preacher, Mr. Kiaga, which attracted the young Nwoye and made him decide to become a missionary teacher. The lines, "And when he got there he found it was a man making a sacrifice. He warmed himself in the fire and ate the entrails," refer specifically to the ministration of Mr. Kiaga among the early Christian converts and the latter-day proselytizing (entrails) which Nwoye, who becomes Mr Isaac Okonkwo, does in *No Longer at Ease* as the catechist of the Church Missionary Society for twenty-five years. The warming-up idea represents the salary he made and the pension of twenty-five pounds a year that followed his retirement (p. 8). Since Nwoye has a natural resentment for Okonkwo, he cannot be attracted towards him; if anything he tries to avoid him. And that is precisely what he does in the novel.

The tale, which the children regard as folk entertainment, is told by Nwoye's mother as an etiological tale to explain the universe and natural phenomena. The tale of the Vulture attempts to explain why Nigeria has two seasons, a rainy season and a dry season; and to describe the effect of seasonal changes on migratory birds like the vulture. In addition, it goes on to explain why the vulture is a scavenger. As a didactic animal tale, the Vulture tale has some morals that parents must inculcate in their children. That is, children should learn to be good emissaries; men and women should learn to live in peace, otherwise their quarrel could result in social disasters for their children, just as children of the Earth suffer because of the quarrel between Earth and Sky.

Nwoye's abandonment of his people's customs and traditions leads him to self-exile. He serves the Christian Church as a catechist—a second rate minister—like the Vulture who eats the entrails after the main meat of the sacrificial animal has been eaten by the man or Master. Ironically, Nwoye likes the tale but, mystified by the rhetoric of the Christian sermons and songs, he ignores the morals of the tale. On the other hand, since Nwoye is pushed into joining the missionaries by the cruel acts of his father, Achebe seems to imply that both the foreign missionaries and the clansmen have contributed equally towards the break up of Umuofia society. Both the traditional Igbo religion and the new and alien religion have basic love as their essence, but the quarrel between their individual agents destroys the love which is inherent in every religion.

Another major tale which Achebe tells is about Mosquito and Ear. The tale is preceded by the opening sentences of Chapter Nine: "For the first time in three nights Okonkwo slept. He woke up once in the middle of the night and his mind went back to the past three days without making him feel uneasy" (p. 68). They are antithetical to the opening sentences of Chapter Eight: "Okonkwo did not taste any food for two days after the death of Ikemefuna. He drank palmwine from morning till night, and his eyes were red and fierce like the eyes of a rat when it was caught by the tail and dashed against the floor" (p. 57). In other words, the tale about Mosquito and Ear interweaves the events of the two chapters.

In Chapter Eight, we find Okonkwo restless and anxious to see the transformation of his effeminate son into a *man*, particularly after Ikemefuna, Nwoye's informal teacher, has been murdered. Nwoye does not go to his drunken father, rather he slips out of the hut as soon as he notices his father dozing. But Okonkwo's beloved daughter, Ezinma, goes in and persuades her father to eat; and he does so but absent-mindedly. Because Ezinma acts responsibly towards her father, "She should have been a boy," Okonkwo thinks as he looks at his ten-year-old daughter. Later in the chapter, when Okonkwo visits his friend Obierika who is expecting his in-laws in his *obi,* he returns to the thought about his son's effeminacy, because

152 | Folk Stories

Obierika's wrestler son, Maduka, has just come in. The following conversation is what the tale about Mosquito and Ear recapitulates:

> "He will do great things." Okonkwo said. "If I had a son like him I should be happy. I am worried about Nwoye. A bowl of pounded yams can throw him in a wrestling match. His two younger brothers are more promising. But I can tell you, Obierika, that my children do not resemble me. Where are the young suckers that will grow when the old banana tree dies? If Ezinma had been a boy I would have been happier. She has the right spirit."
> "You worry yourself for nothing," said Obierika. "The children are still very young."
> "Nwoye is old enough to impregnate a woman. At his age I was already fending for myself. No, my friend, he is not too young. A chick that will grow into a cock can be spotted the very day it hatches. I have done my best to make Nwoye grow into a man, but there is too much of his mother in him" (pp. 59-60).

After the conversation, the death of Ogbuefi Ndulue of Ire village is announced. The talking drums beat. Okonkwo and his friends joke about the taking of the *ozo*-title. (These are all talks about manliness and achievements). They also settle Akueke's bride-price and make bawdy jokes on effeminate men and puns on "the white skin"— leprosy and white man whose ways, like leprosy, contaminate Igbo customs and traditions. Okonkwo participates in these activities with the hope of blotting out of his mind the thought of Nwoye's effeminacy and of the murder of Ikemefuna.

It is against this background that Okonkwo remembers the tale about Mosquito and Ear which his mother, like Nwoye's mother, had told him:

> He slapped the ear and hoped he had killed it. Why do they always go for one's ears? When he was a child his mother had told him a story about it. But it was as silly as all women's stories. Mosquito, she had said, had asked Ear to marry him, whereupon Ear fell on the floor in uncontrollable laughter. "How much longer do you think you will live?" she asked. "You are already a skeleton."

Mosquito went away humiliated, and any time he passed her way he told Ear that he was still alive. (p. 68)

As they apply to the context of the entire novel, Mosquito represents the lingering and nagging fears of Okonkwo which he fails to marry to his conscience, the metaphoric Ear.

After Ikemefuna's sacrifice, Okonkwo obeys his conscience and fasts for two days. But he does not offer any atonement sacrifice as his religious practices demand. Instead, he compounds his mistake by giving his friend, Obierika, the impression that the part he plays is for a pious cause, whereas it is for personal esteem. The more that thought of the evil he did haunts him, the more he suppresses it by regarding his act as a patriotic and pious service done to his people and their goddess, Ani. And when the thought of Nwoye's effeminacy bothers him, he knows that Nwoye resembles his effeminate grandfather, Unoka, but as before, Okonkwo prefers to suppress the truth by saying that Nwoye resembles his mother, Okonkwo's wife (p. 60). Specifically, the tale of Mosquito and Ear tells of sons and fathers, if one uses a psychological approach to analyze Okonkwo's relationship with his dead father on the one hand, and the relationship between him and his sons Nwoye and Ikemefuna on the other. Moreover, it emphasizes how the fear that the two kinds of relationship created motivates and precipitates other abominable acts that will eventuate in the fall of the hero, Okonkwo.

The tale also prefigures the response Okonkwo gives to Ekwefi's audacious and ominous call on Okonkwo:

> "Ezinma is dying," came her voice, and all the tragedy and sorrow of her life were packed in those words.
>
> Okonkwo sprang from his bed, pushed back the bolt on his door and ran into Ekwefi's hut.
>
> Ezinma lay shivering on a mat beside a huge fire that her mother had kept burning all night (p. 69).

Like his fear of Unoka's failure and Nwoye's effeminacy, Okonkwo's latest fear of Ezinma dying of *ogbanje* is a nagging emotion which Okonkwo cannot suppress completely. For, apart from the human misery that the death of Ezinma would create for Ekwefi, Okonkwo knows very well, more than anyone else in the family, the depth of the wound that such a death would inflict on the hero's mind if it is not prevented. For, in spite of her being a woman, Ezinma is becoming "the young sucker that will grow when the old banana tree dies" (pp. 59-60). We find her playing that role very well when Okonkwo and other Umuofia elders are imprisoned on the Government Hill.

Besides using the tale as a structural and artistic prop, Achebe reconstructs an existing Igbo myth which Okonkwo's mother, like other Umuofia mothers, tells to her children as a way of explaining why mosquitoes seem to bite the ear more than they do other parts of the human body; for it is a common experience in any tropical country. Ear fails to marry an eligible suitor, Mosquito, because he looked skinny. Therefore, the story is intended to teach people not to deride their suitors just because of appearance. In addition, children are introduced indirectly to the problems of the social institution of marriage, so that at that early age they are made to realize how dangerous it can be for married people to quarrel constantly.

Ezinma alludes to "the snake-lizard killed his mother" story while she and Ekwefi cook for the diviner, Okagbue, who is busy digging a pit to find where Ezinma had buried her *iyi-uwa* (pp. 76ff). Casually read, the story provides comic relief for mother and child after the former has been overly nervous about losing an only child to *ogbanje*, and the latter has been feverish and tired of running from place to place, pointing at the spots where she buried her *iyi-uwa*. The tale may even be viewed as a routine that accompanies ceremonial cooking. However, read more seriously, the story becomes a reflection of the mood and fears of Ekwefi, about which the narrator says:

> As she buried one child after another her sorrow gave way to despair and then to grim resignation. The birth of her children, which should be a woman's crowning glory, became for Ekwefi mere physical agony devoid of promise. The naming ceremony after seven market weeks became an empty ritual (p. 70).

We can see the metaphoric parallel between the snake-lizard who killed his mother and Ezinma whose sudden death could break the heart of Ekwefi. Up to the point Ezinma remembers the tale, Ekwefi thinks that Ezinma is one of those *ogbanje* children who take pride in inflicting perpetual wounds on their mother's heart and so she shouts: "That is not the end of the story;" whereupon Ezinma says:

> "Oho, I remember now. He brought another seven baskets and cooked them himself. And there were again only three. So he killed himself too" (p. 76).

Ezinma's answer not only completes the "misery-go-round," but it also assures Ekwefi that Ezinma is not going to die like the other heartless ones who, in their pride to inflict pains on their mother, forget that their recurrent infant mortality is also self-destruction.

Apart from being central to the theme of that part of *Things Fall Apart*, the "snake-lizard" story is a folkloric allusion to a popular Nigerian (even West African) folk belief. The traditional Igbo, not having modem medical prevention for recurrent infant mortality, devised a means of explaining the disaster—namely, the myth of *ogbanje*—and also a way to deal with it. That is, it is believed that once the *iyi-uwa* (totemic stone of the dying infant) is divined, dug up, and made impotent by a powerful medicine man, the *ogbanje* can survive. Because many African writers who wrote after Achebe have included the myth of *ogbanje* or *abiku*[6] in their writing, Achebe's tale can be regarded as a source of literary allusions.

Variants of some of the didactic animal tales found in *Things Fall Apart* are cited by Achebe in his other novels. One of those variants is the literary allusion that the narrator makes to "the lizard in the fable who ruined his mother's funeral by his own hand," at the end of *Arrow of God*. It is the same story which Ezinma tells in bits, and

---

[6] Wole Soyinka and John Pepper Clark have treated the myth of *ogbanje* in their poems which they title "Abiku." See Gerald Moore and Ulli Beier (eds.), *Modern Poetry from Africa* (Baltimore, Maryland: Penguin Books, Inc., 1968), pp. 117 and 152.

which we have examined above. Achebe calls it "the snake-lizard," a story which becomes a "fable" in *Arrow of God* (p. 230) in order to make allowances for local variations. That is, some parts of Igboland may tell the story, making Snake the protagonist, while others may use Lizard. It is a variant of the same tale or fable that Odili in *A Man of the People* alludes to when he says, "One day at play another child with whom I had fallen out called me 'Bad child that crunched his mother's skull'" (p. 27). The tale underlines the hazards of childbirth and the special relationship which exists between a mother and her only child. The child becomes a curse to his mother if he turns out to be an *ogbanje* or if his mother dies during labor. Odili explains the attitude of society towards such an ill-fated child:

> Of course as soon as I grew old enough to understand a few simple proverbs I realized that I should have died and let my mother live. Whenever my people go to console a woman whose baby has died at birth or soon after, they always tell her to dry her eyes because it is better the water is spilled than the pot broken. The idea being that a sound pot can always return to the stream (p. 28).

Such "lizards" ruin their mothers' funerals in a peculiar way. They drive the parent to an early grave and thus deny her the expensive rituals and panegyrics appropriate to a mature matron.

Igbo Trickster Tales

Igbo trickster tales come under didactic animal tales, but they are treated separately here in order to emphasize society's attitude towards trickery, especially when someone plays it on his own people. Achebe, like storytellers in traditional Igbo society, makes Tortoise the Igbo trickster. The trickster tale appears in the first three novels, and we quote one tale in full to illustrate how it is told by Ekwefi to Ezinma in *Things Fall Apart*:

> "Once upon a time," she began, "all the birds were invited to a feast in the sky. They were very happy and began to prepare their bodies

with red cam wood and drew beautiful patterns on them with *uli*.

"Tortoise saw all these preparations and soon discovered what it all meant. Nothing that happened in the world of the animals ever escaped his notice; he was full of cunning. As soon as he heard of the great feast in the sky his throat began to itch at the very thought. There was a famine in those days and Tortoise had not eaten a good meal for two moons. His body rattled like a piece of dry stick in his empty shell. So he began to plan how he would go to the sky."

"But he had no wings," said Ezinma. "Be patient," replied her mother, "That is the story. Tortoise had no wings, but he went to the birds and asked to be allowed to go with them.

"'We know you too well,' said the birds when they had heard him. 'You are full of cunning and you are ungrateful. If we allow you to come with us you will soon begin your mischief.'

"'You do not know me,' said Tortoise, 'I am a changed man. I have learned that a man who makes trouble for others is also making it for himself.'

"Tortoise had a sweet tongue, and within a short time all the birds agreed that he was a changed man, and they each gave him a feather, with which he made two wings.

"At last the great day came and Tortoise was the first to arrive at the meeting place. When all the birds had gathered together, they set off in a body. Tortoise was very happy and voluble as he flew among the birds, and he was soon chosen as the man to speak for the party because he was a great orator.

"'There is one important thing which we must not forget,' he said as they flew on their way. 'When people are invited to a great feast like this, they take new names for the occasion. Our hosts in the sky will expect us to honor this age-old custom.'

"None of the birds had heard of this custom but they knew that Tortoise, in spite of his failings in other directions, was a widely-travelled man who knew the customs of different peoples. And so they each took a new name. When they had all taken, Tortoise also took one. He was to be called *All of you.*

"At last the party arrived in the sky and their hosts were very happy to see them. Tortoise stood up in his many colored plumage and thanked them for their invitation. His speech was so eloquent that all the birds were glad they had brought him, and nodded their heads in approval of all he said. Their hosts took him as the king of the birds especially as he looked somewhat different from the others.

"After kola nuts had been presented and eaten, the people of the sky set before their guests the most delectable dishes Tortoise had ever dreamed of. The soup was brought out hot from the fire and in the very pot in which it had been cooked. It was full of meat and fish. Tortoise began to sniff aloud. There was pounded yam and also yam pottage cooked with palm-oil and fresh fish. There were also pots of palm-wine. When everything had been set before the guests, one of the people of the sky came forward and tasted a little from each pot. He then invited the birds to eat. But Tortoise jumped to his feet and asked: 'For whom have you prepared this feast?'

"'For all of you,' replied the man.

"Tortoise turned to the birds and said: 'You remember that my name is *All of you*. The custom here is to serve the spokesman first and the others later. They will serve you when I have eaten.'

"He began to eat and the birds grumbled angrily. The people of the sky thought it must be their custom to leave all the food for the king. And so Tortoise ate the best part of the food and then drank two pots of palm-wine, so that he was full of food and drink and his body filled out in his shell.

"The birds gathered round to eat what was left and to peck at the bones he had thrown all about the floor. Some of them were too angry to eat. They chose to fly home on an empty stomach. But before they left each took back the feather he had lent to Tortoise. And there he stood in his hard shell full of food and wine but without any wings to fly home. He asked the birds to take a message for his wife, but they all refused. In the end Parrot, who had felt more angry than the others, suddenly changed his mind and agreed to take the message.

"'Tell my wife.' said Tortoise, 'to bring out all the soft things in my house and cover the compound with them so that I can jump down from the sky without very great danger.'

"Parrot promised to deliver the message, and then flew away. But when he reached Tortoise's house he told his wife to bring out all the hard things in the house. And so she brought out her husband's hoes, machetes, spears, guns and even his cannon. Tortoise looked down from the sky and saw his wife bringing things out, but it was too far to see what they were. When all seemed ready he let himself go. He fell and fell and fell until he began to fear that he would never stop falling. And then like the sound of his Cannon he crashed on the compound."

"Did he die?" asked Ezinma.

"No," replied Ekwefi. "His shell broke into pieces. But there was a great medicine man in the neighborhood. Tortoise's wife sent for him and he gathered all the bits of shell and stuck them together. That is why Tortoise's shell is not smooth" (pp. 87-90).

In addition to the usual moral tags found in tales of this sort, there are several Igbo folkways that the tale embodies. First of all, there is the allegorical parallel in the relationship between the selfish animal leader, Tortoise, and the other animals, and that between a self-seeking leader and his people. The allegory becomes more vivid when it is realized that the animal feast and menu, the body decorations, the appointment of an orator as a spokesman, the initial submission to the authority of that spokesman, and the bitter grumbling that follows the trickery of the leader, are all characteristic of Igbo folkways. We also notice the sense of community and attendant help which is rendered to Tortoise because other animals have what he lacks; they were prepared to play their "brother's keeper" because he asks for a loan of feathers. In the end, instead of being grateful for their kindness in allowing him to join in their feast and in giving him feathers which enable him to fly, he uses his talent, the power of oratory which no other bird has, to cheat them even as he is beautified with their feathers. Tortoise's ingratitude and selfishness reach a height of insult, which explains why the Igbo can tolerate individuals with limited authority as their leaders but would never accept anybody as king.

The tale also underlines the Igbo folkway of according mutual respect to other people's customs, even if those customs were different and hostile to theirs. It is an attribute that begins with one's preparedness to learn and accept the adequacy of other people's customs as important components of the cultures that practice them. As can be seen in the tale, the people of the sky do not understand the custom of the people of the earth. However, they do not condemn it; rather, they merely observe perhaps to learn about it. It appears that Achebe recommends this kind of attitude to the Igbo and Europe when they first encounter each other and learn about each other's culture for the first time.

The moral of the story is premonitorily summarized by Tortoise's own statement, "I have learned that a man who makes trouble for others is also making it for himself," which he uses to trick the birds into accepting him as a repentant trickster. They believe him. Judging from how easy it is for Parrot to beat Tortoise at his own game, the tale teaches that no one, including the widely-acclaimed trickster Tortoise, has a monopoly on knowledge or tricks. The particular moral of this tale re-emphasizes the general moral of Igbo didactic animal tales, which is that evil is punished but good is rewarded. The birds may have suffered momentary starvation, but Tortoise has to live with a broken and ugly shell throughout his life.

As a myth, the trickster story is told to explain the "why and whereof" of things—namely, why Tortoise's shell is patched and rough; why he has neither feathers like birds nor legs like other animals; why birds peck at bones instead of eating the meat like men and other lower animals. These simple explanations of things may not sound scientific to the modern mind, but they help the children understand the world around them. The stories make them curious as they try to become more observant of the creatures which live in their neighborhood and ask the adults questions about them.

A shorter trickster story involving Tortoise is recorded in *No Longer At Ease:*

> Tortoise went on a long journey to a distant clan. But before he went he told his people not to send for him unless something new under the sun happened. When he was gone, his mother died. The question was how to make him return to bury his mother. If they told him that his mother had died, he would say it was nothing new. So they told him that his father's palm tree had borne a fruit at the end of its leaf. When Tortoise heard this, he said he must

return home to see this great monstrosity. And so his bid to escape the burden of his mother's funeral was foiled' (pp. 148-149).

It is a story told as a folkloric allusion to Obi Okonkwo's refusal to go to Umuofia so he can escape the burden of his mother's funeral. Other members of Umuofia quietly express their disapproval earlier in the scene. For instance, recalling how Obi's father, Mr. Isaac Okonkwo, refused to attend the funeral of Okonkwo Unoka, the President observes that "A man may go to England, become a lawyer or doctor, but it does not change his blood." To add piquancy to his remark, the President proverbializes the situation by saying:

> It is like a bird that flies off the earth and lands on an anthill. It is still on the ground (p. 146).

The result is, we are told, that "Shame and guilt filled his [Obi's] heart," the next day. And since he could not go to Umuofia for the funeral, his "traditionalist" servant, Joseph, arranges a funeral wake for Obi's mother in Lagos at which occasion the "Tortoise story" is told, but it turns out to be an off-color story. Nevertheless, it heightens the sense of guilt felt by Obi for shirking his filial duties.

Finally, in *Arrow of God*, Ezeulu calls himself the tortoise. When he is released from imprisonment on Government Hill at Okperi, Ezeulu plans to leave for home the next morning, defying the inclement weather of the wet season. His companion is John Nwodika who will not hear of Ezeulu's plan to do the journey alone. Ezeulu begs him not to trouble himself but it is all in vain because Nwodika tells him, "It is not a journey which a man of your station can take alone. If you are bent on returning today I must come with you. Otherwise stay till tomorrow when Obika is due to visit." It is at this point that Ezeulu alludes to the tale and proverb of the tortoise:

> "I cannot stay another day," said Ezeulu. "I am the tortoise who was trapped in a pit of excrement for two whole markets; but when helpers came to haul him out on the eighth day he cried! Quick, quick: I cannot stand the stench" (p. 181).

By making a direct comparison of himself with the trickster, tortoise, Ezeulu is admitting openly his planned game of the puff-adder and revenge when he gets home:

> All neighbors were there and every passer-by who heard of his return interrupted his errand to greet him. Ezeulu said very little, accepting most of the greeting with his eye and a nod. The time had not come to speak or to act. He must first suffer to the limit because the man to fear in action is the one who first submits to suffer to the limit. That was the terror of the puff-adder; it would suffer every provocation, it would even let its enemy step on its trunk; it must wait and unlock its seven fangs one after the other. Then it would say to its tormentor: *Here I am!* (p. 184)

Whether as tortoise or puff-adder, Ezeulu is a trickster who willingly undergoes some suffering, though at the provocation of his enemy, in order to justify the revenge he plans to carry out on his people. His people ignorantly sympathize with him for his imprisonment on the Government Hill. He is touched by their gesture, but his mind has been so much eaten up with the thought of revenge that he cannot easily discard his evil plans and reconcile with his people. In the end, he is caught in his own trap. Like other tortoises of Achebe's novels, Ezeulu the biter is bitten.

References to Igbo Legends and Folk Stories

As a nonliterate society, the traditional Igbo depend on their legends (nonhistorical or unverifiable stories handed down by tradition from earlier times and accepted as historical) and folk stories to explain their roots and cultural history. It is for this reason that Achebe refers to the body of stories called legends and folk stories as effective means of commenting on the life and behavior of the Igbo as a particular people, group, or clan. Two such references are made to the destruction of crops and villages in *Things Fall Apart*. The first is the coming of the locusts:

> And the locusts came. It had not happened for many a long year.

The elders said locusts came once in a generation, reappeared every year for seven years and then disappeared for another lifetime. They went back to their caves in a distant land, where they were guarded by a race of stunted men. And then after another lifetime these men opened the caves again and the locusts came to Umuofia.

They came in the cold harmattan season after the harvest was gathered, and ate up all the wild grass in the fields (p.19). The tale foreshadows in particular the actual locusts which destroy Umuofia farm crops, including Okonkwo's; but more importantly the locusts portend the series of natural and man-made disasters that descend on Okonkwo's life—from the drought which bakes his seed yams and nearly makes him lose hope in life, to his exile to Mbanta and to his final suicide—all happening periodically like the cyclic comings and goings of locusts to and from Umuofia.

The next reference is made to a popular story recorded in the same novel and is about the destruction of Abame by the white man's armed forces. When Obierika visits Okonkwo in Mbanta where he is spending his exile, Okonkwo and his uncle, Uchendu, listen to Obierika tell them how the people of Abame killed a white man who was riding a bicycle past their village and how they tied his bicycle on a sacred tree because their oracle had warned that whites will one day dominate them in their homeland. For a long time nothing happened until one market day when Abame market was surrounded by the white men who began to shoot. "Everybody was killed, except the old and the sick who were at home and a handful of men and women whose *chi* were wide awake and brought them out of that market," Obierika concludes and pauses (p. 126). In response to the story, Uchendu grinds his teeth together audibly. Then he bursts out:

> Never kill a man who says nothing. Those men of Abame were fools. What did they know about the man?

He grinds his teeth again and tells a story to illustrate his point:

> Mother Kite once sent her daughter to bring food. She went, and

brought back a duckling. "You have done very well," said Mother Kite to her daughter, "but tell me, what did the mother of this duckling say when you swooped and carried its child away?" "It said nothing," replied the young Kite. "It just walked away." "You must return the duckling," said Mother Kite. "There is something ominous behind the silence." And so Daughter Kite returned the duckling and took a chick instead. "What did the mother of this chick do?" asked the old kite. "It cried and raved and cursed me," said the young kite. "Then we can eat the chick," said her mother. "There is nothing to fear from someone who shouts." Those men of Abame were fools (p. 127).

Okonkwo concurs with his uncle, for he says after a pause:

They were fools. They have been warned that danger was ahead. They should have armed themselves with their guns and with their machetes even when they went to market.

Although this story is about Abame and their foolishness, ironically it applies to Okonkwo and his clansmen, Umuofia, in every detail. Okonkwo murders his adopted son, Ikemefuna, who has become an Umuofia clansman, he offends the Umuofia goddess of morality, Ani. Ani is offended but does not "cry and rave and curse" Okonkwo for his abominable act now. How Okonkwo is punished for the crime has been dealt with elsewhere in the study.

However, the foolishness, which Okonkwo thinks Abame people exhibited when they offended the white man's administration, is what the *egwugwu* of Umuofia exhibit after they have committed arson and wanton destruction of the property of the Christians. In spite of these offenses, Mr. Smith, the priest in charge of the Christian Church in Umuofia, does not fight them physically in fulfillment of his early promise:

"One thing is clear," said Mr. Smith. "We cannot offer physical resistance to them. Our strength lies in the Lord." They knelt down together and prayed to God for delivery (p. 169).

As a result, Okonkwo, who mistakes Mr. Smith's non-physical violence for weakness, thinks that the *egwugwu* have scored a major victory over the Christians. Unfortunately for the band of *egwugwu*, when the District Commissioner returns from his tour, Mr. Smith goes immediately to him and they have a long discussion which the men of Umuofia apparently do not take any notice of. And if they do, they think it is not important. In short, there is quiet diplomacy until the leaders of Umuofia are brought to the District Commissioner's headquarters.

After a seemingly friendly meeting with the leaders of Umuofia, the District Commissioner secretly orders his men to arrest them:

> It happened so quickly that the six men did not see it coming. There was only a brief scuffle, too brief even to allow the drawing of a sheathed machete. The six men were handcuffed and led into the guardroom (pp. 174-175).

To the white men, Okonkwo and his clansmen are "shouting" men; "there is nothing to fear from someone who shouts." But the encounter between the Igbo and the white man requires an answer which is more subtle and delicate than the simple one which Okonkwo's retort seems to offer. This is why even though Obierika seems to agree with Uchendu and Okonkwo that "They [Abame] have paid for their foolishness" (so as not to contradict an elder rudely), he makes an observation which sums up the fears and plight of the Igbo concerning their opposition to the white man's settlement in and domination of Umuofia:

> "But I am greatly afraid. We have heard stories about white men who made the powerful guns and the strong drinks and took slaves away across the seas, but no one thought the stories were true" (p. 127).

Out of experience, the old man, Uchendu, confirms the presence of the white men in Igbo country and other parts of Nigeria to dispel Obierika's belief in that presence as a mere rumor:

"There is no story that is not true," said Uchendu. "The world has no end, and what is good among one people is an abomination with others. We have albinos among us. Do you not think that they came to our clan by mistake, that they have strayed from their way to a land where everybody is like them?" (Ibid)

Hence, the foolishness of Abame which Uchendu talks about is different from what Okonkwo has in mind. Uchendu is referring to the foolishness of Abame in killing a man just because his skin color is different from theirs; but Okonkwo, on the contrary, blames Abame for not being prepared to fight with "their guns and with their machetes." In other words, Okonkwo is recommending suicide to the men of Abame.

Another popular Igbo folktale, which Achebe reconstructs in *Arrow of God* to illustrate his general theme of conflict and aggression resulting from one having a false sense of one's talents and powers, is the story of "the great wrestler whose back had never known the ground."

'Once there was a great wrestler whose back had never known the ground. He wrestled from village to village until he had thrown every man in the world. Then he decided that he must go and wrestle in the land of the spirits, and become champion there as well. He went, and beat every spirit that came forward. Some had seven heads, some ten; but he beat them all. His companion who sang his praise on the flute begged him to come away, but he would not, his blood was roused, his ear nailed up. Rather than heed the call to go home he gave a challenge to the spirits to bring out their best and strongest wrestler. So they sent him his personal god, a little wiry spirit who seized him with one hand and smashed him on the stony earth (p. 26-27).

This story is told to Umuaro men by their Chief Priest, Ezeulu, as an indictment against their appointment of Akukalia as emissary of war. Like the great wrestler, Akukalia is not a man who listens to his "flute player" and stops, once he knows he has the authority of his people, even when he is carrying out his mission wrongly.

Beyond the immediate scene of the novel, the tale applies to both Nwaka and Ezeulu. Nwaka is encouraged by Ezidemili in his opposition to Ezeulu. One does not hear directly from Ezidemili much that can be used to judge the depth of his hatred of the Chief Priest. In effect, it is assumed that Nwaka may have a good reason for opposing Ezeulu, but he does go to great lengths in doing so because Ezidemili has given him initial moral support. And when Nwaka opposes Ezeulu publicly, the people praise him enthusiastically with the praise name, "Owner of Words"—a name which encourages him to wage his war of opposition more and more against Ezeulu, until Ezidemili and Umuaro, like the falconer who loses control of his falcon, can no longer control Nwaka for whom they have been playing the flute of opposition and divisiveness in their *own* clan and against no common clansman. What we find in this situation is a house being divided against itself, as it were. Having been so weakened from within, it cannot stand when outsiders, such as the Christians, mount the campaign for new converts among Umuaro citizens.

On his own part of the conflict, Ezeulu relies on his god, Ulu, for superior intelligence and spiritual security. Again, as in the case of Nwaka and Ezidemili, we do not hear Ulu directly encouraging Ezeulu to fight his clansmen in his war of revenge. Whatever role Ulu is reported to play in the conflict is told us by Ezeulu himself. Unwary readers tend to take the Chief Priest's word for the support he apparently receives from Ulu; but knowing Ezeulu's state of mind and how deep-seated his hatred for his clansmen is, no one should easily believe him. Indeed, Ezeulu, like the legendary great wrestler, scored some victories in the past, including his defiance of the white man's authority at Okperi, but he should not have allowed such victories to delude him to the extent that he determines to fight to the bitter end the very people he was appointed to protect as the Chief Priest of Umuaro. The unmistakable irony becomes more acute when it is recalled that Ezeulu is able, as wise and divine counsellor to his people, to tell the tale of the great wrestler, but is unable to apply the same wisdom when the time comes for him to make the decision of pursuing his plan of wreaking vengeance on his people. Like Okonkwo, he can see clearly through the problems of others during crisis, but cannot use his wisdom to forestall some of his actions which are capable of bringing social and religious disasters to his people. One wonders how wise Ezeulu is if he cannot or chooses not to put his wisdom to practical purposes.

Other legends, included in the novel, concern the marketplaces, where not only buying and selling of goods are carried out but also where important clan meetings are held. Because of this second function, marketplaces are sacred to the people. The legends about them are told on the one hand to explain how they came to be regarded as sacred places, and on the other hand to justify why any decisions made in them have the force of law. One decision made in the marketplace concerns Ikemefuna, whose killing by Okonkwo displeased the Earth-goddess, Ani, and contributed towards Okonkwo's suicide in *Things Fall Apart*. The narrator tells a legend about one of the sacred spots in Umuofia which eventually becomes a market:

> Umuofia was feared by all its neighbors. It was powerful in war and in magic, and its priests and medicine men were feared in all the surrounding country. Its most potent war-medicine was as old as the clan itself. Nobody knew how old. But on one point there was general agreement--the active principle in that medicine had been an old woman with one leg. In fact, the medicine itself was called *agadinwayi*, or old woman. It had its shrine in the center of Umuofia, in a cleared spot. And if anybody was so foolhardy as to pass by the shrine after dusk he was sure to see the old woman hopping about (p. 11).

The passage does not call the shrine a market-place or one situated near it. But there are two other passages recounting legends about market-places which make one believe that all three legends are actually reconstructions of the same legend. The second one also comes from *Things Fall Apart*:

> "The market of Umuike is a wonderful place," said the young man who had been sent by Obierika to buy the giant goat. "There are so many people on it that if you threw up a grain of sand it would not

find a way to fall to earth again."

"It is the result of a great medicine," said Obierika. "The people of Umuike wanted their market to grow and swallow up the markets of their neighbors. So they made a powerful medicine. Every market day, before the first cock-crow, this medicine stands on the market ground in the shape of an old woman with a fan. With this magic fan she beckons in front of her and behind her, to her right and to her left" (p. 103).

And the third is retold in *Arrow of God:*

> As the men of Umuaro passed company after company of these market women they talked about the great Eke market in Okperi to which folk from every part of Igbo and Olu went.
>
> 'It is the result of an ancient medicine' Akukalia explained. 'My mother's people are great medicine-men.' There was pride in his voice. 'At first Eke was a very small market. Other markets in the neighborhood were drawing it dry. Then one day the men of Okperi made a powerful deity and placed their market in its care. From that day Eke grew and grew until it became the biggest market in these parts. This deity which is called Nwayieke is an old woman. Every Eke day before cockcrow she appears in the market-place with a broom in her right and dances round the vast open space beckoning with her broom in all directions of the earth drawing folk from every land. That is why people will not come near the market before cock-crow; if they did they would see the ancient lady in her task.' (p. 19)

As though to confirm our suspicion that all three legends are variants of one Igbo legend concerning their markets, Akukalia's companion adds: "They tell the same story of the Nkwo market beside the great river at Umuru. There the medicine has worked so well that the market no longer assembles only on Nkwo days."

From these legends a number of points about Igbo ways emerges. First, the market is given a mother-figure because it looks after (assembles) the people just like a grandmother does; second, marketing (haggling) is almost a natural behavior to the Igbo, and that breeds conflicts among them; third, haggling and competition leads one to seeking external aid such as medicine and magic to outdo a rival; fourth, the market is attended by both living people and living-dead ancestors, hence it has a spiritual significance for the people. And when a leader shouts, "Umuofia kwenu," and receives the response of "Yaa!" he knows that he has obtained the consensus of men and their ancestors. To back away from a decision made on a course of action to be taken could be regarded as treason, depending on the seriousness of the case at hand. This is why at the last meeting in the market before his suicide, Okonkwo keeps his word of "I shall fight [the white man] alone if I choose" (p. 181), and kills the head messenger. But it is also why Okonkwo's hearing of voices asking: "Why did he do it?" makes him commit suicide (p. 184). That is, his condemnation in a sacred place has the consensus of men and the living-dead ancestors.

Other Tales

The story about Dimaragana in *Things Fall Apart* is an example of single-motif tales about human beings. Obierika cites it to his friend Okonkwo as subtle criticism of some of his people's customs. He favors a change of some Umuofia laws which restrict the freedom of titled individuals, but Okonkwo wants the customs to be as unreformed as they were handed down to them through many generations:

> "Sometimes I wish I had not taken the *ozo* title," said Obierika. "It wounds my heart to see these young men killing palm trees in the name of tapping "
>
> "It is so indeed," Okonkwo agreed. "But the law of the land must be obeyed."
>
> "I don't know how we got that law," said Obierika. "In many other clans a man of title is not forbidden to climb the tall tree. Here we say he cannot climb the tall tree but he can tap the short ones standing on the ground. It is like Dimaragana, who would not lend his knife for cutting up dog-meat because the dog was taboo to him, but offered to use his teeth." (p. 63)

We learn from the tale the different attitudes of both men towards their customs, namely: Obierika is progressive but Okonkwo is conservative. The difference in their attitudes is what makes the former to reflect on the impact of the white man's presence in Umuofia, adjust to the change which that presence brings, and live; it also makes the latter determine to fight the white man in order to preserve the dignity of his culture, but in the process of achieving his aim he makes costly mistakes and dies. Dimaragana's act in the tale can be compared with Ezeulu's mistake in *Arrow of God*; he apparently avoids being converted by the Christians, but sends his son Oduche to the white man's church and school.

In addition, there are jocular tales in the novels which, while entertaining as folk humor, make subtle remarks or pass a moral judgement on the behavior of people in society. In *No Longer at Ease*, Christopher and Obi are arguing a point about bribery as a common social evil in Lagos. Obi is shocked that men could take advantage of young innocent girls in order to give them jobs. To prove to Obi that many innocent-looking little girls are not what they appear to be, Christopher tells a jocular story:

> A girl who comes the way she did is not an innocent little girl. It's like the story of the girl who was given a form to fill in. She put down her name and her age. But when she came to sex she wrote: "Twice a week." Obi could not help laughing (p. 110).

Although the author presents the story as a joke, yet it is a succinct remark on the central theme of the novel—bribery and corruption in Nigeria. Whether the bribe is money or sexual favors, both the giver and the taker are equally guilty of the crime. But when it comes to moral turpitude, men should be blamed more since the looks and age of the girls tend to portray them as defenseless victims of a corrupt society. Initially, Obi resists the idea of taking bribes, especially the one which is offered in form of sex, but in the end he accepts a bribe from the same girl, but in another form, twenty pounds.

In the first edition of *Arrow of God* (London, 1964), Achebe includes a fairy tale about two jealous wives, but he merely refers to the story without telling it in full in the second edition (revised, London, 1974) of the novel. Commenting on the omission, Robert M. Wren observes that:

> Achebe has cut the story, leaving only the bare beginning, that the story is about two wives, of whom "the senior wife was wicked and envious"—these quoted words being added to the revised edition. Many readers still find the cut—four and a half pages—inconsequential, unless they assumed that the story, placed so crucially, must have had relevance to Ezeulu's state of mind; such readers have asked what the relevance is. Achebe has answered the question: the story is not consequential, it is not relevant to the priest's state of mind, and we can all forget about it—except as a very good folktale, well told, merely out of place.[7]

Since some readers felt (contrary to Achebe's opinion) that the story is relevant to the priest's state of mind (even as a mere allusion in the revised edition of the novel), we shall look at the story again. Bernth Lindfors wrote a detailed critical essay, "The Folktale as Paradigm in Chinua Achebe's *Arrow of God*,"[8] which appraises how generally "Achebe, like many a fireside raconteur, often uses proverbs and folktales to comment indirectly on eccentricities of human behavior which have been observed or manifested recently by his audience. The lore thus serves a moral purpose, interpreting as well as reflecting contemporary social realities"[9] generally, and points out in particular the thematic function of the fairy tale in the novel. According to Lindfors, many regard the tale as a variant of the widespread "Tale of the Kind and the Unkind Girls" (No. 480 in the Aarne-Thompson tale type index). His main argument is that when the morphology and placement of the story within the novel are

---

[7] Robert M. Wren, "Achebe's Revision of *Arrow of God*," *Research in African Literatures* 7 (1976), p. 54.

[8] Bernth Lindfors, *Folklore in Nigerian Literature* (New York: Africana Publishing Company, 1973), pp. 94-103.

[9] *Ibid*, p. 94.

examined, we realize its relevance to Ezeulu's tragedy. Lindfors's examination of the story reveals structural and thematic parallels between Ezeulu's non-submission to Ulu's authority with its disastrous consequence and that of the boy. Finally, Lindfors sees parallels between the farm as demi-world and Ezeulu as demi-god. His argument leads him to conclude that:

> Achebe's sensitive handling of this tale in *Arrow of God* suggests that his art is far more subtle and sophisticated than it appears on the surface. And to this it should be added that some of his techniques seem to be more African than European. For example, his ability to utilize folktales as relevant social commentary in symbolic form is surely something he acquired at home, not abroad (*Ibid*, p. 102).

Mary Ellen B. Lewis is one of those who regard Achebe's fairy tale about two jealous wives as a variant of the "Tale of the Kind and the Unkind Girls."[10] But it should be pointed out that Achebe's tale is not a variant of the so-called African reaction AT 480, "The Tale of the Kind and Unkind Girls." Rather, it is a variant of a known Igbo fairy tale which Ernest Emenyonu calls "Ngeleagun 'egbu", and which he includes in his book, *The Rise of the Igbo Novel*.[11]

Nevertheless, Lewis uses Achebe's tale to demonstrate how a critic should go "beyond content in the analysis of folklore in literature," in order to obtain a better and rewarding result than what one gets by merely identifying folklore materials found in an author's works. Her analysis of that tale makes her to say:

> Essentially, Ugoye tells a story to please her children and to alleviate her own anxiety over her relationship with the senior wife. Lindfors suggests that the tale is a paradigm for the novel as a whole, but I

---

[10] Mary Ellen B. Lewis, "Beyond Content in the Analysis of Folklore in Literature: Chinua Achebe's *Arrow of God,*" *Research in African Literatures* 7 (1976), pp. 44-52.

[11] Ernest Emenyonu, *The Rise of the Igbo Novel*, (Ibadan: Oxford University Press, 1978), pp. 12-15.

prefer to see the tale as a paradigm for the recurrent theme of Ugoye's relationship with Matefi—the novel itself depicting culture conflict, and in this case, the largely negative power of the dominant, intrusive culture on the delicate, yet strong fabric of the traditional pattern of life. Through the tale, Ugoye works out her hostility for, as in the tale, the senior wife will get her due because of her own flawed character—her pride, her selfishness, her envy. Ugoye need do nothing, for envy brings its own reward, ideal advice perhaps to a young woman caught in a tension-filled, tradition-bound relationship. Thus the telling of the tale both releases Ugoye's hostility, enabling her to find relief in fictive therapy, and entertains her children, instructing them, as Ibo tales are said to do, about proper behavior, in this case warning them against envy; and in taking the time to tell them that all is well in their world, lately in upheaval.[12]

Because envy is an important theme of the novel, Ugoye's tale could be regarded as either a paradigm for the novel as a whole, as Lindfors suggests, or a paradigm for the recurrent theme of Ugoye's relationship with Matefi, as Lewis prefers to regard it. Indeed, the novel itself depicts culture conflict, but the envy between Ezeulu and Nwaka is stronger and poses more national danger than that between Ugoye and Matefi. Furthermore, as brothers they quarrelled and allowed strangers to inherit their father's home. In general, story-telling sessions in traditional Igbo home settings are poised between folk entertainment and cultural initiation, verbally transmitted. Children listen to the stories as pastimes while they wait for the women to finish cooking the evening meals; they can also have a few laughs which well-told jocular tales provide. But on a more serious note, parents tell the folk stories to inculcate in their children good behavior, manners, hard work, contentment, obedience, fairness, and submission to the authorities of the elders and ancestors—virtues which constitute the bedrock of and lessons in Igbo social, political, religious, and ethical morality.

---

[12] Lewis, *op. cit.*, p. 48.

Legends, anecdotes, single-motif tales, and even trickster stories about other people are told either to warn against wicked behavior or to inspire young people to lead a virtuous life, thereby preparing them for adulthood. As "a fireside raconteur," Achebe either quotes or reconstructs Igbo folk stories in his novels to recapitulate, interweave, or foreshadow major events of the novels, while making subtle commentary on the lives of his characters and the Igbo fictional society. The way he handles the stories emphasizes the Igbo people's love and use of folk stories as pragmatically educational verbal art. It is to this finer Igbo folkway that Leopold Senghor referred when he said, "The traditional African narrative is woven out of everyday events. In this it is a question neither of anecdotes nor of things 'taken from life.' All the events become images, and so acquire paradigmatic value and point beyond the moment."[13]

---

[13] Quoted in Janheinz Jahn, *Muntu: The New African Culture* (New York: Grove Press, Inc., 1961), p. 211.

8 | Folk Songs and Chants

> On the face of it there was no kind of logic or meaning in the song. But as Obi turned it round in his mind, he was struck by the wealth of association that even such a mediocre song could have.
> —Achebe's narrator in *No Longer at Ease*.

The folk songs and chants that we find in Chinua Achebe's novels, if analyzed critically, can yield crucial cultural information about the Igbo, their world-view and principal concerns, some of which we have touched upon in other sections of this study. As will be demonstrated, Achebe's employment of folk songs and chants to recreate Igbo culture in its complexities and the norms which differentiate and sharply characterize it from other cultures is one of the attractions of his novels.

A folk song, as viewed in this study is simply a song originating from the country folk and handed down from generation to generation, and is used, as a group communication device, to focus the attention of groups on important issues, to organize them for joint response, and to produce consensus.[1] That is why the songs are

---

[1] See Lomas and Halifax, "Folk Song Texts as Culture Indicators," in Alan Lomas, *Folk Song Style and Culture*. (Washington, D.C.: American

repetitive and choric in form, and didactic functionally. Achebe is neither a folk song creator nor its singer; therefore, the folk songs and chants that we find in his novels are not created by him. Rather he has borrowed them from his culture and ingeniously reconstructed them to aid the structural and thematic developments of his novels and his craftsmanship. For this latter reason, this study does not address the poetics of the folk songs or the elusive matter of melody, rhythm and phonotactic structure[2]—redundant song features which are usually the concern of textual song analysts of literate societies. Also, we avoid the poetics of folk songs and chants because Achebe does not concern himself with scoring the songs in his novels so as to make formal prosodic evaluation of them easy and necessary; but for him and for his fictional Igbo societies, the importance of folk songs and chants as Igbo oral tradition lies primarily in their didactic function and oral performance. In fact, underlining the differences between written songs of literate societies and orally transmitted folk songs of nonliterate societies, Bruno Nettl once observed:

> In less technical language, oral tradition means simply that music (like stories, proverbs, riddles, methods of arts and crafts, and, indeed, all folklore) is passed on by word of mouth. Songs are learned by hearing; instrument making and playing are learned by watching. In a sophisticated culture, music is usually written down, and a piece conceived by a composer need never be performed at all during his lifetime; it can be discovered centuries later by a scholar and resurrected. But in a folk or a nonliterate culture, a song must be sung, remembered, and taught by one generation to the next. If this does not happen, it dies and is lost forever. Surely, then, a piece of folk music must in some way be representative of the musical taste and the aesthetic judgement of all those who know it and use it, rather than being simply the product of an individual, perhaps

---

Association for the Advancement of Science, Publication No. 88, 1968), p. 275, whose definition of folk song I borrowed.

[2] *Ibid.*, p. 276.

isolated creator.[3]

Put simply, the Igbo folk songs and chants, as recreated in Achebe's novels, have a wealth of associations that requires our evaluation. However, for lack of necessary equipment, the evaluation will be done in terms of the function rather than the poetics of the songs. Hence in this chapter, we aim to discover what the songs and chants mean to their singers and their listeners; and to Achebe who introduces them for special artistic effects, wherever they appear in his novels.

To begin with, the folk songs and chants found in the novels are here classified and examined under the following groups: panegyric songs, homiletic songs, bridal songs, lullabies, play songs, work songs, dirges, and general songs.

Panegyric Songs

Since the Igbo revere achievements, there abound in the society many panegyric songs which express people's admiration for the efforts of achievers. While the songs are used to praise achievers they are also sung to incite aspirant men to action, especially manly actions such as wrestling and head-hunting.

During burial ceremonies, title-taking celebrations, emergency meetings, and other public activities which involve the presence of warlike men, praise singers and talking drums sing the praises of individuals and their ancestors who have done praise-worthy things. On their part, women sing the praises of men who have brought honor and recognition to their villages and clans. They are at times especially hired to sing during celebrations and festivals. Achebe knows about the role of panegyric songs and so has incorporated them in his novels. For example, in *Things Fall Apart*, women sing a panegyric song in praise of Okafo who throws Ikezue in what the narrator describes as "a fierce wrestling contest" (p. 45). As they sing

---

[3] Bruno Nettl, *Folk and Traditional Music of the Western Continents* (Englewood Cliffs, New Jersey: Prentice-Hall, Inc., 1965). p. 3.

his praise, young children clap their hands:

> Who will wrestle for our village?
> > Okafo will wrestle for our village.
>
> Has he thrown a hundred men?
> > He has thrown four hundred men.
>
> Has he thrown a hundred Cats?
> > He has thrown four hundred Cats.
>
> Then send him word to fight for us. (p. 46)

From the song, we realize the importance of victory in inter-village wrestling matches. Victory brings fame to both the Cat and his village. In Umuofia society, which is full of esoteric ceremonies, a wrestling match is one of those few honor-giving contests that are open to the general public: men and women, boys and girls, the rich and the poor. The matches attract such large crowds that a representative of a village must have gone through local "play-offs" before he is chosen to represent his village at the "semi-final". That means when a contestant wins, he wins big, and when he loses, he loses much. It is such a contest that brings honor to Okonkwo's village, and fame to the hero as a young man of eighteen, when he threw Amalinze the Cat—Amalinze the great wrestler who for seven years was unbeaten, from Umuofia to Mbaino (p. 3).

Wrestling matches are such important sports for the Igbo that all through the novel, great wrestlers are highly respected and rewarded spiritually and materially. An example of rewarded contestants is Okonkwo who, more than anyone else in his society, has enjoyed fame throughout the nine villages of Umuofia and even beyond; in addition, through wrestling, he won the heart of his lovely wife, Ekwefi:

> The second day of the new year was the day of the great wrestling match between Okonkwo's village and their neighbors. It was difficult to say which the people enjoyed more—the feasting and fellowship of the first day or the wrestling contest of the second. But there was one woman who had no doubt whatever in her mind. She was Okonkwo's second wife, Ekwefi, whom he nearly shot. There

was no festival in all the seasons of the year which gave her as much pleasure as the wrestling match. Many years ago, when she was the village beauty Okonkwo had won her heart by throwing the Cat in the greatest contest within living memory. She did not marry him then because he was too poor to pay her bride-price. But a few years later she ran away from her husband and came to live with Okonkwo. All this happened many years ago. Now Ekwefi was a woman of forty-five who had suffered a great deal in her time. But her love of wrestling contests was still as strong as it was thirty years ago (p. 36).

Ekwefi's love of wrestling contests is that strong because of the panegyric song the women sang in praise of Okonkwo—a song which helps her to cope with her problem of losing her babies to *ogbanje*. We imagine this to be so because, according to Pete Seeger,

> Some songs mainly help people forget their troubles. Other songs help people understand their troubles. Some few songs inspire people to do something about their troubles. Occasionally these different roles are present in one song.[4]

Panegyric songs sung to young wrestlers like Obierika's son help Okonkwo to understand his troubles, particularly as they remind him of Nwoye's lack of enthusiasm for manly activities.

The numbers, hundred and four hundred, in the panegyric song the women sing to Okafo refer to the traditional numbers of men who are sent to fight other villages in inter-tribal wars, as well as standard denominations in Igbo counting—*ogu ise* (100) and *nnu* (400). Military officers in charge of men of those numbers have special honors conferred on them at the end of military campaigns. That is why the women are urging the *faceless* elders in charge of war logistics to "send [Okafo] word to fight for us"; Okafo has demonstrated a wrestling prowess which can enable him to lead

---

[4] Peter Seeger, *The Incomplete Folksinger* (New York: Simon and Schuster, 1972), p. 5.

their men successfully through any wars at all.

In *Arrow of God*, Ezeulu and his household celebrate the marriage feast of his son, Obika. The narrator reports that the feasting which follows lasts till sunset because there are pots of yam pottage, foofoo, bitter-leaf soup and *egusi* soup, two boiled legs of goat, two large bowls of cooked *asa* fish taken out whole from the soup and kegs of sweet wine tapped from the raffia palm. By local standards, the provision is plenty enough to rouse the women to sing one of their panegyric songs. Hence, "whenever a particular impressive item of food was set before the women their song-leader raised the old chant of thanks"[5]:

Kwo-kwo-kwo-kwo-kwo
    Kwo-o-o-oh!
We are going to eat again as we are wont to do!
    Who provides?
Who is it?
    Who provides?
Who is it?
    Obika Ezeulu he provides
Ayo-o-o-o-o-oh! (*Ibid.*, p. 117)

The chanting is done so loudly that every villager who hears it is drawn to the scene of feasting. Some come to observe the amount of food that the bridegroom and his family provide; others come to eat some of the food; yet a third group may come to enjoy the songs and dances that characterize every feast, such as the present one. For the two families of the bride and bridegroom, the marriage feast breeds mixed emotions because it is a time of merriment and celebration, and a time to part with what one treasures very highly; the parents of the bride go home unsure of having entrusted their daughter to the proper parental care of their in-laws, and the mother of the bridegroom is not sure either that she will ever have the full opportunity of enjoying the love of her son, since a new kind of love

---

[5] *Arrow of God*, p. 116.

has come into her son's life. The narrator makes a remark on the the bride's feelings:

> But in the end her mother and all the protecting company from her village set out for home again leaving her behind. Okuata felt like an orphan child and tears came down her face. Her mother-in-law took her away into her hut where she would stay until Sacrifice at the crossroads was performed (p. 117).

Those who attend the marriage feast go home to tell stories about what they saw. Usually the rich homes, such as Ezeulu's, are expected to provide more items of food than the poorer ones. And since the women chant their praises according to what provisions they find, there is always an unspoken competition among bridegrooms over who would outspend the other in order to earn more praises from the praise-chanters. Thus the overall effect of praise-singing is stratification of society into the "have's" and the "have-nots," or *ogaranya na ogbenye*.

Marriages are often prearranged by parents, who make sure that their daughters are given in marriage to rich people, without any consideration for love. Okonkwo is an example of the men who, obsessed with social status, would never allow their daughters to choose their husbands freely. On the other hand, girls who eventually marry rich men are assured of good social and emotional security, even after their husbands are long dead. They may also find love if they are as hardworking as members of their rich husbands' families, whose basic idea of marriage is that love is gradually cultivated, not necessarily a pre-marital qualification.

The rivalry between rich homes in Achebe's novels is exemplified by the appearance of Nwaka's household and (with sharp contrast) that of Ezeulu.[6] Nwaka is of the opinion that he should receive more praise for being richer than Ezeulu whose fame does not depend on personal achievements but on ascribed powers of the Chief Priest of Ulu. Both men have admirers who call them praise

---

[6] For full discussion of this subject, see Chapter Five of this study.

names from time to time.

Praise songs can also be sung to describe the beauty of a person in public places; such songs are intended to draw an audience's attention to the person being described. For instance, Odili reports in *A Man of the People* how women sang a song to describe and praise their politician, Chief the Honorable M. A Nanga, M. P.:

> Five or six dancing groups were performing at different points in the compound. The popular 'Ego Women's Party' wore a new uniform of expensive accra cloth. In spite of the din you could still hear as clear as a bird the high-powered voice of their soloist, whom they admiringly nicknamed 'Grammar-phone.' Personally I don't care too much for our women's dancing but you just had to listen whenever Grammar-phone sang. She was now praising Micah's handsomeness, which she likened to the perfect, sculpted beauty of a carved eagle, and his popularity which would be the envy of the proverbial traveller-to-distant-places who must not cultivate enmity on his route. Micah was of course Chief the Honorable M. A Nanga, M. P. (p. 1).

To the women, the singing of praise songs is an artistic expression—the lead-singer or soloist's ability to weigh the festal occasion, realize the importance of the *august* visitor, including his physical appearance, and comment appropriately on them. In this scene, "Grammar-phone" functions like a village minstrel. Give her the name of Nanga, tell her what he is coming to do, and she will compose and sing you a spontaneous, unrehearsed song about the man, which the other women and men in the audience can easily echo and dance to.

However, beneath the apparent good time the people and their visitor, Nanga, are having lies the subtle satirical criticism of the whole festival. The narrator, Odili, condemns the whole occasion as a phony exercise because it has been organized by local leaders of Nanga's political party to praise a man who is too corrupt to represent his constituency and help shape the destiny of his nation. The rally is also designed to give Nanga a cheap popularity that will eventually make it impossible for any candidate with a better political vision to campaign against Nanga and succeed. That is why the narrator, who turns out to be one of Nanga's rivals in the end, says:

> As I stood in one corner of that vast tumult waiting for the arrival of the Minister I felt intense bitterness welling up in my mouth. Here were silly, ignorant villagers dancing themselves lame and waiting to blow off their gunpowder in honor of one of those who had started the country off down the slopes of inflation. I wished for a miracle, for a voice of thunder, to hush this ridiculous festival and tell the poor contemptible people one or two truths. But of course it would be quite useless. They were not only ignorant but cynical. Tell them that this man had used his position to enrich himself and they would ask you—as my father did—if you thought that a sensible man would spit out the juicy morsel that good fortune placed in his mouth (p. 2).

The "miracle or voice of thunder" that the narrator "wished for, to hush the ridiculous festival" finally came at the end of the novel, when

> the Army obliged us by staging a coup at that point and locking up every member of the Government. The rampaging bands of election thugs had caused so much unrest and dislocation that our young Army officers seized the opportunity to take over. We were told Nanga was arrested trying to escape by canoe dressed like a fisherman (p. 147).

These lines "prophesied" the Nigerian Military Coup of January 15, 1966, which marked an end to the first Republic of Nigeria and promised a better future for all Nigerians. In fact, rivalry, fuelled by praise names, is also found in the modern society of *A Man of The People*. Praise songs and chants are known to have caused feuds and rivalry among political opponents in Africa. For this reason one agrees with Lindfors that "the ending [of *A Man of the People*] was meant to be true to Africa and not merely truthful about Nigeria.

The coup was an African parable, not a Nigerian prophecy."[7]

As a general thematic concern, Achebe recognizes that praise-songs and chants are an important Igbo folkway, especially because they form an important aspect of Igbo festivals and celebrations. Nevertheless, praise-singing incites undue competitions and envy that are capable of destroying both the men being praised and their praise-singers. In *Things Fall Apart,* for example, part of Okonkwo's problem is that whenever he achieves something like throwing Amalinze the Cat, women and men alike sing his praises. The result is that he kills five men in inter-clan wars, thereby qualifying to act as Umuofia's emissary of war to Mbaino; his military fame makes it easier for him to bring back from Mbaino two children as restitution for a murdered Umuofia woman. In the same manner, when he kills his adopted son, Ikemefuna, he regards his act as another praise-worthy thing to do, even though his conscience troubles him. He thus expects his son, Nwoye, to be as blood-thirsty as he is. And when Nwoye fails to act according to his expectation, Okonkwo has no patience with him, just as he has none for other less successful men of Umuofia. At last, his violent action, which Umuofia promotes through constantly singing his praises, turns out to be ironically what pushes Okonkwo to commit suicide and throws his society into confusion—a confusion that weakens the society and makes it easier for the white men to gain administrative control of Umuofia clan.

Similarly in *Arrow of God,* Ezeulu and Nwaka wrestle to find out who will throw the other and break his anklet; their clansmen are the "flute players". Nwaka draws spiritual strength for his opposition to the Chief Priest from Ezidemili, and Umuaro men publicly applaud him uproariously and call him the praise-name "Owner of Words", not necessarily because he is always right but because he is very rich. On one occasion, the narrator remarks:

There were murmurs of approval and of disapproval from the

---

[7] Bernth Lindfors, "Achebe's African Parable" *Critical Perspectives on Chinua Achebe,* (Washington, D.C.: Three Continents Press, 1978), p. 254.

assembly of elders and men of title. Nwaka walked forward and back as he spoke; the eagle feather in his red cap and bronze band on his ankle marked him out as one of the lords of the land—a man favored by Eru, the god of riches (p. 16).

Certainly Ezeulu cannot receive a fair hearing from such interest group of titled men. But to fight Nwaka and his henchmen, Ezeulu resorts to scheming in order to build his own interest group of majority of the intelligentsia. Both groups fight at last, weaken their society and allow Mr. Goodcountry, the Christian missionary in Umuaro, to make converts of the Igbo men.

Homiletic Songs

Homiletic songs are those songs in Achebe's novels which tend to preach or embody the religious and moral philosophies of the Igbo. Some of the moral which the songs preach derives from the Bible read in Igbo societies which have accepted Christianity, while other moral lessons are drawn from traditional Igbo religion. Like any other homiletics, Achebe's homiletic songs are sung to teach, admonish or persuade those who are the subjects of the songs. In other cases people sing homiletic songs as a means of expressing their faith and prayerful wishes.

After Uchendu has spoken to Okonkwo on how to adopt a new way of life in order to survive the depression caused by exile in Mbanta, Uchendu closes his long talk by asking Okonkwo and other members of the agnatic family the question, "Have you not heard the song they sing when a woman dies?" He follows up the question with the homiletic song:

> For whom is it well, for whom is it well?
> There is no one for whom it is well;

and like a preacher he ends his homily by saying,

> I have no more to say to you. (*TFA*, p. 122)

Okonkwo is not required to answer the question asked in the song. Rather, he is required to say "Amen!" to Uchendu's sermon and then meditate on the words of advice he has just heard. From his attitude after the meeting, it is clear that Uchendu's advice had a good effect on Okonkwo; it helped him to triumph over his calamity. The homiletic song recommends that man endure what he cannot prevent or cure. Behind that attitude towards human existence is the latent belief in the force which controls the destiny of man, a force to which man must resign himself, drawing sustenance from the fate of other people in adversity.

When we come to *No Longer at Ease,* the nature of the homiletic songs changes from one which is drawn from folk philosophy of life to one taken from the Bible, because the novel is dramatizing primarily the life and problems of a man born and bred in a Christian home, Obi Okonkwo. In the first chapter of the novel, Obi's father, Mr. Isaac Okonkwo, organizes a send-off party in which Obi is counselled on how to behave himself overseas. Towards the end of the party, a guest thanks Mr. Okonkwo for inviting them, and he also thanks other guests for answering Mr. Okonkwo's call, adding 'If you had not answered his call, our brother would become like the king in the Holy Book who called a wedding feast.' Such a Biblical allusion inspires Mary, one of the Christian guests, to sing a homiletic song:

> Leave me not behind Jesus, wait for me
> When I am going to the farm.
> Leave me not behind Jesus, wait for me
> When I am going to the market
> Leave me not behind Jesus, wait for me
> When I am eating my food.
> Leave me not behind Jesus, wait for me
> When I am having my bath.
> Leave me not behind Jesus, wait for me
> When he is going to the White Man's Country,
> Leave him not behind Jesus, wait for him (p. 10).

Looked at superficially, it would seem as if the song carries no philosophy. But if one meditates on it, one will be struck by the wealth of association that even such a mediocre song can have. For instance, Christian converts are taught that Jesus is omnipresent, omnipotent and omniscient. So they call on him to protect them in all activities of life. The two major traditional Igbo occupations are farming and marketing of farm products, hence the singer invites Jesus to be with her in those places where she does her work. At the end of each day's work, Christians take a bath, eat their food and go to sleep. That is why "farm", "market", and "bath" are important words of the song. The choric line, "Leave me not behind Jesus, wait for me," conveys the inherent struggles found in those Igbo activities that Mary enumerates, especially farming and marketing. The converts realize the inadequacy of their own strength and so must solicit the assistance of a strongman, Jesus, who must lead the way and also look behind to ensure that the followers are following suit.

Nevertheless, the song inspires derision in the reader, when he considers the tone of the song generally. What we find here is "Jesus of Nazareth" being domesticated in Umuofia, Eastern Nigeria, by a village woman so that Jesus can be real to her. It is only in this way that "the mad logic of the Trinity"[8] which the new dispensation preaches can become acceptable to a mind which is used to making practical association of things, but not contemplating abstract ideas. Mary personalizes Jesus, which is the best way to accept God and his surrogates.

The song itself is an example of native inventiveness: essentially, it is a reconstructed version of the hackneyed Christian song, "Pass me not, oh gentle Jesus," which is as old and weather-beaten as "Rock of Ages" itself. In its new form, the song can be tolerated a few more years before Obi returns from the White Man's Country to create a new opportunity for another reconstruction. Indeed, what has happened to the original Christian song demonstrates how Christianity is being Africanized in all parts of the continent. Achebe has reconstructed the song in the same way he "reconstructs" the British English language in order to fully express his African messag-

---

[8] *Things Fall Apart*, p. 137.

es and thoughts in his novel; how he does it will be the subject of the next chapter.

Another homiletic song that Achebe records in *No Longer at Ease* is "The Song of the Heart" (p. 117). The song is so titled because it is about Obi (literally, heart), and also talks about kinship which is a matter of the heart. The narrator reports that the song is sung by "a band of young women who had been making music at a funeral" on the evening when Obi returns from Lagos to Umuofia. They have just decided to go in and salute Obi when his father, opposed to all heathen songs, decides to drive them away; but Obi persuades him that the women could do no harm. To emphasize the function and place of the song in the novel, the narrator says:

> It was ominous the way he [Isaac Okonkwo] gave in without a fight and went to shut himself up in his room. Obi's mother came out to the *pieze* and sat on a high chair by the window. She liked music even when it was heathen music (p. 116).

That is, the song foreshadows the verbal fight that Obi and his parents will later engage in over Obi's marriage proposal to Clara, an *osu*, and his parent's quiet disappointment and resignation; it also ominously foreshadows the death of Obi's mother and his failure to return for her funeral. Here is the song:

> A letter came to me the other day. I said to Mosisi: "Read my letter for me." Mosisi said to me: "I do not know how to read." I went to Innocenti and asked him to read my letter. Innocenti said to me: "I do not know how to read." I asked Simonu to read for me. Simonu said: "This is what the letter has asked me to tell you:
>
>> *He that has a brother must hold him to his heart*
>> *For a kinsman cannot be bought in the market*
>> *Neither is a brother bought with money.*"

Is everyone here?
(*Hele ee he ee he*)
Are you all here?
(*Hele ee he ee he*)

> The letter said
> That he who has brothers
> Has more than riches can buy.
> (Hele ee he ee he) (p. 117)

One of Obi's problems throughout the novel is his failure to appreciate fully the depth and importance of kinship in the lives of Umuofia at home and abroad. As a way of life, the Igbo believe that since blood relationship is not a common commodity, it should be guarded and preserved cautiously. Also they believe that the help which a kinsman gives, especially in times of trouble, is more invaluable than material riches which may not last. We find a demonstration of the wisdom of that principle of life which the song preaches in Obi's own life. Until his arrest and conviction for taking bribes, Obi keeps to himself as a reaction to Umuofia people's opposition to his marriage with Clara in Lagos. As a part of his Western orientation, he prefers individualistic living to communal living which Umuofia people everywhere practice. To Obi, communal living constricts one's individual freedom of choice. He does not realize that his people's opposition is meant to save him, his children and grandchildren from the stigma of being labelled and ostracized as *osu* for life. The people, as Obi's elders, could not "be in the house and see the she-goat suffer in her parturition."[9] Hence they "must hold [Obi] to [their] heart, for a kinsman cannot be bought in the market"; they know that they cannot buy him with money!

As it applies to the particular incident in the novel, the song gives Obi a warning which he fails to heed. Obi knows that once he loses his mother he cannot replace her with another bought from the market, and that no amount of money he makes can play the role of a mother in his life. Yet he does not stop to think over his mother's warning:

> I did not tell anybody about the dream in the morning. I carried it in my heart wondering what it was. I took down my Bible and read

---

[9] *Arrow of God*, p. 26.

the portion for the day. It gave me some strength, but my heart was still not at rest. In the afternoon your father came in with a letter from Joseph to tell us that you were going to marry an *osu*. I saw the meaning of my death in the dream. Then I told your father about it.... I have nothing to tell you in this matter except one thing. If you want to marry this girl, you must wait until I am no more. If God hears my prayers, you will not wait long.... But if you do this thing while I am alive, you will have my blood on your head, because I shall kill myself (p. 123).

If Obi were a bit careful, he should have told his mother that he was not going to "do the thing" so as to save her from dying. Instead he fails to reassure her, boycotts his family's evening prayers, and lies that he was ill—a rejection of his family's ideals. And finally, he decides to return to Lagos in two days time instead of spending a week with his family as he had told them earlier on. That is why Obi regrets his action; upon hearing the news of his mother's death, "something caught in his throat. He got out of bed and stood gazing at the light coming in through the louvres. Shame and guilt filled his heart" (p. 146). He cannot say "Had I known," because the women singers gave him a good warning which is contained in the words of the first stanza of the song and re-emphasized in the second stanza, after they had made sure everybody heard their message: "Is everybody here? Are you all here?" Indeed, the target of the song, Obi, was there. He, in fact, welcomed them at the displeasure of his father. But if "The Song of the Heart" was not warning enough to Obi, he cannot say he does not appreciate the danger of displeasing his mother at the point of death. His not-too-careful act cannot be forgiven easily when his unusual blood relationship (apart from their biological relationship) with his mother[10] is put into consideration.

The role of the letter in the song should be emphasized: "The

---

[10] For a full analysis of Obi's unusual relationship with his mother, see Rosemary Comer, "The Start of Weeping is Always Hard: The Ironic Structure of *No Longer at Ease*" in *Literary Half-Yearly*, 21, 1 (1980), pp. 121-135. See also *No Longer at Ease*, pp. 68-69.

Song of the Heart" is actually the content of the letter which Moses and Innocent fail to read but which Simon finally reads. Obi's mother also reads the meaning of her ominous dreams from a letter sent to her by Joseph, Obi's townsman in Lagos. Thus, the letter is not just a means of conveying warnings that Obi fails to heed, but it also serves as a communication link between Umuofia at home and abroad, between the city and the countryside, and between Obi's immediate family in Umuofia and his extended family in Lagos. Although the "Song of the Heart" is not Achebe's composition, he exploits it to reflect Obi's situation. This power of composing ready-made elements into imaginatively significant pattern is one of Achebe's great gifts.

Play Songs

Play songs are simply songs that people, especially children, sing as they play. However, when read closely they offer more than "playful" insights into the themes of the novels. Wherever they appear in all four novels, play songs appear to force readers to stop, sing the songs and reflect on them, if they can; or they read the songs as poetry.

At the end of Chapter Four of *Things Fall Apart*, there is the play song,

> The rain is falling, the sun is shining,
> Alone Nnadi is cooking and eating,

sung by children who, because "the rain fell in thin, slanting showers through sunshine and quiet breeze," no longer stayed indoors but ran about playing. Actually, the song describes the weather condition at the time that the children are playing—rain and sun in a single combat—conveyed in the words of the first line of the song. However, what does not belong in the context of the song is Nnadi who is cooking and eating alone, the words of the second line. Obviously, something is wrong somehow and somewhere. That is why some children must stop to think. According to the narrator,

Nwoye always wondered who Nnadi was and why he should live all by himself, cooking and eating. In the end he decided that Nnadi must live in that land of Ikemefuna's favorite story where the ant holds his court in splendor and the sands dance forever (p. 32).

Nwoye's explanation makes sense to a boy of his age, and the song as folk story has performed its duty, which is to make its listener think. But for adult readers, the song must mean more than what Nwoye offers. The song reflects Ikemefuna's mood. Just before the song is sung, we are told that "Ikemefuna had began to feel like a member of Okonkwo's family." But he still thought about his mother and his three-year-old sister and he had moments of sadness and depression. In other words, his moments of joy and sorrow fluctuate like "the rain is falling, the sun is shining." As it relates to Ikemefuna, "Alone Nnadi is cooking and eating" refers to his mother who cooks and eats without him. Both son and mother are constantly depressed by their "aloneness" in the midst of company—Ikemefuna in Nwoye's company and Ikemefuna's mother in her three-year-old daughter's company. Neither Nwoye nor the little girl is capable of understanding the loneliness of their companions. It is this lack of understanding which heightens the plight of mother and son, who are victims of and separated by the jungle law of Umuofia and Mbaino.

Another play song, which also relates to Ikemefuna, is:

Eze elina, elina!
    Sala
Eze ilikwa ya
Ikwaba akwa oligholi
Ebe Danda nechi eze
Ebe Uzuzu nete egwu
    Sala (p. 54)

Although we treat this song as play song, it is essentially an *interior monologue* that reproduces the course and rhythm of consciousness just as it occurs in Ikemefuna's mind, with no (or at any rate, with minimal) intervention by the author.[11] Ikemefuna recalls the play song from the memory of one of his play sessions and actually acts it out:

> He sang it in his mind, and walked to its beat. If the song ended on his right foot, his mother was alive. If it ended on his left, she was dead. No, not dead, but ill. It ended on the right. She was alive and well. He sang the song again, and it ended on the left. But the second time did not count. The first voice gets to Chukwu, or God's house. That was a favorite saying of children. Ikemefuna felt like a child once more. It must be the thought of going home to his mother (*TFA*, p. 54).

The song, with the ensuing narrator's commentary on it, is really sentimental and heightens the reader's feeling for Ikemefuna who is about to face imminent, heartless murder by Okonkwo. As Ikemefuna walks to the song's beat, readers imaginatively watch him to find out on which foot the song ends. Ikemefuna's explanation of the result of the game may sound both childlike and childish, yet it gives readers insight into Igbo children's folk beliefs. The nostalgic feeling the song generates in Ikemefuna is terminated as his adopted father murders him; Okonkwo's act warrants the immediate condemnation of the sensitive reader and the punishment of the Earth-goddess, Ani.

Read in its translated form, we find that the song may also have a bearing on Okonkwo. Robert M. Wren reports that Ernest Arinze Agbogu translated the song as follows:

> King don't eat, don't eat!
>   Sala
> King if you eat it
> You will weep for the abomination
> Where Danda (ant) installs a king

---

[11] M. H. Abrams, *A Glossary of Literary Terms* (New York: Holt, Rinehart and Winston, Inc., 1971), p. 165.

Where uzuzu (dust or sand) dances (literally, obeys the drum)
   Sala[12]

The song is a sung hindsight of Ezeudu's warning to Okonkwo before he actually kills Ikemefuna: "That boy calls you father. Do not bear a hand in his death" (p. 51). The word, "king", aptly describes Okonkwo whose roles in the novel qualify him as a lord of his clan; for, since the Igbo knew no kings (*Arrow of God*, p. 28), the word *king* connotes lord. And Okonkwo's fate after he flouts the warning and kills Ikemefuna is that he dies at the end of the novel; his corpse finally becomes a toy for Danda (ants) and Uzuzu (dust) in the grave. Thus, Okonkwo becomes the proverbial fly that follows the corpse into the grave (*AOG*, p. 27). His over-ambition is the poison that kills him, despite the warning of the elders. His life is thus cut short. Hence Achebe gives Okonkwo's life an appropriate ending— death by suicide towards which his abominable acts in the novel have often gravitated.

In *No Longer at Ease* the play song, "Otasili Osukwu,"[13] is not directed to the principal character, Obi. Rather, it is a song that makes a statement on the war of words between two opposed adherents of the white man's religion. The narrator observes that

> They [the C. M. S. Central School Umuofia] had also played an old evangelical tune which in Obi's school-days Protestant schoolchildren had sung to anti-Catholic words, especially on Empire Day, when Protestants and Catholics competed in athletics
>
> "*Otasili osukwu Onyenkuzi Fada*
> *E misisi ya oli awo-o.*"
>
> which translated into English is as follows:

---

[12] Robert M. Wren, *Achebe's World: The Historical and Cultural Contexts of the Novels of Chinua Achebe* (Washington, D.C.: Three Continents Press, Inc., 1980), p. 156.

[13] *No Longer at Ease*, pp. 45-46.

Palm-fruit eater, Roman Catholic teacher,
His missus a devourer of toads. (pp. 45-46)

The white missionaries who came first to Umuofia society of *Things Fall Apart* acted as amour-bearers of Christianity in their "holy war" waged against "paganism." But having firmly entrenched their presence in Umuofia society of *No Longer at Ease*, their religious war became one fought between Catholics and Protestants which are denominations of the same religion. In fact, it was the inherent quarrelsome nature of Christianity, which traditional Igbo people carefully observed, that made them call every Christian, *"onye uka"* (literally, quarrelsome person) in *Arrow of God*. Of course, they avoided such persons. For example, we are told that when Nwafo and Obiageli were reciting *"Eke nekwo onye uka"* ("Python, run. There is a Christian here") outside Ezeulu's *obi*, "it ran away *fiam*[14] like an ordinary snake" (pp. 204-205). Perhaps, it is the aggressive nature of the Christian religion as opposed to the passivity of traditional religion of Umuaro that fascinated Ezeulu and made him send his son, Oduche, to the Christians, so he can fight his archenemy, Ezidemili, whose god, Idemili, is represented by the python. Python is very scared at the mention of a Christian. In a word, the play song, "Otasili osukwu Onyenkuzi Fada" has an association with the religious unrest in Umuofia and elsewhere in Nigeria, which is alluded to in the title of the novel, *No Longer at Ease*.

Commenting on the play song, "Mili zobe ezobe! / Ka mgbaba ogwogwo!" (*AOG*, p. 182) Wren says:

"Mili zobe ezobe! / Ka mgbaba ogwogwo!"
Water, rain and rain! So I can play
(or dance) around happily (or healthfully?

---

[14] *Fiam* (onomatopoeic); the sound the python makes as it scuttles away from a Christian. According to Wren, "the royal python ... is a docile, sluggish snake that preys on small animals" (p. 167); therefore for it to scuttle away implies that it concedes superior power to the Christian.

ogwogwo may be a nonsense word). Ar XVI 182.[15]

But what Wren may have regarded as "a nonsense word" is the key to the meaning of the play song. *Ogwogwo* is an Igbo onomatopoeic name for the swift flood which forms as tropical torrential rains fall and rage throughout the land. Courageous children play merrily in it as a way of showing off their courage to the weaker ones. It is a hazardous play which could be rewarding in fame to those who go through it successfully; but sometimes children have been swept off their feet playing the game. The song is like a war song which alluringly invites one to a dangerous game. The idea of danger is borne in the narrator's qualifying phrase, "the *heady* feeling which sent children naked into the rain singing" [my emphasis].

Considering Ezeulu's frame of mind, it seems to me that a more accurate translation of the song is, "Come down, rain! / So I can play in the torrential flood." The question is, why should Ezeulu invoke the elements on himself? In part, by courageously wading through the physical flood Ezeulu proves to his companion, John Nwodika, that he is made of sterner stuff. He plays the same game whenever he shakes hands with younger people (*AOG*, p. 2). More importantly, Achebe has an answer which exposes Ezeulu's latent preparedness to challenge Umuaro elders in a conflict which eventually rocks the social and religious foundations of his clan like the *ogwogwo* he is here invoking to form:

> But Ezeulu's elation had an edge of bitterness to it. This rain was part of the suffering to which he had been exposed and for which he must exact the fullest redress. His mind sought out new grievances to pile upon all the others (p. 182).

He knows the risk involved in such a play, but he takes his chance and perishes in it.

The one major play song we find in *A Man of the People* is sung in pidgin English. The name of its target is probably a Christian for

---

[15] Wren, *op. cit.*, p. 162.

he is named Sunday, and a few of the words of the song come from the Bible. This is so because the society of the novel has accepted both Christianity and Western education as a way of life. The song reads:

> Sunday, bigi bele Sunday
> Sunday, bigi bele Sunday
> Akatakata done come!
> Everybody run away
> Sunday, Alleluia! (pp. 96-97)

Rendered in edited English, the song reads like this:

> Sunday, the big-bellied Sunday
> Sunday, the big-bellied Sunday
> The big one has come your way!
> Everybody run away
> Sunday, Alleluia!

Thus rendered, however, the "danceability" and comicality of the song are lost because those are the twin features of the song which make it suitable for the festal occasion of Christmas.

The song describes the children's Mask who, though tame and unaggressive, must be feared like any other masked spirit. At least if the Mask is incapable of *Akatakata* (aggressive act), its praise-singers can verbally create one for him if only to remind their audience that a Mask is a Mask. Moreover, the song refers contextually to Odili who is gradually creating a lot of trouble for himself as he goes to seduce Edna, Chief the Honorable M. A. Nanga's fiancee. The shout of Alleluia which follows the warning embodied in the song is the usual shout of faith and agreement that follows a preacher's admonition.

Work Songs

The difference between play songs and work songs lies in the kind of exercise that their singers do. That is, play songs are sung as people play, and work songs when they work. The two kinds of songs function alike in the novels: they serve primarily as folk entertainment; but behind the entertainment is the serious voice of the narrator making subtle comments on incidents, events, episodes, and certain situations in the novels; the songs foreshadow, recapitulate and interweave events of the novels in the same manner that other verbal types such as folk stories function. Achebe records one of his work songs in Chapter Twenty of *Things Fall Apart*:

> Kotma of the ash buttocks,
>   He is fit to be a slave.
> The white man has no sense,
>   He is fit to be a slave. (p 158)

It is sung by enraged Igbo men who have been imprisoned by white men and supervised by corrupt and cruel court messengers. To express their pent-up emotion of anger, the prisoners curse their oppressors as they cut grass in the mornings, pretending that they "sing in time with the strokes of their machetes."

The song reinforces the narrator's comment on the crudities of colonial methods of administering justice in Igboland:

> But apart from the church, the white men had brought a government. They had built a court where the District Commissioner judged cases in ignorance. He had court messengers who brought men to him for trial. Many of these messengers came from Umuru on the bank of the Great River, where the white men first came many years before and where they had built the center of their religion and trade and government. These court messengers were greatly hated in *Umuofia* because they were foreigners and also arrogant and high-handed. They were called *kotma,* and because of their ash-colored shorts they earned the additional name of Ashy-Buttocks.... They were beaten in the prison by the *kotma* and made to work every morning clearing the government compound and fetching wood for the white Commissioner and the court messengers. Some of these prisoners were men of title who should be above such mean occupation (p. 158).

Here then is the rationale of the work song. The same criminal collaboration between the white Commissioner and his corrupt court messengers is what drives Okonkwo crazy as he is imprisoned alongside five other Umuofia titled men and elders. Here, the prisoners curse and wish enslavement for the white man and his court messengers because they are men of words, but later in the novel Okonkwo, a man of quick and violent action, swears vengeance and cuts down the head messenger.

The prisoners' work song in *Arrow of God* does not contain the hate and fury we find in "*Kotma* of the ash buttocks," neither are its targets the white man and his court messengers. The song,

> When I cut grass and you cut
> What's your right to call me names? (p. 55)

is mild and playful because it is addressed to the passer-by who feels superior to the prisoner although he too clears his farmlands.

The next work song in *Arrow of God*,

> Lebula toro
>   A day
> Lebula toro
>   A day (p.76),

is a subtle Igbo workmen's protestation against the low wages of "three pence a day" they were paid by a white road-builder, Mr. Wright. Hence its targets are the white man and his agents. The narrator alludes to a line in the Bible to underline the injustice of treating the natives as slaves when he says: "The natives cannot be an exception to the aphorism that the laborer is worthy of his hire." Since the colonization of the Igbo came about through Christianity, trade and government, the white administrative officers were expected to be as moral in their dealings with the natives as the Bible preaches. Regrettably, most of them were far from being fair in their dealings with the natives.

Lullabies

There is only one Igbo lullaby in *Arrow of God*. It is sung by Obiageli Ezeulu on two occasions. Apparently she sings it to a younger child, but the import of the cradlesong is more than just to lull Amechi to sleep. The song reads thus:

> *Tell the mother her child is crying*
> *Tell the mother her child is crying*
> *And then prepare a stew of uziza*
> *And also a stew of uziza*
> *Make a watery pepper-soup*
> *So the little birds who drink it*
> *Will all perish from the hiccup*
> *Mother's goat is in the barn*
> *And the yams will not be safe*
> *Father's goat is in the barn*
> *And the yams will all be eaten*
> *Can you see that deer approaching*
> *Look! he's dipped one foot in water*
> *Snake has struck him!*
> *He withdraws!*
> *Ja-ja kulo!*
> *Traveller Hawk*
> *You're welcome home*
> *Ja-ja kulo!*
> *But where's the length*
> *Of cloth you brought*
> *Ja-ja kulo!* (p. 124)

M. M. Mahood calls this song "a song of vigilance like 'The sheep's in the meadow, the cow's in the corn'"; and she quotes lines 8-11 of the lullaby as the relevant lines of the song of vigilance.[16] Indeed,

---

[16] M. M. Mahood, "Idols of the Den: Achebe's *Arrow of God*," *Critical Perspectives on Chinua Achebe* (Washington D.C.: Three Continents Press,

we agree with Mahood that the lullaby is a song of vigilance because only a vigilant baby-nurse can carefully observe and report when the child is crying, name various recipes that a nursing mother uses to prepare several kinds of Igbo food, report when a goat goes to eat her father's yams in the barn, notice the movement and withdrawal of a snake, and characterize a traveller as "Traveller Hawk."

Obiageli sings the song the first time to hush up Amoge's sick child because she has insisted on valiantly carrying her burden—the sick child on her back—in submissive violation of Ezeulu's command, "I know you can, but he is sick and should not be shaken about. Take him to your mother" (p. 123). Obiageli's insistence is a way of proving her earlier claim, "But I can carry him. See." It also proves that Obiageli is a true Ezeulu child, because "the offspring of a hawk cannot fail to devour chicks"; she resembles her father in stubbornness (p. 128).

The same lullaby is sung by Obiageli a second time, when Ezeulu has just returned from his imprisonment at Okperi and people had gathered in his *obi* to greet him (pp. 186-187). Mahood introduces the significance of the song as she comments:

> Villagers crowd into the family circle of Ezeulu's *obi*; and as they join in laughing at his grandson's insistence that he be carried by the priest's youngest daughter, Obiageli, a child scarcely bigger than himself, Ezeulu's resolution to challenge his community begins to weaken. Once again, the children in the story are made to serve an integral purpose.... As she disappears, immensely proud of her burden, there revives in Ezeulu that pride in his own burden which once made him the trusted carrier of Ulu. And when Ofoka, a man who is neither friend nor enemy, comes to congratulate him on having gone out and wrestled alone with the white man, Ezeulu's pride in his responsibility brings back an ancestral memory of the priest's function.[17]

1978), p. 196.

[17] *Ibid.*, pp. 196-197.

Also, Mahood quotes Achebe's reproduction of Ezeulu's memory of that function which appears in the novel as an interior monologue:

> Yes, it was right that the Chief Priest should go ahead and confront danger before it reached his people. That was the responsibility of his priesthood. It had been like that from the first day when the six harassed villages got together and said to Ezeulu's ancestor: *You will carry this deity for us.* At first he was afraid. What power had he in his body to carry such potent danger? But his people sang their support behind him and the flute man turned his head. So he went down on both knees and they put the deity on his head. He rose up and was transformed into a spirit. His people kept up their song behind him and he stepped forward on his first and decisive journey, compelling even the four days in the sky to give way to him (p. 189).

Whether or not it is the combined "flute-playing" of Ofoka and Obiageli's insistence on carrying her burden that triggered Ezeulu's conceived vengeance on his people, Obiageli's lullaby contains phrases which reveal that Ezeulu had already resolved to punish his people before he returned.

The friendly welcome the people accord him merely "begins to weaken" but does not change his resolution. He bides his time to find a suitable way of carrying out his resolution without appearing to be doing so consciously. That is why when his enemies accuse him rightly of punishing Umuaro for not supporting him, in his fight against the white man, his friend Akuebue ignorantly says:

> I know Ezeulu better than most people. He is a proud man and the most stubborn person you know is only his messenger; but he would not falsify the decision of Ulu. If he did it Ulu would not spare him to begin with. So, I don't know (p. 212).

Yes, Akuebue does not know that the man he is vouching for is a schemer who said on his way home, "*Mili zobe ezobe! / Kamgbaba ogwogwo*" (p. 182); the same man who is thinking of delaying his fight with his people for three more months, playing with alternatives such as to dissolve his resolution and at the right time form it again and asking himself, "Why should a man be in a hurry to lick his fingers; was he going to put them away in the rafter?" (p. 191)

Obiageli's song describes indirectly Ezeulu as a mother (Chief Priest) who makes "a watery pepper-soup / So the little birds (Umuaro people) who drink it / Will all perish from the hiccup (the local political fight that results in the non-announcement of the day of the New Yam Feast which in turn results in the starvation of children)." Ezeulu is also "Traveller hawk" whose return to Umuaro is compared to "Father's goat is in the barn." Whether as "Hawk" or "Goat," Ezeulu is welcome home, but what follows his return is destructive to Umuaro children just as the swoop of a hawk is to chickens. Words and phrases which add up to imagery of destruction include: pepper soup, perish, hiccup, will not be safe, will all be eaten, struck, and hawk. Also, the "traveller hawk's" failure to bring home a length of cloth—gesture of goodwill—is quite ominous. In the end, to avoid the total destruction of their children by starvation, Umuaro men send their sons with yams "to offer to the new religion and to bring back the promised immunity. Thereafter any yam harvested in [their] fields was harvested in the name of the son" (p. 230).

Bridal Songs

The few Igbo bridal songs Achebe includes in his novels are sung in the evenings of wedding days. They tease the women as well as poke bawdy jokes at the bride, incite phallic dances from both the bride and the bridesmaid, and introduce the bride into a new social status; she is transformed from girlhood into womanhood—a necessary *rite de passage.*

Before Achebe recreates the existing bridal song of the early forties,

> "If I hold her hand
>   She says, 'Don't touch!'
> If I hold her foot
>   She says, 'Don't touch'

> But when I hold her waist-beads
> She pretends not to know" (*TFA*, pp. 107-108),

he first of all introduces the time, mood, occasion and circumstance of the celebration:

> As night fell, burning torches were set on wooden tripods and the young men raised a song. The elders sat in a big circle and the singers went round singing each man's praise as they came before him. They had something to say for every man. Some were great farmers, some were orators who spoke for the clan; Okonkwo was the greatest wrestler and warrior alive. When they had gone round the circle they settled down in the center, and girls came from the inner compound to dance. At first the bride was not among them. But when she finally appeared holding a cock in her right hand, a loud cheer rose from the crowd. All the other dancers made way for her. She presented the cock to the musicians and began to dance. Her brass anklets rattled as she danced and her body gleamed with cam wood in the soft yellow light. The musicians with their wood, clay, and metal instruments went from song to song. And they were all gay (p. 107).

What we find here is an atmosphere of merry-making and celebration that precedes bridal singing and dancing. Although male praise-singers set the scene, the actual bridal song and dance are performed by a band of girls who support their kind as she gets ready to leave them and join her husband. In a way, the song is a farewell song to the bride from her compeers.

The song tells of the pretended anger and coyness of the bride as it also makes a statement about the sex life of the people. That is, in spite of the apparent lack of equality between men and women in Umuofia, couples do have time for romance in which they listen to their body language which tells them where and where not to touch. The bridal song, therefore, whets the sexual appetite of both the bride and her man; but the couple must wait for seven "market" weeks to have the proper initiation and purification rituals performed before they start making love.

Folk Songs and Chants

On page 116 of *Arrow of God*, a similar bridal singing and dancing is described by Achebe, but he does not write out the bridal song, *Ifeoma*, being performed for the bride, Okuata. His description of the dance is followed by a full description of the marriage feast that followed the bridal song and dance and which we evaluated as folk entertainment in Chapter Five. But later in the novel, Achebe describes the feeling of Okuata after her first sexual encounter with her husband, Obika:

> Although Okuata emerged at dawn feeling awkward and bashful in her unaccustomed loin-cloth it was a very proud bashfulness. She could go without shame to salute her husband's parents because she had been "found at home" [a virgin]. Her husband was even now arranging to send the goat and other presents to her mother in Umuezeani for giving him an unspoilt bride. She felt greatly relieved for although she had always known she was a virgin she had had a secret fear which sometimes whispered in her ear and made her start. It was the thought of the moonlight play when Obiora had put his penis between her thighs. True, he had only succeeded in playing at the entrance but she could not be too sure (p. 122).

Once again Achebe makes a comment on the sex life of the Igbo. Traditionally, pre-marital sex is condemned vehemently. Many girls remain virgin for fear of being publicly disgraced if after the first night of love making their husbands did not "find them at home." They also fear that they could suffer prolonged labor during childbirth if they failed to confess their sin of fornication before the oracle. Whether a bride's pre-marital sexual infidelity is discovered directly by her husband or known through her confession before the oracle, usually the penalty for fornication is great; it ranges from public disgrace to annulment of the marriage contract. The fear of discovery alone is a potent social and moral control of the brides. Nevertheless, Achebe provokes a laugh in the reader as he creates folk humor about the sexual inexperience of children at play!

Dirges

Dirges, as Achebe describes them in his novels, are not just songs sung at the burial (first funeral rite) or in commemoration (second funeral rite) of the dead, but also they are sung during funeral feasts. Dirges have both meanings in Igbo society because death is never regarded by them as the end of human existence; rather it is a transition from human existence in the physical world to human existence in the spirit world. People may mourn temporarily for the absence of their loved ones who leave them behind and go to *alammo* (spirit world), but there is hope of resurrection and reincarnation which alleviates the sorrow and trauma of death, except in the cases of *ogbanje*. Like bridal songs, therefore, Igbo dirges are *au revoir* songs. They are encomiastic of the dead, whose heroic exploits are talked about by funeral drums; and the esoteric messages of the drums provide occasions for feasting and dancing.

In *Things Fall Apart*, Achebe describes funeral celebrations and merely refers to the dirges without writing them down. For example, one such description occurs in Chapter Thirteen. (See our description of it in Chapter Two of this study). However, he has a few written down in *Arrow of God*. One of them is about Umuaro. As Ofoedu and Obika draw nearer to the work site, where men of their age group are working on the white man's road, they hear "the dirge with which a corpse was taken":

> Look! a python!
> Look! a python!
> Yes, it lies across the way. (p. 81)

Considering that the narrator does not mention that the python was dead and was to be buried before he introduces the dirge, we may wonder about the relevance of the funeral song where it appears. Or should we accept without question the narrator's remark which follows the song?:

> The two men recognized it now and also recognized the singers as men of their age group. They burst out laughing together. Someone

had given the ancient song a new and irreverent twist and changed it into a half familiar, half strange and hilarious work-song. Ofoedu was certain that he saw the hand of Nweke Ukpaka in it; it was the kind of malicious humor he had (p. 81).

Indeed, on its face value, the dirge, now transformed into half strange and hilarious work-song, provides malicious humor. Yet, if we question the transformation very seriously we realize its symbolic import and relevance to the general theme of the novel; that is, the traditional society of Umuaro is now being *killed* and replaced by the new one under the British Administration. So a dirge is in order.

The road they are building is the white man's road which is built to replace the people's traditional footpaths. Eventually, it will serve as a route through which the clan's agricultural products such as palm-oil will be carted out of Umuaro; and with the movement of trade comes corruption of the city into the rural community. The men of Obika's age group are forced to build the road and this is different from the voluntary communal service they are used to giving to their society. Their task master is Mr. Wright, a white road-builder, who is assisted by his Igbo stooge, Moses Unachukwu. The whipping of the late-comers, Obika and Ofoedu, represents definitive challenge to and probable defeat of the highest spiritual authority of Umuaro, for Obika is the son of the Chief Priest, Ezeulu. That means that once the native authority is challenged from the head, the rest of the people will be cowed into easy submission; after all, the Bible says "If the foundation be destroyed, what can the righteous do?"

Two symbols in the road episode tell of death: the red clay they dig off the road symbolizes interment; and while Mr. Wright gives Obika half a dozen more lashes on his back, we are told, "He did not struggle at all; he only shivered like the sacrificial ram which must take in silence the blows of funeral dancers before its throat is cut. Ofoedu trembled also, but for once in his life he saw a fight pass before him and could do nothing but look on" (p. 82). Having been so humiliated, what the age group initially regarded as Nweke Ukpaka's malicious humor is indeed a dirge for the traditional order which began giving way to the new at the time that the clan was defeated militarily—the breaking of guns incident. So the dirge is not just malicious humor; it is the consummation of national mourning which takes place towards the end of the novel.

Achebe repeats the dirge on page 221 as a part of Ezeulu's dream vision about the death of Obika, the sacrificial ram. He follows it up with a longer dirge:

> I was born when lizards were in ones and twos
> A child of Idemili. The difficult tear-drops
> Of Sky's first weeping drew my spots. Being
> Sky-born I walked the earth with royal gait.
> And mourners saw me coiled across their path.
> But of late
> A strange bell
> Has been ringing a song of desolation:
> Leave your yams and cocoyams
> And come to school
> And I must scuttle away in haste
> When children in play or in earnest cry:
> Look! a Christian is on the way.
> Ha ha ha ha ha ha ha ha ha ha ha ha.... (p. 222)

We have elsewhere in this study referred to Ezeulu's mother as the demented solitary singer. However, from the words of the song, it appears it is a sung *soliloquy* of a humiliated and "killed" python, the totem of the Umuaro snake-cult. The snake tells the story of its origin, the culture conflict between Christian and traditional Igbo religions, and the triumph of Christianity because Igbo children have been taught to look down on their religion. The dirge presages both the death of Obika and the defection of traditional Igbo suppliants to the Christian camp which helps Mr. Goodcountry to win more native converts.

General Songs

The songs we regard here as general songs are so called because they do not belong to the same genres as some of the ones we have examined above, neither are they as traditional as the others. They appear mainly in the novels which treat of modern Nigerian societies. Nevertheless, Achebe uses them to make some of the points he is concerned about in the novels.

In *No Longer at Ease*, it is the popular Nigerian "High-life" dance:

Nylon dress is a lovely dress,
Nylon dress is a country dress
If you want to make your baby happy
Nylon is good for her.

If you want to make your baby happy
Go to the shop and get a doz'n of nylon.
She will know nobody but you alone
Nylon is good for her.

I was playing moi guitar jeje,
A lady gave me a kiss.
Her husband didn't like it,
He had to drag him wife away.

Gentlemen, please hold your wife
Father and mum, please hold your girls.
The calypso is so nice,
If they follow, don't blame Bobby (pp. 101-103).

The lyric of the song makes a social comment on Lagos life which in the sixties was too fast for visitors from the countryside. The society is that of "those who had started the country off down the slopes of inflation."[18] To play "big men", the corrupt civil servants and politicians steal the nation's money to buy their "babies" or mistresses nylon dresses, attend expensive night clubs in which a lot of "sinful" acts are committed. We notice in the song such words as *moi* (French), *jeje* (Yoruba) and *calypso* (foreign

---

[18] *A Man of the People*, p. 2.

music), which indicate that "Gentleman Bobby" was the Lagos-based musician that composed the song, and played often at the Ambassadors Hotel, Yaba. The total effect of such exotic words is that the soloist makes the dancers feel high and "modern" for the acceptance of their mistresses. The phrases and imagery of their conversations are appropriately contemporary; you can hear cries of "Anchor! Anchor!," a corruption of the French word *encore!* and No petrol, no fire, "which clearly meant no beer, no dance" (p. 103).

The C. P. C. party-members, led by Max and Eunice in *A Man of the People*, have their own old schoolmate chant and song to perform as they warm up to launch their new political party in Odili's village:

Hip, hip-hip—
Hurrah!
HIP, HIP-HIP—
Hurrah!
For they are jolly good fellows
For they are jolly good fellows
For they are jolly good fellows
And so say all of us.
And so say all of us, hurrah!
And so say all of us, hurrah!
For they are jolly good fellows
For they are jolly good fellows
For they are jolly good fellows
And so say all of us (p. 122).

The "jolly good fellow-feeling" among old schoolmates is not only exhilarating to the singers, but also it is enticing to passers-by for Achebe comments that "The singing and laughter and the sight of so many cars brought in neighbours and passers-by until [they] had a small crowd." The party is formed by the intelligentsia hence their song comes from foreign lands. Those who cannot understand them or what the meaning of the song is are attracted at least by the laughter and expression of camaraderie of the campaigners.

One last general song we should examine which appears in *No*

Longer at Ease is "Oyiemu—o":

> An in-law went to see his in-law
> Oyiemu—o
> His in-law seized him and killed him
> Oyiemu—o
> Bring a canoe, bring a paddle
> Oyiemu—o
> The paddle speaks English
> Oyiemu—o (p. 42)

Benjamin DeMott explains the significance of the song both to Obi's situation and to Achebe's general thematic interests in *Things Fall Apart* and *No Longer at Ease,* including one item that molds Achebe's satiric themes—"a theory of history linking the fall of man with the advent of civilization, and rehabilitating the metaphor of the noble savage—is one that civilized people themselves do not always treat with favor."[19] DeMott finds a link between the falls of Okonkwo *pere* and Okonkwo *fils* [Obi] in the sense that both heroes live in two worlds where physical "environment" and the unassailable white man's religion and government constitute a threat to their two societies which both heroes attempt to fight but are destroyed by the forces. He adds that the folk song, "Oyiemu—o" is used by Achebe to prove how "the younger Okonkwo is an introspective University graduate who hopes to elevate ethical standards among public servants, and in telling of the ruin of Obi's hopes, and of his decline into graft, the novelist seems bent upon showing him forth as a victim of a general cultural situation, rather than as a figure of personal weakness." Finally, DeMott declares:

> Laboring hard to translate the refrain into English, he comprehends at length that it is a comment on two great "betrayals"—the murder of an in-law ("a man's in-law was his *chi,* his personal god"), and the

---

[19] Benjamin DeMott, "An Unprofessional Eye: Oyiemuo-o?" *American Scholar,* 32 (1963), p. 292.

snapping of the bond of language that united the tribe: the "burden of the song was 'the world turned upside down.'" In so far as it crystallizes incertitude, ambivalence and probing doubt, the translated tag stands as a key passage for both of Achebe's novels (Ibid., p. 294).

Besides the resemblances in the fates and worlds of Okonkwo and his grandson, Obi, the song also predicts what may happen to Obi if he marries Clara, an *osu*. Clara became an *osu* because she is the daughter of an *osu;* and if Obi becomes an in-law to an *osu* father, by marriage he becomes an *osu*, therefore he is figuratively killed by his in-law since the Igbo dread the *osu* caste like poison. English in the song is symbolic of white culture and education which makes Obi to dare to do the unimaginable. The intentional attempt to marry an *osu* and the decision to study English instead of Law are Obi's two great betrayals of his people.

It is not an accident that Achebe has included so many folk songs and chants in his novels. As a people who are very fond of their religion, rituals, ceremonies, folktales, feasts and battles, the Igbo sing the songs to praise, satirize, eulogize, indict, sermonize and tell stories as occasions may warrant. Achebe, being a well-informed member of that culture, exploits folk songs and chants as valuable thematic and structural materials to aid his artistry. We have therefore examined the thematic and structural functions as well as the significance of the songs to the novels without going to their prosodic evaluation. From our evaluation we can conclude that Achebe uses folk songs and chants to create situation, medium and mood of the dramatic actions of his novels which manifest the Igbo culture that he is reevaluating for his audience's appreciation.

9 | Language and Imagery

> But it will have to be a new English still in full communion with its ancestral home but altered to suit its new African surroundings.
> —Achebe in *Morning Yet on Creation Day*

Chinua Achebe, an Igbo novelist, writes in English because he feels that the English language will be able to carry the weight of his African experience. But it will have to be a new English, still in full communion with its ancestral home but altered to suit its new African surroundings.[1] Probably other writers of English in most Third World Countries are doing the same for the sake of communication and wider readership of their works; for, according to Dell Hymes,

> ... Communication cannot be equated with a "common" language. A term such as "the English language" comprises all linguistic varieties that owe their basic resources to the historical tradition known as English. That "language" is no longer an exclusive possession of the English, or even of the English and the Americans—there are perhaps more users of English in the Third World, and they

---

[1] Chinua Achebe, *Morning Yet on Creation Day* (Garden City, New York: Anchor Press/Doubleday, 1975), p. 84.

have their own rights to its resources and future. Many varieties of "English" are not mutually intelligible within Great Britain and the United States as well as elsewhere. In fact, it is an important clarification if we can agree to restrict the term "language" (and the term "dialect") to just this sort of meaning: identification of a historically derived set of resources whose social functioning—organization into used varieties, mutual intelligibility, etc.—is not given by the fact of historical derivation itself, but is problematic, needing to be determined, and calling for other concepts and terms.[2]

The passage reemphasizes the points that many progressive African critics and writers, including Achebe himself, have made in the past—namely, that the African writer's continued use of English as a mode of expression does not make his work less African because he writes in *a foreign* language; and that although he alters the English language to suit its new African surroundings, his new variety of English should not be branded quaint because it is different from British or American English. What is more important is that Achebe has conducted a successful language experiment in his novels to make him one of Africa's foremost novelists. How he does it and what that experiment is comprised of are examined below.

The language used in Achebe's novels is characterized by such Igbo linguistic elements as proverbs, pidgin, folk stories and imagery which enable the author to describe his Igbo characters and explore his theme very fully. Perhaps it is because of Achebe's vivid portrayal of Igbo thought pattern, imagery, humor and philosophy—all expressed in readable English—that R. Angogo says that "In his books, *Things Fall Apart* and *Arrow of God*, Achebe uses a language

---

[2] Dell Hymes, "Speech and Language: On the Origins and Foundations of Inequality Among Speakers," *Language as a Human Problem*, edited by Einar Haugen and Morton Bloomfield (New York: W.W. Norton & Company, Inc., 1974), pp. 51-52

I would like to refer to as 'Ibo in English.'"[3] Albeit, what Angogo implies by "Ibo in English" is that Achebe manipulates English language in such a way that the varieties of language that he gives to his individual Igbo characters are probable, a quality which we could term language realism.

Achebe's description of how Christopher, one of his characters in *No Longer at Ease,* uses language can be read as a comment on how he as an author assigns a particular kind of language to a character to suit a particular occasion. The narrator says:

> Whether Christopher spoke good or 'broken' English depended on what he was saying, where he was saying it, to whom and how he wanted to say it. Of course that was to some extent true of most educated people, especially on Saturday nights. But Christopher was rather outstanding in thus coming to terms with a double heritage.
> (p. 100)

Christopher's "double heritage" could also apply to Achebe's training (as a novelist) in the conventions and rules of the novel as a *genre* as well as to his acquisition of the art of convention as an Igbo storyteller. Secondly, it refers to the Igbo novel as a hybrid genre: a marriage of foreign and written form and indigenous and oral tradition. In fact, it is to aid readers' understanding of the second set of characteristics of the Igbo novel that this study in the folkways of Chinua Achebe's novels is undertaken.

Imagery

Imagery is a part of language. But in this chapter the title, "Language and Imagery," is used to emphasize—even overemphasize—the importance of imagery as a distinguishing feature in the language of Achebe's novels. We adopt one of M. H. Abram's three definitions of the use of imagery which is that "most commonly, imagery is

---

[3] R. Angogo, "Achebe and the English Language," *Busara,* 7,2 (1975), p. 2.

used to signify *figurative* language, especially the vehicles of metaphors and similes."[4] Achebe's novels are full of Igbo similes and metaphors because such figures of speech characterize the speech patterns of the Igbo characters.

Furthermore, a good selection of imagery from all four novels indicates that Achebe is a conscious artist: when he is writing novels about traditional societies, his similes and metaphors become *ethnic* but they become *cosmopolitan* in the novels with urban settings. To illustrate, the narrator in *Things Fall Apart* says:

> Okonkwo ... had brought honor to his village by throwing Amalinze the Cat [metaphor] (p. 3).

and

> He laughed loud and long and his voice rang out clear as the *ogene* [simile]... (p. 7).

The ethnic images in the two sentences—Amalinze the Cat, and, [as] clear as the ogene—are selected, among others, from ethnic experience such as hunting, farming, wrestling, tribal wars, moonlight plays and from tropical animals, diseases, and weather. Similar images are found in *Arrow of God*, another novel with a rural setting:

> The moon he saw that day was as thin as an orphan fed grudgingly by a cruel foster-mother [simile] (p. 1).

and

> He reached for a few sticks of firewood stacked in the corner, set them carefully on the fire and placed the yam, like a sacrifice, on top [simile] (p. 3).

---

[4] M. H. Abrams, *A Glossary of Literary Terms*, 3rd Edition (New York: Holt, Rinehart and Winston, Inc., 1971), p. 77.

However, as he writes about people of the city in *No Longer at Ease* and *A Man of the People,* Achebe uses images which realistically represent modern Nigerian artifacts, activities, and social behavior. For example, the narrator in *No Longer at Ease* says:

> Whenever Mr. Justice William Galloway, Judge of the High Court of Lagos and the Southern Cameroons, looked at a victim he fixed him with his gaze as a collector fixes his insect with formalin [simile] (p. 1).

and

> He had expected it and rehearsed this very scene a hundred times until it had become as familiar as a friend [simile] (p. 2).

Both sentences are selected from a court scene in Lagos but the images they contain are drawn from chemistry and drama, respectively.

A Man of the People, a novel whose narrative action is predominantly urban, contains images similar to those found in *No Longer at Ease:*

> In spite of the din you could still hear as clear as a bird the high-powered voice of the soloist, whom they admiringly nicknamed "Grammar-phone"[5] [metaphor] (*AMOP,* p. 1).

and

> I had no mother to buy head-ties for, and although I had a father, giving things to him was like pouring a little water into a dried-up well [simile] (p. 27).

---

[5] "Grammar-phone," a corruption of Gramophone, a machine for reproducing music, was very popular in Nigerian villages in the 1960s hence the woman lead singer and soloist, whose voice was as melodious as gramophone, was called by others "Grammar-phone."

Three factors account for Achebe's good use of ethnic imagery; he was brought up in a society that uses the images so effectively that they became part of his own linguistic acquisition; he did extensive research which enabled him to know so much about traditional Igbo similes and metaphors; and he is an observant creative writer, who learned directly from the behavior of rural communities at work, including observing animal behavior and listening to folktales about them. All three ways of acquiring linguistic folklore have together made Achebe such an observant and sensitive writer that he could write a sentence as descriptive as:

> Ekwefi screwed her eyes up in an effort to see her daughter and the priestess, but whenever she thought she saw their shape it immediately dissolved like a melting lump of darkness. (TFA, p. 96).

It is only a solitary walk in a tropical night that can observe and respond to the kind of feeling the sentence evokes. The same feeling is evoked by a similar sentence:

> A vague chill had descended on him and his head had seemed to swell like a solitary walker at night who passes an evil spirit on the way. (p. 56)

On the other hand, his cosmopolitan images are drawn from the urban life he experienced in cities such as Enugu, Ibadan (as a college student) and Lagos where he lived and worked. Again, his realistic use of images gathered from various corners of urban life attests to his meticulous observation of people and his acquisition of their linguistic and social habits. We find that the sentence, "'There is no darkness there,' he told his admiring listeners, 'because at night the electric shines like the sun, and people are always walking about, that is, those who want to walk,'" (NLAE, p. 11) not only contrasts the darkness of the countryside with the perpetual light of the city, but it also makes a social comment on the uneven development of several parts of Nigeria, the behavior of the peoples who live in them, and the difference between natural phenomena such as sun and moon, and artifacts such as electricity, machinery, shilling and gramophone.

To illustrate the difference between ethnic and cosmopolitan images, we consider here two sentences drawn from *Things Fall Apart* (rural setting) and *No Longer at Ease* (urban setting):

> Ikemefuna told him that the proper name for a corn-cob with only a few scattered grains was *eze-agadi-nwanyi*, or the teeth of an old woman (TFA, p. 32).

and

> He had very bad teeth blackened by cigarettes and kolanuts. One was missing in front, and when he laughed the gap looked like a vacant plot in the slum (NLAE, p. 60).

In the first sentence, the simile is drawn from farming. Ikemefuna, a country boy, is making a comparison between a corn-cob with few scattered grains and the teeth of an old woman who is also found in a rural community. But in the second sentence the image seems to have come from another Igbo community, Ajegunle in Lagos, a slummy outskirts of Lagos which was developing when the novel was written. "Vacant plot" would be a familiar image to city-dwellers.

Whereas Achebe uses purely ethnic images in *Things Fall Apart* and *Arrow of God*, he includes some of them as complements to the cosmopolitan ones in *No Longer at Ease* and *A Man of the People*. This is so because the village life of the rural novels has a great influence on the urban societies of the urban novels. When such ethnic images are used in the urban novels, Achebe usually says something like "He is like the little bird, *nza* who after a big meal so far forgot himself as to challenge his *chi* to single combat,' *said another Ibo*" (NLAE, p. 148) [my emphasis], to remind his readers that although the image is used by a city-dweller, yet the speaker borrowed it from his Igbo people in the countryside. Or, Achebe may use an Igbo proverbial allusion to indicate the origin of an image:

> He wrote the kind of English they admired if not understood: the

kind that filled the mouth, *like the proverbial dry meat* (NLAE, p. 29) [my emphasis].

The author's allusion to the proverbial dry meat should be understood by an average Igbo man and by anyone who has read *Things Fall Apart*[6].

In sum, Achebe uses images to beautify his prose style, make comments on the linguistic habits of the people of his novels, and reveal the life-style and philosophy of the characters who use the images in their speeches. Also, textual critics can look at the images and tell which of the novels have rural or urban settings. The images used in *Arrow of God*, alongside the themes of the novels, for example, can persuade such critics to regard the events of Achebe's third novel as having taken place between those of the second novel, *No Longer at Ease*, in spite of the publication dates of the novels.

Literal Translation and Phraseology

According to Obiechina, West African writers attempt to recapture traditional speech by translating fairly literally from the vernacular to English (extending to the syntax in Okara's *The Voice*). They do this chiefly by rendering the proverbs and characteristic turns of phrase used in rural communities; this gives authenticity to the writing.[7] Achebe's novels, especially those with rural settings, are full of literal translations and phraseology which, rendered in any other forms, would not give adequate expression to the lives, speech-patterns and linguistic habits of the characters whose Igbo vernacular language Achebe realistically attempts to recapture in his

---

[6] The allusion is to Igbo smoked meat which Igbo elders offer to their visitors as "kola" in small pieces. Though small, the dry meat proves more filling and delicious to eat than bigger but unsmoked pieces of meat.

[7] Emmanuel Obiechina, *Culture, Tradition and Society in the West African Novel* (Cambridge: Cambridge University Press, 1975), p. 155

novels. Some readers[8] have in the past criticized Achebe's phraseology, but he has defended it thus:

> From a natural to a conscious artist: myself, in fact. Allow me to quote a small example from *Arrow of God*, which may give some idea of how I approach the use of English. The Chief Priest in the story is telling one of his sons why it is necessary to send him to church:
>
>> I want one of my sons to join these people and be my eyes there. If there is nothing in it you will come back. But if there is something there you will bring home my share. The world is like a Mask dancing. If you want to see it well you do not stand in one place. My spirit tells me that those who do not befriend the white man today will be saying *had we known tomorrow*.
>
> Now supposing I had put it another way. Like this, for instance:
>
>> I am sending you as my representative among these people— just to be on the safe side in case the new religion develops. One has to move with the times or else one is left behind. I have a hunch that those who fail to come to terms with the white man may well regret their lack of foresight.
>
> The material is the same. But the form of the one is *in character* and the other is not. It is largely a matter of instinct, but judgement comes into it too.[9]

Indeed, Achebe's peculiar use of language is one of the distinguishing characteristics of characters in his Igbo novels. Achebe may have given a language variety appropriate to a college graduate like Obi of *No Longer at Ease* to the Chief Priest of Ulu, Ezeulu, had he

---

[8] See Elizabeth Pryse "Getting into Perspective," *Nigerian Magazine* 74 (September 1962), and Ernest Emenyonu, "African Literature: What Does It take to be its Critic," *African Literature Today* 5 (1971), pp. 1-11.

[9] Achebe, *op. cit.*, pp. 82-83.

used the second instead of the first version of Ezeulu's counsel to his son, Oduche.

A few of the literal translations of Igbo phrases into English are examined below to emphasize why Achebe includes them in his novels:

The narrator says, "'Ekwefi!' a voice called from one of the huts. It was Nwoye's mother, Okonkwo's first wife. 'Is that me?' Ekwefi called back'" (*TFA*, pp. 37-38). The literal translation is "Is that me?" instead of "Is it me [that you are calling]?" Achebe defends his choice by saying, "That was the way people answered calls from outside. They never answered yes for fear it might be an evil spirit calling" (*TFA*, p. 38). His explanation touches upon the Igbo folk belief that a spirit calls human beings once and that if they answered yes, they would die. Therefore, to ensure that the call came from fellow humans, people always asked the caller, "Is that me?" But in Igbo "Is that me?" (trans. *O bu mu?*) is syntactically correct. That is why the novelist would neither choose "Are you calling me," or "Is it me you are calling?"

Another literal translation is:

"It is true indeed, my dear friend. I cannot yet find a mouth with which to tell the story." (*TFA*, p. 48)

[*O bu eziokwu nezie, ezi enyim. E nwebegbi m onu m ji ako akuko ahu*]

If one tries to rewrite the statement, he loses its Igbo idiomatic implication, which is that Ekwefi is so baffled and stunned by Okonkwo's firing at her that she is incapable of relating her scary experience to Chielo. Ekwefi's escape is so miraculous that it can only be explained theologically by the priestess, Chielo, who says:

"Your *chi* is very much awake, my friend" (p. 44).

[*Chi gi mu anya, enyi m*]

That is, Ekwefi is saved by her spirit-double or guardian angel—a statement which expresses the Igbo cosmological belief in *chi*. And even though it is a cosmic intervention, the guardian angel is anthropomorphized in that he must be as awake and vigilant as a human being to prevent *Ekwensu* (Devil, to whom all evil is attributed by the Igbo) from completing the evil work he started, using Okonkwo.

What follows in the conversation leads to the exposition of another Igbo folk belief in *ogbanje* (spirit-child):

"... And how is my daughter, Ezinma?"
"She has been very well for some time now. Perhaps she has come to stay."
"I think she has. How old is she now?"
"She is about ten years old."
"I think she will stay. They usually stay if they do not die before the age of six."
"I pray she stays," said Ekwefi with a heavy sigh.
The woman with whom she talked was called Chielo. She was the priestess of Agbala, the Oracle of the Hill and the Caves. In ordinary life Chielo was a widow with two children. She was very friendly with Ekwefi and they shared a common shed in the market. She was particularly fond of Ekwefi's only daughter, Ezinma, whom she called "my daughter." Quite often she bought bean-cakes and gave Ekwefi some to take home to Ezinma. Anyone seeing Chielo in ordinary life would hardly believe she was the same person who prophesied when the spirit of Agbala was upon her (p. 44).

Ezinma and Chielo are so friendly because the former is *ogbanje*, who must be presented from time to time to Agbala by the latter, who is Agbala's priestess. Their relationship is more spiritual than social. Later in the novel (pp 90ff), when the spirit of Agbala is upon Chielo, she takes Ezinma to the oracle.

As in the case of Ezeulu, Achebe gives an appropriate level of language to his rural characters—illiterate Igbo women, Ekwefi and Chielo. Their language not only portrays them as such, but also reveals how Achebe avoids anglicizing their speech pattern in order to gain language realism.

Other literal translations of Igbo sentences into English for the same effects are:

From *Things Fall Apart*

"Everyday I tell you that *jigida* and fire are not friends. But you will never hear. You grew your ears for decoration, not for hearing. One of these days your *jigida* will catch fire on your waist, and then you will know" (p. 65).

"You might as well say that the woman lies on top of the man when they are making the children" (p. 67).

From *No Longer at Ease*

"If you follow its sweetness, you will perish" (p. 75).

"You think white men don't eat bribe? Come to our department. They eat more than black men nowadays" (p. 30).

From *Arrow of God*

"Today I shall kill the boy with my own hands" (p. 45).

"I have already said that what this new religion will bring to Umuaro wears a hat on its head" (p. 45).

And, from *A Man of the People*

"My brother, when those standing have not got their share you are talking about those kneeling" (p. 87).

"You have to listen to my irritating voice until the day comes when you stop answering Odili Samalu or else until you look for me and don't see me any more" (p. 120).

In a word, a lot of Achebe's literal translations of Igbo phrases into English have to do with Igbo philosophy of life, morality, pedagogy and rhetoric, which are essential Igbo folkways that Achebe presents to his audience. Had he expressed some of the phrases in a more "novelistic" way in order to "delete the kind of anthropological material which often filled novels of cultural assertion during the independence period at the expense of narrative speed and focus,"¹⁰ then his novels would have lost their Igbo character. We will illustrate the importance of literal translations in the novels as we examine the poetic qualities of proverbs below.

Proverbs as Imagery

We have already examined proverbs in Chapter VI of this study and discovered how Achebe uses them dexterously to comment subtly on the activities of the characters, and to express the moral and ethical principles of the various societies of his novels. In the present chapter, however, proverbs are examined briefly as a distinguishing feature of Achebe's language and imagery, and as a form of literal translation.

The proverbs beautify speeches of such Igbo orators as Ezeulu and Nwaka, because such proverbs contain rich imagery, allusions, and folk humor drawn from interesting areas of life that are familiar to the people. Obiechina underscores the poetic quality of Igbo proverbs when he says that proverbs "derive their effectiveness and force from the underlying connection between a literal fact and its allusive amplification and which vivifies an experience by placing it beside another which bears the stamp of approval."¹¹ To demonstrate the importance of imagery in the proverbs found in Achebe's novels, we examine a proverb from Chapter Thirteen of *Arrow of God*:

Ezeulu has summoned his people to inform them that he had been invited the previous night to visit the white man at Okperi. He notices some opposition from the crowd, among whom is his archenemy, Nwaka. He senses that they would accuse him of failing to give them the traditional wine before addressing them. So he quickly says:

So I said to myself: Tomorrow I shall summon *Umuaro and tell them.*

---

[10] See Bruce King, "The Revised *Arrow of God,*" *Echos du Commonwealth*, 5 (1979), p. 95.
[11] Obiechina, *op. cit.*, p. 156.

Then one mind said to me: *Do you know what may happen in the night or at dawn?* That is why, although I have no palm wine to place before you I still thought I should call you together. If we have life there will be time enough for palm wine (p. 142).

Then Ezeulu concludes with a proverb:

"Unless the penis dies young it will surely eat bearded meat."

Achebe could have used an English proverb such as:

"A patient dog eats the fattest bone,"

but obviously that would have destroyed both the effect of the proverb in the priest's speech and the wealth of associations the proverb contains.

The proverb, "Unless the penis dies young it will surely eat bearded meat," could be analyzed to yield the following poetic and rhetorical values: (a) It contains the metaphor, "bearded meat," which stands for female genitals. It is a more elegant way of saying vagina, which, if so bluntly mentioned would have lowered the speech and manners of the high priest. (b) In spite of the wrong impression foreigners have about the place of women in Igbo society, in many ways Igbo women are respected more than men; for every woman is a potential mother, and "mother is supreme" in Igboland. Hence it is easier for men to crack bawdy jokes about their own genitals than it is for them to do so with women's. (c) The proverb also expresses the Igbo virtue, patience, which leads to one enjoying better and greater things later on. The Igbo being a very ambitious people can easily accept Ezeulu's appeal, for are they not the people who said that "If you want to eat a toad you should look for a fat and juicy one?" Bearded meat is the genitalia of a mature and experienced woman, not the type that would make one play at the entrance until he is exhausted. (d) Penis in the proverb is a synecdoche which stands for a young man, who is counselled to wait until he is mature enough to enjoy sex more fully. It is advice that is given against premarital sex; one can avoid fornication only by being patient. (e) And the proverb is said as folk humor to lighten the grimness of the occasion and condone Ezeulu's oversight of not providing the traditional palm-wine for libation. It produces the intended rhetorical effect because the narrator says that "for a long time no one stood up to reply. Instead there was general talking (which sometimes sounded like murmuring) among the assembled rulers of Umuaro" (p. 142).

Thus, in a simple proverb such as this, one finds sex education and morality; Igbo pedagogy which comes in the form of proverbs, folk songs and folktales, and their appropriate moral tags; rhetorical persuasion which is essential to Igbo oratory; and folk humor which helps Igbo men to keep their sanity in times of crises. As we have observed earlier on, Achebe could have used the hackneyed English proverb, "A patient dog eats the fattest bone," but that would not have had all the associations we have pointed out above. Also, Igbo dogs eat bones, but the majority of them, like Nwanku in *Arrow of God*, eat feces and foofoo as their regular meals. Hence, Ezeulu has used a proverb more appropriate to his rhetorical needs. When analyzed the way we have done, most of the Igbo proverbs found in the novels can yield the same kinds of poetic imagery, allusiveness, and cultural and linguistic beauty.

Pidgin English

It happens that to communicate with each other, two or more people use a language in a variety whose grammar and vocabulary are very much reduced in extent and which is native to neither side.[12] Such a language is the "pidgin" found in Achebe's *No Longer at Ease* and *A Man of the People*. Both novels are set in cities inhabited by people from different ethnic groups of Nigeria as well as foreigners, and characters communicate with each other in pidgin, which is not native to any of its users. Also, in this case the pidgin is English-based because it is collateral to English, the language of

---

[12] See Robert A. Hall, Jr., *Pidgin and Creole Languages* (Ithaca, New York: Cornell University Press, 1966), p. xii.

the colonialists.

Among the chief users of pidgin in the novels are domestic servants, laborers and small-scale businessmen who need a smattering of English as a lingua franca but have not been instructed in English. However, educated people can use pidgin as a means of communicating with uneducated speakers. That is why policeman, soldiers and even foreigners speak pidgin whenever the right occasion demands it.

At any rate, there are conditions under which pidgin is spoken in the two novels. These are: (a) Speakers of "standard" British English often switch code into pidgin when they find that they are not communicating with "less educated" audience. This is because the grammar and vocabulary of pidgin are much reduced in extent. (b) A speaker may use pidgin only as "occasional remarks" because, as the narrator in *No Longer at Ease* says, certain words are easier to say in English than in Igbo. (c) Some public officers sometimes use pidgin to solicit bribes, hence pidgin could be regarded as an "unrespectable" language. The prime examples of such corrupt users of pidgin being some corrupt politicians and policemen. (d) And when speakers want to be jovial they speak pidgin. The narrator reports that Christopher uses pidgin when he wants to be jovial; and when he switches code and tells Bisi in pidgin "this na Africa, you know," this is to soften the effect of his placing women low in society.[13]

To know the outlined conditions under which pidgin is spoken is to enable one appreciate the rhetorical stance of a good speaker: he must know his audience, the occasion, and the subject at hand before selecting a suitable medium of communication. For instance, on Saturdays, Lagos night clubs are varied in nature. Some are parties for Ambassadors, others are for clan unions such as Umuofia Progressive Union, and yet a third type may just be a "good-time" party in which a "Nylon dress is a lovely dress" highlife record is

---

[13] The conditions under which pidgin is spoken are outlined following those found in Kofi Yankson, "the Use of Pidgin in *No longer at Ease* and *A Man of the People*," *Asemka*, 1,2 (1974), pp. 68-79.

played. In the first kind of party, "Queen's English" is expected to be spoken, an ethnic language such as Igbo is used in the second, and in the third kind, the obvious language is pidgin English, which is more appropriate to the mixed audience. In all three audiences, communication is the key to the selection of language that a good speaker makes.

Obi made his "Mistake Number Two"—speaking the English which was full of 'is' and 'was'—because he did not make any rhetorical preparation like Christopher. That is, he failed to take his cue from the Secretary of the Union whose written Welcome Address contained "the kind of English they admired if not understood: the kind that filled the mouth, like the proverbial dry meat" (p. 29). The author is not condemning Obi's English in this instance, but he does represent the people's disappointment in Obi who failed to "beat the drum according to how they danced." In fact, Achebe satirizes the Secretary's ridiculous choice of English words that never communicate, when he says, "the kind of English they admired if not understood."

When we turn to *A Man of the People* we find that pidgin is given a comparatively dignified status, because one of the two principal characters, Chief Nanga, belongs to the linguistic group that uses pidgin English around a city such as Lagos; and being "a man of the people" he has got to learn to use pidgin. The second chief character, Odili, belongs to a linguistic group that uses English, and like Obi he rarely uses pidgin because he does not belong to the former linguistic group. Chief Nanga always speaks English or pidgin because he belongs to both groups. His political strength is due in part to his ability to use both varieties as weapons of manipulation.

There is no question about Odili speaking pidgin as a language of conversation; but as we have argued in the case of Christopher and Obi in *No Longer at Ease*, Odili's conversation is not a less serious matter. We may recall that one of the reasons why Odili decided to run for election is that Chief Nanga took away his girlfriend from him—a serious point in the novel. To illustrate how pidgin could be used to comment on serious matters, let use examine the following conversation:

'How the go de go?' I asked.
'Bo, son of man done tire.
'Did you find out about that girl?' I asked.
'Why na so so girl, girl, girl, girl been full your mouth. Wetin? So person no fit talk any serious talk with you. I never see.'
'O.K., Mr. Gentleman,' I said, pumping the lamp.
'Any person way first mention about girl again for this room make him tongue cut. How is the weather?'
He [Andrew] laughed (pp. 20-21).

In fact, many people, when they first read the conversation, are carried away by the apparent joke it contains. That is all right, and perhaps those are the people who do not see the seriousness of the conversation. Nevertheless, its seriousness would dawn on us if we stopped and asked ourselves, "Why is Odili telling us this story?" Then one will realize that Achebe uses Odili to expose his own character in the form of a flashback which foreshadows the conflict of interest that will eventually arise between him and Chief Nanga.

The conversation exposes another kind of linguistic problem that Nigerian college graduates encounter: that is, the difficulty they have in speaking pidgin English fluently. For, they cannot make a complete sentence in pidgin without inserting in it a "grammatical" phrase or clause. That is why anybody who knows a little bit about pidgin would certainly not accept the above conversation as good pidgin for it breaks all the rules of phonology, morphology, and syntax, just as it lacks the vocabulary and idiom that make pidgin a viable language.[14] This is not a criticism of Achebe who records the conversation as he hears it from his "educated" characters, but rather a criticism of those who do not speak pidgin English very well. Such characters are often times unable to switch code easily and so cannot mingle with people as easily as Chief Nanga, a man of the people, does.

---

[14] For details of structure and relationship of these elements of pidgin language, see Hall Jr., *op. cit.*, pp. 25-102.

Achebe's use of pidgin matches the characterization, subject matter, and occasions in those novels where it becomes a viable language variety. More pidgin is used in *A Man of the People* than in *No Longer at Ease* because the society of the former novel is more diversified than that of the latter. Also, because of the presence and influence of the white men in *No Longer At Ease,* "standard" English is still very much a language of business and government but their absence in *A Man of People* means the destruction of the language hegemony of British English. To the British, that destruction signalled the "corruption" of the language which they had established as a possible lingua franca for a country they created; and with the "corruption" of the language came the corruption of the society!

Religious Terminology and Allusions

It should be recalled that the first white men ever to gain any foothold in the Igbo societies of Achebe's novels were Christian missionaries. They brought a new and alien religion which paved the way for government and trade. Their entry produced enormous conflicts because the people the missionaries attempted to convert were even more religious than the missionaries because religion permeated every aspect of Igbo life—namely: marriages, festivals, politics, government, education and social life. We know all this because Achebe has described the events for us in religious terms, alluding to the scriptures of the two parties in the various tragic conflicts he explores in his novels.

In *Things Fall Apart,* for example, Achebe uses Igbo religious terms to describe Okonkwo's fears of failure:

> But his whole life was dominated by fear, the fear of failure and of weakness. It was deeper and more intimate than the fear of evil and capricious gods and of magic, the fear of the forest, and of the forces of nature, malevolent, red in tooth and claw (pp. 12-13).

This sounds like a description of Satan and his angels, variously called the Serpent, Dragon, Devil and Evil Forces in the Bible, making their appearances trying to seduce children of God. Achebe selects words such as Igbo men use in describing the forces of evil before the white missionaries came. What that proves is that each religion has its own ideas about the nature and physical appearance of the malevolent spirit or god, or Satan, as well as where he may be found. Christians talk of Heaven and Hell, but the Igbo talk of *Ala-mmo* (spirit-world) and Evil Forest. The Christians believe that the spirits of dead men remain in the grave awaiting the last trumpet sound before resurrection. The Igbo believe in *Ala-mmo,* where the ancestors remain before reincarnation. Hence in the novels, some characters make comparative references to both religions, traditional Igbo religion and Christianity, in order to explain why in spite of the obvious attractions of Christianity, only the "dregs" of Igbo society initially joined the new dispensation. Both religions have one essence but their practices are different. This idea is expanded in the conversation between Akunna and Mr. Brown which has been examined in a previous chapter.

Religious terminology is rife in *Things Fall Apart* because, apart from the culture conflict between the two peoples being to a large extent religious (and to a lesser degree administrative), Achebe is concerned with the materialistic over-ambition of Okonkwo in a society known generally for its spirituality. The quest for material things by the Igbo heroes is further expanded in *Arrow of God.* Achebe's noted concern about the situation is borne in one of his interview remarks:

> Ibo society has always been materialistic. This may sound strange because Ibo life had at the same time a strong spiritual dimension—controlled by gods, ancestors, personal spirits or *chi* and magic. The success of the culture and the balance between the two, the material and the spiritual .... Today we have kept the materialism and thrown away the spirituality which should keep it in check.[15]

Ezeulu and Nwaka would not have been such deadly enemies had

---

[15] Achebe, "The role of the Writer in a New Nation," *Nigeria Magazine,* 81 (1964), p. 158

they remembered their religious duties to their gods, to the ancestors, and to the people at large. The dramatic action of the novel is concentrated on the Chief Priest who, for the purpose of wreaking vengeance on his people and thereby earning more praise from his admirers, forgets his religious duties and responsibilities. Conversely, Nwaka is insolent even to a high priest just because he is wealthy and highly titled. They both seek the praise of men and earn the wrath of their gods.

At the end of *Arrow of God*, the narrator says:

> The Christian harvest which took place a few days after Obika's death saw more people than even Goodcountry could have dreamed. In his extremity many a man sent his son with a yam or two to offer to the new religion and to bring back the promised immunity. Thereafter any yam harvested in his fields was harvested in the name of the son (p. 230).

The passage echoes the words, "In the name of the Father, Son, and Holy Ghost," which Catholics say as they re-enact the sign of the cross during mass. To the Christians, "in the name of the son" is all right; but to the Igbo, it is not. Thus, we find Achebe's use of language, which arises from his double religious heritage, creating a seeming ambiguity to readers who are foreign to Achebe's culture. For instance, when asked, "what is the meaning of 'son' when you write, at the very end of *Arrow of God*. 'Thereafter any yam that was harvested in the man's fields was harvested in the name of the son'?," (1965 ed.) Achebe explains:

> ... There is a suggestion of Christian ethics in "the name of the son," nearly in a caricatural sense. There is a bit of parody there, but it is not really parody because Christianity is not a joke, and suddenly what will happen to the Ibo culture is not going to be a joke. But there is an even deeper possibility in which the harvest in the name of the son becomes a reversal of the natural order. In the society we have been looking at [i.e., Igbo] in this story, you do not do things in the name of the son but in the name of the father. The legitimacy is with the elders, the ancestors, with the tradition and

age. We now have a new dispensation in which youth and inexperience earn a new legitimacy. This is something new and different. Wisdom belongs to the elders, but the new wisdom is going to belong to the young people. They are going to go to school, to go to church, and will tell their fathers what it is. This almost amounts to turning the world upside down.

I think that Ezeulu himself sensed it coming; he had some kind of psychic vision. This is why he sent his son to the British. Something told him that it might be necessary. He found some other explanations for doing it, but in fact he sensed what he was doing. This was confirmed the first time he was interviewed by the English administrator Clarke, and Ezeulu looked up and the image in his mind was that of a puppy, something unfinished, half-baked, too young; and yet there was authority.

Now, this reversal itself is tied up with the colonial situation. There is no other situation in the world where power resides with inexperience and young people. A young man would not approach the seat of power in England, but in a colonial situation he is given power and can order a chief around. In a very deep sense this reversal is the quintessence of colonialism. It is a loss of independence. These are some of the ideas that are implied at the end of the novel.[16]

Achebe's answer reveals how a familiar theological allusion can be used stylistically to relate and unify the general thematic preoccupations of all this novels. That is, the tragic conflicts between sons and fathers, between unfriendly elders, villages, clans, gods, between the Igbo and the white men, and between the cultures of both peoples, which led to things falling apart in the societies, and the people who hitherto had some measure of peace are now no longer at ease.

Whereas traditional Igbo religion preaches that sons should obey their fathers, elders and ancestors—a basic teaching of most reli-

---

[16] Michel Fabre, "Chinua Achebe on *Arrow of God*," *Echos du Commonwealth*, 5 (1979-1980), p.78.

gions—the Christian missionaries read and emphasize to young, callow minded Igbo converts like Nwoye those Biblical verses which bring about division in the family thereby destroying those ideals which emphasize family unity in Igbo societies. That is why Nwoye, when asked about his father, Okonkwo, could stand before Ogbuefi Obierika and impudently say, "I don't know. He is not my father" (*TFA*, p. 131); and when his father dies and he is informed of his death by hanging, Nwoye merely says, "Those who live by the sword must perish by the sword," echoing the word of Jesus Christ (*NLAE*, p. 125). It is this same Nwoye, now turned catechist in the second novel, who advises his own son, Obi, against marrying an *osu*. However, he fails because he cannot reconcile his Christian principles with his ethnic religious practices so as to persuade his son to stop loving Clara, an *osu*. The disobedience and disrespect he showed to his father, Okonkwo, under the aegis of Christianity is now being used as a weapon against him. The same problem of disobedience and disrespect is also found in *Arrow of God*—between Ezeulu and Oduche—and in *A Man of the People* between Samalu and Odili and between Chief Nanga and Odili. All four cases "almost amount to turning the world upside down" because the young men are encouraged by the alien church and school to disobey their fathers and elders. The situation is that the new order tries to force the old to give way.

Furthermore, there are instances of Achebe localizing a Biblical story and imagery in order to discuss, in the form of analogy, an Igbo problem. For instance, in *No Longer at Ease,* he says:

> There was a long silence. The lamp was now burning too brightly. Obi's father turned down the wick a little and then resumed his silence. After what seemed ages he said: 'I know Josiah Okeke very well.' He was looking steadily in front of him. His voice sounded tired. 'I know him and I know his wife. He is a good man and a great Christian. But he is an *osu*. Naaman, captain of the host of Syria, was a great man and honorable, he was also a mighty man of valor, but he was a leper.' He paused so that this great and felicitous analogy might sink in with all its heavy and dreadful weight.

'Osu is like leprosy in the minds of our people. I beg of you, my son, not to bring the mark of shame and of leprosy into our family. If you do, your children and your children's children unto the third and fourth generations will curse your memory. It is not for myself I speak; my days are few. You will bring sorrow on your head and on the heads of your children. Who will marry your daughters? Whose daughters will your sons marry? Think of that, my son. We are Christians but we cannot marry our own daughters' (NLAE, p. 121).

The stylistic merits of this passage are many. It contains two Biblical allusions, one to the story of Naaman and the other to "The Ten Commandments;" there is cultural explanation of the word, osu; there is a reference to incest; and also there is language realism: when Ezeulu advises his sons and Umuaro people, he talks like the Chief Priest of Ulu, using proverbial analogy and imagery which is familiar to his audience. In the present passage, Isaac Okonkwo talks like a catechist. He, like his traditional counterpart, uses proverbial analogy and imagery known to his listener. As the son of a preacher, Obi must have been familiar with the words of the prophets and therefore cannot say they are untrue, unless he is deliberately revolting against his father's ways. Of course, he knows that Igbo fathers must tell their sons the truth as a matter of parental duty and cultural responsibility, unless such a parent has been influenced to the contrary by alien culture.

Achebe's religious terminology and allusions suggest some correspondence, analogy, opposition, even indebtedness, between the two warring religions once we can identify their sources. Nevertheless, when the religious echoes and allusions are contextually analyzed in relation to particular and general thematic concerns of the author, we could be overwhelmed by a battery of ideas and meanings that they are capable of yielding. Knowing the sources of the religious allusions Achebe uses in his novels is not as important as discovering how well he has used them to aid his narrative action.

Language and Style

The language features we have been examining—literal translations of Igbo phrases into English, proverbs, pidgin and religious terminology and allusions—all add local color or a quality of Africanness to Achebe's novels. Through the combination of all four features Achebe is able to portray very vividly traditional Igbo culture, which had its dignity before the coming of the white men into Igboland. The peculiar use of language, especially in *Arrow of God* has been described as a "dignified but racy—occasionally bawdy—language" by Danielle Bonneau, who also gives instances of where picturesque periphrases are used to describe people and gods, and where allusions to sex and excrement are made.[17]

Achebe's language and style in *Things Fall Apart* are so admired by B. I. Chukwukere that he describes them in a paragraph which summarizes what he calls *the essential Achebe*:

> Part of the greatness of Achebe, part of the pleasure we get from reading him, lies in the very fact that he has a sure and firm control of English, exemplified particularly in his rendering of Ibo language-process-idiom, imagery, syntax and so forth—into English. He effortlessly, as it appears, leaps across an enormous gulf dividing the basic sources of literary creativity: feeling or thought, the stimulus of vision, and expression, the externalization in words of the vision. His achievement in *Things Fall Apart* deserves emphasis and emulation. The characters speak in a manner any Ibo or allied language - speaker would easily recognize as *natural* to them—rhythm, verbal nuances and the like. The most admirable feature of this *tour de force* is that Achebe neither rudely shocks nor seriously wounds the basic English sentence-pattern or sentence-structure, and at the same time he does not reduce the fundamentals of Ibo language idiom, sound and flow, to obscurity. Consequently a non-Ibo, or to be more precise any native English speaker, would have no good

---

[17] Danielle Bonneau, "Approaches to Achebe's Language in *Arrow of God* "*Echos du Commonwealth*, 5 (1979-1980), p. 78.

ground for antagonism. It would be wrong for him or her to grumble that the English of the novel is un-English. A native Ibo speaker, on the other hand, would acknowledge the fact that although the conversations or narrations are in English, yet Ibo speech-patterns and speech-flow are evident. To look for the planning and effort that went behind the erection of this almost indescribable bridge across a wide cultural gap is a step towards discovering what one might call *the essential Achebe*.[18]

Chukwukere's commendatory remark indicates the overall critical reception of Achebe's language and style in his novels, especially in the scenes and episodes depicting Igbo characters in action. For example, Eldred Jones regards Achebe's sensitive use of English to reflect the African environment as one of the significant successes of *Things Fall Apart*, adding that environment is used more subtly to symbolize theme and crystallize character. Also, Jones includes Achebe's presentation of life and belief in Umuofia in the idiom of people who believed in it, and his refusing to obtrude his own personality upon the material of the novel, as other good qualities of the author.[19] Kofi Awoonor remarks that the novelty of Achebe's work lies in his use of African themes in the creation of an African past, dignified yet unromantic, and in his fresh Igbo-derived English style.[20]

Furthermore, apart from the literary and linguistic merits of Achebe's language and style in his novels, there is also the political merit to consider. In his preface to Frantz Fanon's *Wretched of the Earth*, Jean Paul Sartre notes the fundamental irony of the ex-colonial's literature: "An ex-native, French-speaking, bends that language to new requirements, makes use of it, and speaks to the

---

[18] B. I. Chukwukere, "The Problem of Language in African Creative Writing," *African Literature Today*, 3 (1969), p. 19.

[19] Eldred Jones, "Language and Theme in *Things Fall Apart*," *Review of English Literature* 4,4 (1964) pp. 40-41.

[20] Kofi Awoonor, *The Breast of the Earth*, (Garden City, New York: Anchor Press/Doubleday, 1976), p. 280.

colonized only."[21] The bending of English in Achebe's novels, "to new requirements" is a kind of irony, perhaps ingenuity, because through the bending of the colonial language Achebe gains literary independence. It is with this understanding that Lloyd W. Brown asserts that:

> The Nigerian's [Achebe's] fiction demonstrates his preoccupation with language, not simply as a communication device, but as a total cultural experience. At this level, language is not merely technique. It is the embodiment of its civilization and therefore represents or dramatizes modes of perception within its cultural grouping. Accordingly, the white man's failure to understand African customs in *Things Fall Apart* is bound up with his ignorance of the African's language. In other words, Achebe seizes upon the perceptual values represented by an alien European culture and its language, then exploits these criteria to portray external conflicts between the African and the white colonialist, or to project the internal crises of African society.[22]

Achebe's peculiar use of the English language, as he plays the role of a novelist as teacher, makes him a spokesman for his people, but he does not "speak to the colonized people only." He also speaks to the colonizers and to other spectators of the colonial conflicts between the Igbo and the white men, particularly spectators in Europe and America, where his novels are read. That means that the variety of English used in the novels and which were originally regarded as "a tongue for sighing"[23] against colonialism has now become a tongue for singing the beauty and dignity of Igbo—indeed

---

[21] Frantz Fanon, *Wretched of the Earth*, trans. Constance Farrington,(New York: Evergreen, 1968), p. 10.

[22] Lloyd Brown, "Cultural Norms and Modes of Perception in Achebe's Fiction," *Critical Perspectives in Nigerian Literatures*, ed. Bernth Lindfors (Washington, D.C.: Three Continents Press, 1976), p. 133.

[23] For full argument of this point, see Chinua Achebe "The African Writer and the English Language," *Morning Yet on Creation Day*, pp. 74-84.

African—culture. The outcome of such an experiment in language is that Achebe's means of communication has accommodated and expressed to the fullest Igbo and African thought-patterns and behavior.

10 | Conclusion

> This theme—put quite simply—is that African peoples did not hear of culture for the first time from Europeans; that their societies were not mindless but frequently had a philosophy of great depth and value and beauty, that they had poetry and, above all, they had dignity.
> —Achebe in "The Role of the Writer in a New Nation"

What is there at last to be said about Igbo folkways in Chinua Achebe's novels? And what final words can we say about Achebe the propagator of the folkways? One can say, for one thing—curiously—that issues have been raised and questions asked about Igbo culture and its celebration; and, also, that an attempt has been made to test the validity, even the necessity, of Achebe including such folkways in his novels which are a foreign literary genre. Indeed, our appreciation of the folkways validates Achebe's assertion that "African peoples did not hear of culture for the first time from Europeans; that their societies were not mindless but frequently had a philosophy of great depth and value and beauty, that they had poetry and, above all, they had dignity."[1]

Furthermore, our investigation has so far proved that Achebe's mastery of Igbo art of story-telling and his formal education in the European art of novel-writing together produce a model fictional experiment in the African writer. Ironically, however, Achebe's sensibility is profoundly conservative in the sense that he has been able to write novels that fit very well into the European pattern, even as he maintains his Igbo culture and oral performance. His achievement in this literary experiment is a matter of good artistry.

Thematically, Achebe's novels are considered great because they recreate the folkways of a people who were happy with their music and dances, rituals and ceremonies, marriage, and other religious, social, political and economic instutitions. The Igbo people had a dignified culture and, above all, they had no imperial ambitions because their gods could never have allowed them to fight "a war of blame" against other people. However imperfect their institutions were, the Igbo societies knew how to deal with their own problems because they thought and acted like one people, we are told in the novels, until the white men came to their societies and "put a knife on the things that held us together and we have fallen apart" (*TFA*, p. 160).

One of the things that held the Igbo people together was their traditional religion which the white man attempted to replace with Christianity. This is why religion is such an important Igbo folkway explored in this study. The way Achebe exploited traditional religion and other folkways shows that Achebe, out of relative obscurity, discovered his mission and chose the novel as a competent means of presenting the view that Igbo culture, like many other African cultures, was rich and worthy of celebration. Hence novel-writing has proved for him a vital cultural and literary necessity. That is, his novels indicate that Achebe's role is that of a cultural interpreter to his foreign readers. In fact, his fictional ancestors, Okonkwo and Ezeulu—major characters of his novels—played similar roles but

---

[1] Chinua Achebe, "The Role of the Writer in a New Nation," *Nigeria Magazine*, 81 (June 1964), p. 158.

perished in the process because they had made too may decisions that one considers moral mistakes.

Choice of Medium of Expression

Achebe needed a medium through which he could communicate with those who misjudged Igbo culture, apparently because they did not understand the Igbo language. So he chose the English language—a medium that is as international as his audience. That selection of a suitable medium has increased his readership, even within his country, Nigeria. Thus Achebe is enabled to speak to the colonized and the colonizers as well as to their spectators, the non-participants in the tragic encounter between Europe and Africa. Achebe, as a responsible literary emissary, would have failed his Igbo ancestors had he delivered their message in the language of the oppressors, in British English that is, without manipulating it to accommodate Igbo thought-patterns, idioms, aphorisms, proverbs, metaphors, and general philosophy of life. His peculiar use of English as a novelistic medium required that he should first learn "how to write with his right hand"—the art of Igbo conversation and the acquisition of their proverbs which are "the palm-oil with which words are eaten," and then learn "how to write with his left hand"—the art of writing fiction which is a part of his colonial heritage. Both forms of education constitute his double-heritage which he has used to advantage. He underscores the importance of acquiring both skills, and recommends the skills to any African writer, who uses English language as a medium, when he says:

> For an African, writing in English is not without its serious setbacks. He often finds himself describing situations or modes of thought which have no direct equivalent in the English way of life. Caught in that situation he can do one of two things. He can try and contain what he wants to say within the limits of conventional English or he can try to push back those limits to accommodate his ideas. The first method produces competent, uninspired and rather flat work. The second method can produce something new and valuable to the English language as well as to the material he is

trying to put over. But it can also get out of hand. It can lead to bad English being accepted and defended as African or Nigerian. I submit that those who can do the work of extending the frontiers of English so as to accommodate African thought-patterns must do it through their mastery of English and not out of innocence.[2]

The language of his novels attests to his mastery of English and to the ingenious exploitation of it to address the issues of great concern to him and to his people. Achebe's successful language experiment opened a new thoroughfare where hitherto there was a wilderness for subsequent Igbo authors such as Onuora Nzekwu, John Munonye, and Elechi Amadi who appear to have been influenced by "Achebe's sensitive sociological approach to the novel, with all its vision of history."[3]

Achebe's Audience

Turning to the question of Achebe's audience, we may simply ask, "For whom does Achebe writes?" From our discussion of folkways in his novels, the answer is quite clear: that he writes, in the main, for the African but non-Africans are not excluded. Achebe himself was the first to suggest this answer when he stated his overall thesis: that his novels were intended to teach his readers that the African past, though not that perfect, "was not one long night of savagery" from which Europeans delivered the Africans. And in some other situation he said:

> A couple of weeks ago I read a lecture at the University of Massachusetts in which I said that Joseph Conrad is a bloody racist. It was only necessary to say so because *The Heart of Darkness*, I discovered, was the most popularly read book in the English department there.

---

[2] Achebe, *op. cit.*, p. 160.

[3] Ernest Emenyonu discusses in detail Achebe's influence on his contemporaries in Chapter 8 of his *The Rise of the Igbo Novel* (Ibadan: Oxford University Press, 1978), pp. 164-185.

And some people jumped up and cried, 'He is not talking about Africa. This is literature. You have no sense of humor.' This response shows you the world is actually divided in two. To them a book which is completely, totally offensive, which dehumanizes the African, is entertainment. For me, it is not. It is a monumental untruth unsaved by ornate turgidity.[4]

The deduction we make from the pronouncements is that Achebe is unhappy about the misrepresentation of Africa by early European writers. In that sense his novels are novels of "protest" and reeducation. Despite such writers' misrepresentation of the African image in their novels of Africa, the white-controlled schools and examination bodies went ahead and recommended them to African students as compulsory textbooks: an indirect but sure way of forcing the Africans to accept a non-existent inferiority which the colonialists invented to rationalize colonialism through religion, government, and trade. Fortunately, since independence, various African governments have taken over the control of their schools and examination bodies. Most of them have adopted Achebe's books as texts. It is hoped that in this way Achebe's re-education of his people has started. In fact, some heads of African Colleges and Universities have realized that African literature is more important than the European and are now Africanizing their departments of language and literature—a change made possible by the availability of African texts, including Achebe's novels.

The international audience is equally important because it too needs re-education. One is encouraged by the news that Achebe's "novels have been translated into some thirty languages,"[5] which may mean that more and more willing readers are getting his message. Some may have been attracted by the sociological and anthropological information they get out of the novels. Yet others

---

[4] Chinua Achebe, "Chinua Achebe Et L'Engagement Dans La Literature (an interview)," *Echos du Commonwealth*, 5 (1979-1980), p. 180.

[5] See Innes and Lindfors, *Critical Perspectives on Chinua Achebe* (Washington, D.C. 1978), p. 1.

read the novels for their literary merits. For whatever reason they are read, Achebe's novels are important for the re-education service they offer to both the foreign and domestic audiences.

Historical Validity of the Fictive Creations

Achebe's novels contain literary re-evaluation of the historical past of his people because, "there is a saying in Ibo that a man who can't tell where the rain began to beat him cannot know where he dried his body. The writer can tell the people where the rain began to beat them."[6] Achebe sees the problems of the present Igbo, Nigerian, and African societies and knows that they derive from the historical past. His investigation into that historical past reveals that both the Africans and the white men are to blame for the tragic encounter of Europe and Africa. Until Africans are prepared to see the mistakes of their ancestors and avoid repeating the same mistakes, they will continue to suffer. Furthermore, contrary to an erroneous popular view which a misreading of Achebe's novels has produced—that Africa was an Edenic society until the white men came in—our evaluation of the Igbo folkways reveals that the narrators blame Africans more than they do the white intruders. The situation is so because, as an author, Achebe seeks the truth. He, therefore, stresses the importance of maintaining the truth, while adopting a historical approach in his novel-writing:

> The question is how does a writer re-create this past? Quite clearly there is a strong temptation to idealize it—to extol its good points and pretend that the bad never existed. This is where the writer's integrity comes in. Will he be strong enough to overcome the temptation to select only those facts which flatter him? If he succumbs he will have branded himself as an unworthy witness. But it is not only his personal integrity as an artist which is involved. The credibility of the world he is attempting to recreate will be called to

---

[6] Achebe, "The Role of the Writer in a New Nation," *Nigeria Magazine*, 81 (June 1964), p. 158.

question and he will defeat his own purpose if he is suspected of glossing over inconvenient facts. We cannot pretend that our past was one long, technicolor idyll. We have to admit that like other people's pasts ours had its good as well as its bad sides.[7]

Through narrating the activities of the major characters and of the citizens of the fictive Igbo societies, Achebe introduces the weaknesses and the strengths of those societies. Age is respected, but achievement is revered, we are told. Hence, achievement is religiously pursued and becomes a temptation, even obsession, which makes Okonkwo insult, physically assault, and even kill others. Battering of women is a recurrent social offense. Twins and their mothers are branded as abominable people; therefore, they must be thrown away into the forests and ostracized. And there are so many "superstitious" folk beliefs which literally constitute the cosmology of the people. And yet Achebe does not shy away from recreating the ugly picture of his ancestral home; rather he tells things the way they are. What is more, bad readers only recognize the bad pictures without noticing the impression that citizens have of their culture; they forget to read the characters' own responses to the weaknesses of their society.

To rephrase that, the cursory reader does not realize that Achebe is saying "Yes, there is battering of women, but the elders of *egwugwu* also met and condemned it in the Mgbafo-Uzowulu case; Okonkwo beat his wife, and Ezeani made him offer a propitiation sacrifice." There is unnecessary killing in the novels, which men and their gods condemn. For example, Okonkwo wantonly kills people twice and he is twice reprimanded by his best friend and his people, and is summarily punished and killed by Ani, the Earth-goddess in charge of morality.

When we come to the urban novels, *No Longer at Ease* and *A Man of the People*. Achebe reports social indiscipline like bribery and corruption. But what is more, the citizens who commit these offenses are capable of self-criticism. Obi, the hero of *No Longer at*

---

[7] *Ibid*, p. 158.

Ease, is secretly but vehemently condemned for taking bribes, by his people. But they defend him publicly because of their basic philosophy of life, that "the fox must be chased away first; after that the hen might be warned against wandering into the bush" (p. 5). In their fair-mindedness, they can say proverbially that "it is not right to ask a man with elephantiasis of the scrotum to take on smallpox as well, when thousands of other people have not had even their share of small diseases;" so they cannot start asking Obi to repay his loan in the face of his immediate financial problems (p. 90). They can appreciate Obi's dilemma because inwardly they know that one of the reasons why he took bribes from people was because of the financial demands his people, including Umuofia Progressive Union in Lagos, made on him. Therefore, it behooves them to support him as he stands trial for the crime they indirectly made him commit.

In *A Man of the People*, the political mistakes of the Nigerian (and African) societies are exposed without mincing words. The novel is regarded as one of the best political satires ever to come out of Africa. But as in the cases of the first three novels, Achebe also records disinterestedly the people's responses to crime. Take the case of Josiah, a local shopkeeper, who was suspected by his fellow villager of calling Azoge, a blind beggar, to his shop and giving him rice to eat and plenty of palm-wine to drink. Azoge thought he had met a kind man and accepted his hospitality. While he was eating and drinking, Josiah took away his stick and put a new stick like the old one in its place thinking that Azoge would not notice. But if a blind man does not know his own stick, who would?, they asked. As Azoge shouted, the people *knew* that Josiah had taken the beggar's stick "to make medicine for trade, of course" (p. 85). So, one of the villagers, Timothy, expressed his disapproval proverbially thus:

> "Josiah has taken away enough for the owner to notice," he said again and again. "If anyone ever sees my feet in this shop again let him cut them off. Josiah has now removed enough for the owner to see him." (p. 86)

Odili, who wants political reform of the nation, later quotes

Timothy's words, expanding it a little to give us what becomes the main quotable quote of the novel:

> "Koko had taken enough for the owner to see," said my father....
> My father's words struck me because they were the very same words the villagers of Anata had spoken of Josiah, the abominated trader. Only in their case the words had meaning. The owner was the village, and the village had a mind; it could say no to sacrilege. But in the affairs of the nation there was no owner, the laws of the village became powerless (p. 148).

We can now see why Achebe and some other African writers hold the white men partially responsible for making things fall apart for African countries—the colonizers destroyed the mind and authority of the village. In its *civilized* form, the village can no longer say no to sacrilege. The colonial judicial and law-enforcement agents, aided and abetted by corrupt *kotma* and interpreters, can set abominated men like Josiah free on technical legal grounds, even when the immorality of the suspect is quite apparent. And sons can stand up and impudently shout orders to their fathers and elders just because they are educated in the Western system.

The point of the African protest is not that Africa was a Utopia spoiled by the coming of the white men. Surely, there were many social, political, religious, and economic institutions which were bad but they would have been gradually changed with time. In fact, there are indications of evolutionary change in the novels:

> "It was only this morning," said Obierika, "that Okonkwo and I were talking about Abame and Aninta [both Igbo clans], where titled men climb trees and pound foo-foo for their wives."
> "All their customs are upside-down. They do not decide brideprice as we do, with sticks. They haggle and bargain as if they were buying a goat or a cow in the market."
> "That is very bad," said Obierika's eldest brother. "But what is good in one place is bad in another place ..." (TFA, pp. 66-67).

"It has not always been so," he said. "My father told me that he had been told that in the past a man who broke the peace was dragged on the ground through the village until he died. But after a while this custom was stopped because it spoiled the peach which it was meant to preserve." (Ibid, p. 29)

Admittedly, some of the men such as Okonkwo were very conservative but they could not have resisted change forever. Change must come when it will and that gradually too! Africans would have loved to *change* from their so-called primitive stage to a developed one at their own rate, for it is a basic Igbo maxim that "the time a man wakes up is his morning." (AOG. p. 111)

Interpretative Perspective

So far, we have commented on Achebe's choice of medium of communication, the subject matter of his novels, his audience, and the historical validity of his fictive creations. All four rhetorical preoccupations affected his presentation of the Igbo folkways that we have examined in this study. He uses some of these folkways as literary devices which enable him to develop his themes; and at other times he uses the stories he tells as a means of re-enacting Igbo folkways he wants his audience to see and appreciate.

Our evaluation of these folkways has been literary because in spite of their folk quality, we regard Achebe's novels as essentially creative writing or written literature, even though portions of the novels could be readapted and performed orally. Indeed Achebe has adapted and used the verbal arts of the Igbo in his novels, but the fact remains that the folk materials remained raw until they were transmitted imaginatively into goods we can now handle and appreciate as novels.

The re-fashioning of the Igbo folk materials (oral tradition) by Achebe (the novelist) into novels (the foreign form) was necessary because the old order (traditional Igbo societies) had given way to the new (modern Nigerian and African societies) in which the moon was no longer sufficient to illuminate their nights. They needed electricity in the modern cities just as the village minstrels and bards needed to make way for modern African writers to sing the praise and dirge of their past and present heroes, not only with cannons and long drums, but also with the *uli* (the written form) that never fades.

This study, which has deliberately concentrated on Igbo folkways, has demonstrated that the success of Achebe as a novelist depended on how well he was able to interpret the native material in the foreign mode of expression—the fictional style and technique. Thus, "one can say with some justification that even though the coming of Europeans caused problems of social, cultural, and psychological adjustment, it has at least brought some positive gains, chief of which is the liberation of the African from ethnic isolation: one result is the emergence of the novel, the art-form best fitted to represent his new life and experience."[8]

Achebe has, however, modified his borrowed art-form through the structural manipulation of Igbo folkways to explore his themes and explain his culture to his audience. At first, his style appeared "quaint" to some indiscreet critics who could not identify with the folk elements of the novels; however, the so-called quaint elements are now acknowledged, by more careful critics, as innovations. The mistakenly maligned writer has, in effect, become rightfully the conscious artist.

---

[8] Emmanuel Obiechina, *Culture, Tradition and Society in The West African Novel* (Cambridge: Cambridge University Press, 1975), p. ix.

Bibliography

Primary Sources

Achebe, Chinua. *Things Fall Apart*. London: Heinemann Educational Books, Ltd., 1958; Reprinted 1966.

———. *No Longer at Ease*. London: Heinemann Educational Books, Ltd., 1960; Reprinted 1978.

———. *Arrow of God*. London: Heinemann Educational Books, Ltd., 1964; Second Edition 1974 and reprinted 1977.

———. *A Man of the People*. London: Heinemann Educational Books, Ltd., 1966; Reprinted 1978.

Secondary Sources

Abrams, M. H. *A Glossary of Literary Terms*, 3rd Edition. New York: Holt, Rinehart and Winston, Inc., 1971.

Achebe, Chinua. "The Black Writer's Burden." *Presence Africaine*, 31, 59 (1966), 135-40.

———. *Morning Yet on Creation Day* (Essays). Garden City, New York: Anchor Press/Doubleday, 1976.

———. "The Role of the Writer in a New Nation." *Nigeria Magazine*, 81 (1964), 157-160.

Angogo, R. "Achebe and the English Language." *Busara*, 7,2 (1975), 1-14.

Arinze, Francis A. *Sacrifice in Ibo Religion*. Ibadan: Ibadan University Press, 1978.

Ashley, Leonard R. N. "Names Into Words, And Other Examples of The Possibilities of Extending The Boundaries of Literary Onomastics." *Literary Onomastics Studies*, VII (1980), 1-24.

Awoonor, Kofi: *The Breast of The Earth*. Garden City, New York: Anchor Press/Doubleday, 1976.

Bascom, William. "Folklore and Anthropology." *Journal of American Folklore*, 66 (1953), 283-290.

Beum, Robert, ed. *Edmund Spenser's Epithalamion*. Columbus, Ohio: Charles E. Merrill Publishing Company, 1968.

Bonneau, Danniell. "Approaches to Achebe's Language in *Arrow of God*. "*Echos du Commonwealth*," 5 (1979-80), 68-88.

Brown, Lloyd. Cultural Norms and Modes of Perception in Chinua Achebe's Fiction." *Critical Perspectives on Nigerian Literatures*. Ed. Bernth Lindfors. Washington, D.C.: Three Continents Press, 1976.

Bulfinch, Thomas. *Bulfinch's Mythology*. New York: Avenel Books, 1978.

Carroll, David. *Chinua Achebe*. New York: Twayne Publishers, Inc. 1970.

Chukwukere, B. I. "The Problem of Language in African Creative Writing." *African Literature Today*, 3 (1969), 15-26.

Colmer, Rosemary. "The Start of Weeping is Always Hard: The Ironic Structure of *No Longer at Ease*." *Literary Half-Yearly*, 21, 1 (1980), 121-135.

DeMott, Benjamin. "An Unprofessional Eye: Oyiemu-o?" *American Scholar*, 32 (1963), 192, 294, 296, 298, 300, 302, 304, 306.

Echeruo, Michael. "Chinua Achebe and His Critics." *A Celebration of Black and African Writing*. Ed. Bruce King and Kolawole Ogungbesan. Zaria and Ibada: Ahmadu Bello University Press and Oxford University Press, 1975, pp. 150-163.

———. *The Conditioned Imagination From Shakespeare to Conrad*. London: The Macmillan Press Ltd., 1978.

———. "The Dramatic Limits of Igbo Rituals." *Critical Perspectives on Nigerian Literatures*. Ed. Bernth Lindfors, Washington, D.C.: Three Continents Press, 1976. pp. 75-85.

Emenyonu, Ernest N. "Ezeulu: The Night Mask Caught Abroad by Day." *Pan-African Journal*, IV, 4 (1971), 407-419.

———. "African Literature: What Does It Take to Be Its Critics?" *African Literature Today* 5 (1971), 1-11.

Fanon, Frantz. *The Wretched of the Earth.* New York: Grove Press, Inc., 1968.

Finnegan, Ruth. *Oral Literature in Africa.* Nairobi, Kenya: Oxford University Press, 1976.

Firor, Ruth A. *Folkways in Thomas Hardy.* Philadelphia: University of Pennsylvania Press, 1931.

Fraser, Robert. "A Note on Okonkwo's Suicide." *Kunapipi,* 1,1 (1979), 108-113.

Furguson, Paul F. "By Their Names You Shall Know Them: Flanner O'Connor's Onomastic Strategies." *Literary Onomastics Studies,* VII (1980), 87-105.

Gassner, John and Ralph G. Allen. *Theater and Drama in the Making,* Vol. 1. Boston: Houghton Mifflin Company, 1964.

Griffiths, Gareth. "Language and Action in the Novels of Chinua Achebe." *African Literature Today,* 5 (1971), 88-105.

Hall Jr., Robert A. *Pidgin and Creole Languages.* Ithaca, New York: Cornell University Press, 1966.

Harris, Wilson. *Palace of the Peacock.* London: Faber and Faber, 1973.

Hoffman, Daniel G., et al. "Folklore in Literature: A Symposium." *Journal of American Folklore.* LXX: 275 (Jan.-March 1957), 1-24.

Hymes, Dell. "Speech and Language: On the Origins and Foundations of Inequality Among Speakers." *Language as a Human Problem.* Ed. Einar Haugen and Morton Bloomfield. New York: W. W. Norton & Company, Inc., 1974. pp. 45-71.

Innes, C. L., and Bernth Lindfors, eds. *Critical Perspectives on Chinua Achebe.* Washington, D.C.: Three Continents Press, 1978.

Jahn, Janheinz. *Muntu: The New African Culture.* New York: Grove Press, Inc., 1961.

Johnson, John W. "Folklore in Achebe's Novels." *New Letters.* 40, 3 (1974), 95-107.

Jones, Eldred. "Language and Theme in *Things Fall Apart. "Review of English Literature,* 4,4 (1984), 39-43.

Killam, G. D. *The Novels of Chinua Achebe.* London: Heinemann Educational Books Ltd., 1971.

King, Bruce, ed. *Introduction to Nigerian Literature.* Lagos, Nigeria: University of Lagos and Evans Brothers Ltd., 1971.

———. "The Revised *Arrow of God.*" *Echos du Commonwealth*, 5 (1979-1980), 89-98.

Lewis, Mary Ellen B. "Beyond Content in the Analysis of Folklore in Literature: Chinua Achebe's *Arrow of God.*" *Research in African Literatures*, 7 (1976), 44-52.

Lindfors, Bernth. "Achebe's African Parable." *Presence Africaine*, 66 (1968), 130-136.

———. *Critical Perspectives on Nigerian Literatures*. Washington, D.C.: Three Continents Press, 1976.

———. "The Blind Men and the Elephant." *African Literature Today*, 7 (1975), 53-64.

———. *Folklore in Nigerian Literature*. New York: Africana Publishing Company, 1973.

Lomax, Alan. *Folk Song Style and Culture*. Washington D.C.: American Association for the Advancement of Science, Publication No. 88, 1969.

Madubuike, Ihechukwu *A Handbook of African Names*. Washington, D.C.: Three Continents Press, 1976.

Mahood, M. M. "Idols of the Den: Achebe's *Arrow of God.*" *Critical Perspectives on Chinua Achebe*. Ed. C. L. Innes and Bernth Lindfors. Washington D.C.: Three Continents Press, 1978, pp. 180-206.

Mbiti, John S. *African Religions and Philosophy*. New York: Frederick A. Praeger, Publishers, 1969.

Moore, Gerald. "Achebe's New Novel: *Arrow of God.*" *Transition*, 14 (1964), 52.

Moore, Gerald, and Ulli Beier, eds. *Modern Poetry from Africa*. Baltimore, Maryland: Penguin Book, Inc., 1968.

Morton, Richard. *Ulysses*. Lincoln, Nebraska: Cliff's Notes, Inc., 1972.

Nettl, Bruno. *Folk and Traditional Music of the Western Continents*. Englewood Cliffs, New Jersey: Prentice-Hall, Inc., 1965.

Njaka, Mazi Elechukwu Nnadibuagha. *Igbo Political Culture*. Evanston: Northwestern University Press, 1974.

Nnolim, Charles E. "A Source for *Arrow of God.*" *Critical Perspectives on Chinua Achebe*. Ed. C. L. Innes and Bernth Lindfors. Washington, D.C.: Three Continents Press, 1978.

———. "Achebe's *Things Fall Apart:* An Igbo National Epic." *Modern Black Literature.* Ed. S. Okechukwu Mezu. Buffalo, New York: Black Academy Press, Inc., 1971.

Nwoga, Donatus I. "The Chi Offended." *Transition,* 15 (1964), 5.

———. *The Supreme God As Stranger in Igbo Religious Thought.* Ekwereazu in Imo State, Nigeria: Hawk Press, 1984.

Obiechina, Emmanuel. *Culture, Tradition and Society in The West African Novel.* Cambridge: Cambridge University Press, 1975.

———. "Introduction." *The Conch,* III. 2 (1971), 1-15.

Ogbaa, Kalu. "An Interview with Chinua Achebe." *Research in African Literatures,* 12, 1 (1981), 1-13.

Okigbo, Christopher. *Labyrinths.* London: Heinemann Educational Books Ltd., 1971.

Opoku, Kofi Asare. *West African Traditional Religion,* Accra: FEP International Privated Ltd., 1978.

Pevear, Richard, trans. *Alain/The Gods.* New York: New Directions Publishing Corporation, 1974.

Rajec, Elizabeth M. "Franz Kafka and Philip Roth: Their Use of Literary Onomastics (Based on The Professor of Desire)." *Literary Onomastics Studies,* VII (1980), 69-86.

The Random House College Dictionary. Ed. Jess Stein. New York: Random House Inc., 1975.

Roscoe, Adrian A. *Mother is Gold: A Study in West African Literature.* Cambridge: Cambridge University Press, 1971.

Rotimi, Ola. "Traditional Nigerian Drama." *Introduction to Nigerian Literature.* Lagos: University of Lagos and Evans Brothers Ltd., 1971.

Seeger, Pete. *The Incomplete Folksinger.* New York: Simon and Schuster, 1972.

Seitel, Peter. "Proverbs: A Social Use of Metaphor." *Genre,* 2 (1969), 143-161.

Shelton, Austin J. "The Offended Chi in Achebe's Novels." *Transition,* 13 (1964), 36-37.

Societe d'Edutes des Pays du Commonwealth (France). "Chinua Achebe: *Arrow of God* et ses Critiques." *Echos du Commonwealth* 5, 1979-1980.

Taylor, Archer. *The Proverb.* Cambridge, Massachusetts: Harvard

University Press, 1931.

Thiong'o Ngugi wa. "Chinua Achebe: A Man of the People." *Critical Perspectives on Chinua Achebe.* Ed. C. L. Innes and Bernth Lindfors, Washington, D.C.: Three Continents Press, (1978), pp. 279-282.

Thompson, Stith. *The Folktale.* Berkeley: University of California Press, 1977.

Trench, Richard C. *Proverbs and Their Lessons.* London: Kegan, Paul, Trench Trubner and Co.,Ltd., 1905.

Uchendu, Victor C. *The Igbo of Southeast Nigeria.* New York: Holt, Rinehart and Winston, 1965.

Wali, Obi. "The Dead End of African Literature." *Transition,* 4, 10 (1963), pp. 13-15.

Weinstock, Donald, and Cathy Ramadam. "Symbolic Structure in *Things Fall Apart.*" *Critique: Studies in Modern Fiction,* XI, 1 (1969), 33-41.

Winters, Marjorie. "An Objective Approach to Achebe's Style." *Research in African Literatures,* 12, 1 (1981), 55.

———. "Morning Yet on Judgement Day: The Critics of Chinua Achebe." *Journal of the Literary Society of Nigeria,* 1: forthcoming.

Wren, Robert M. *Achebe's World: The Historical and Cultural Context of the Novels of Chinua Achebe.* Washington, D.C.: Three Continents Press, 1980.

———. "Achebe's Revision of *Arrow of God*" *Research in African Literatures,* 7 (1976), 53-58.

Yankson, Kofi. "The Use of Pidgin in *No Longer at Ease* and *A Man of the People.*" *Asemka,* 1, 2 (1974), 68-79.

Index

Abam, 28, 84
Abame, 44-45, 163-6, 250
abiku, 155
Abrams, M. H., 194, 216-7
Achebe, Chinua, 771-8, 11, 13,
  16, 22-5, 27, 32-6, 39, 56, 61,
  63-7, 75-7, 83, 86, 88, 94, 96-
  97, 100-1, 103, 108-9, 113,
  118-9, 128-9, 138-40, 143,
  144-6, 148,151, 154-6, 160,
  166, 171-3, 175, 177-8, 185,
  188-9, 203-4, 206-7, 209-10,
  214-6, 219-20, 233, 236-9,
  250, 252
  art, 5
  artistic form, 7
  attitude towards traditional
    religion, 59-60
  audience, 245-7
  homiletic songs, 186
  language and imagery, 214
  language and style, 238-41
  literal translations, 225
  novels, 9, 24, 32, 61-4, 87,
    89-90, 96, 100, 109, 111,
    116, 145, 162, 176, 182,
    186, 216-7, 221, 226, 232,
    238, 242-3, 246-7, 251
  on bribery, 125
  on English language, 216, 222
  on Igbo cosmology, 60
  on Igbo didactic animal tales,
    145-6
  on legends and folk stories,
    162
  on praise songs and chants,
    185
  on proverbs, 111-2, 143
  on sex life of the Igbo, 206
  phraseology, 222
  role, 243
  satire, 141
  treatment and use of *chi*, 14-7
  use of English, 238
  use of ethnic images, 219-220
Afo, 64, 80, 104-5
Africa, 2, 3, 8, 184, 229, 244,
  246-7, 249
  emancipation of, 2
  image of, 3
African, affairs, 63
  character, 122
  colleges and universities, 246
  countries, 250
  cultures, 4, 72, 243
  customs, 240
  folktale, 6
  governments, 246
  literature, 108, 246
  parable, 185

260 | Index

past, 239, 245
peoples, 3, 242
problems, 22
protest, 250
societies, 247, 249, 251
themes, 239
thought-patterns, 245
writers, 155, 243-4, 250-1
Africanness, 238
Africans, 2, 61, 71, 73, 245-7, 251
Agaba, 86
agadinwanyi, 168
agbala, 47, 69, 78, 118-9
Agbala, the Oracle of the Hills and Caves, 46, 70-1, 115, 119, 224
Agbogu, Ernest Arinze, 194
Aghadike, 70
Agu, 65, 84
Akatakata, 198
Akuebue, 69, 117, 131, 136, 203
Akueke, 68, 95
Akukalia, 13, 78-9, 166, 169
Akunna, 11-4, 233
ala mmo, 22, 54, 207, 233
Allen, George, 63
Alusi, 105
Amadi, Elechi, 245
Amadioha, 26
Amalinze the Cat, 74, 81, 146, 179, 185, 217
Amalu, 54
Ambassadors Hotel, 211
Amechi, 201
America, 72, 142, 240
American English, 215
Americans, 214
American University, 72
Amoge, 202
Anata, 250

ancestors, 14, 19-24, 35, 37, 54, 84, 87, 103, 170, 174, 233-5
Andrew, 231
Anglo-Saxon, 62
Angogo, R., 215-6
Ani, the earth goddess, 17, 26, 30-1, 33, 38-9, 41-43, 47, 49, 54-5, 57, 60, 77, 120-1, 135, 153, 164, 168, 248
  authority and functions of 31-32
  shrine of, 39
animal tale, didactic, 145, 156
Aninta, 29, 250
Anosi, 133
anwansi, 31
Anyanafummo, 70
Anyanwu, 26
Armah, Ayi Kwei, 3
Arrow of God, 1, 5-6, 9, 16, 25, 28, 31-3, 35, 47-8, 60, 62, 69-70, 73-4, 77-8, 85, 88, 90, 92, 96-8, 104, 106-7, 118, 128-30, 134-5, 138, 143, 156, 161, 166, 169, 171-2, 181, 185, 190, 195-7, 200-1, 206-7, 215, 217, 220-2, 225-6, 228, 233-6, 238
art(s), 3-4, 8; *see also* Achebe's art
artistic form; *see also* Achebe's artistic form
Awoonor, Kofi, 2, 239
Azoge, 140-1, 249

Bible, 186-7, 190, 198, 200, 208, 232
Bisi, 229
black peoples, 3
bondage, 2
Bonneau, Danielle, 238

Braddeley, Mr., 18
Bridal songs, 204-6; *see also* songs
bride price, 152, 180
Britain, 62
British, the 128, 235
   Administration, 18, 48, 63, 72-3, 130, 208
   Commissioner, 45
   English, 188, 223, 229, 232, 244
Brown, Lloyd W., 108, 240
Brown, Mr., 11-4, 95, 233

Caliban motif, 108
Cambridge degrees, 71
Cameroons, Southern, 218
Carroll, David, 19, 56
caste, 33
Catholics, Roman, 195-6, 234
ceremonies, 8, 51, 69, 88-90, 93, 95-99, 104, 106, 110, 178-9, 243; *see also* folk songs and chants
Chapayev, Vasily Ivanovich, 6
Chartier, Emile (alias Alain), 58
chi, 4, 20, 22, 24, 35, 78-81, 118-20, 146, 163, 212, 223, 236
   meanings, functions, and roles of 14-8
Chielo, 223-4
Chika, 119
Chineke, 9-10, 21
Chinese Noh play, 6
Choice of Medium of Expression, 244-5
Christ, Jesus, 49, 187-8, 236
Christian camp, 146
   church, 50, 129, 151, 164
   converts, 62, 150, 188
   missionaries, 186, 232, 236
   religion, 29, 50, 94, 121, 196
Christians, 23, 29, 34, 45, 49, 62, 66, 107, 133, 138, 164-5, 167, 171, 188, 196, 233-4
   as secret agents, 129
Christmas, 198
Christopher, 171, 216, 229-30
Chukwu, 9-14, 17, 20-2, 24-6, 30
Chukwuka, 12, 68, 76
Chukwukere, B., 238-9
Church Missionary Society, 62, 150, 195
civilians, 4, 8
clan(s), 18, 28, 35, 39, 41, 46-7, 50, 54, 56-7, 62, 64, 69, 82-5, 87, 90, 94-5, 107-8, 132, 167
Clara, 18-9, 34-5, 189-90, 213, 236
Clark, John Pepper, 155
Clarke, Mr., 63, 73, 235
C. M. S., *see* (Church Missionary Society)
Colonialism, 235, 240, 246
Commonwealth literature, 2
Conrad, Joseph, 5, 222, 245
cosmic force, 9
cosmology, 7,9; *see also* Igbo cosmology
court messengers, 11, 45, 199, 200
C. P. C., 81, 211
cultural mestizos, 2
culture, 2-3, 6, 8; *see also* Igbo culture
customs, 4
   burial, 6

Daily Chronicle, The, 71
deities, 10-12, 19-20, 26-8, 64, 203

Index

DeMott, Benjamin, 212
destiny, 15-6, 20
Dimaragana, 170-1
Dimgba, 65
Dimkpa, 65
Dirges, 207-9
District Commissioner, 6, 11, 47-9, 165, 199
District Officer, 72-3
divination, 3, 27, 32-33
division of labor, 28
dramatic elements, 8
drums, talking 85

Echeruo, M.J.C., 89-90
Edenic Society, 244
Edna, 143, 198
Edogo, 33, 133
Education Officer, 73
efulefu, 34
Ego Women's Party, 183
egwugwu, 27, 44, 94-5, 97, 101-3, 164-5, 248
Egwu na Amu, 110
Eke, Chief Ogbonnaya, 16, 18, 20-1, 97, 141
ekwe, 91, 108
Ekwefi, 66-7, 70, 153-6, 159, 179-80, 219, 223-4
Ekwensu, 94, 224
elders, 35, 45, 53, 67-70, 98, 112, 115-7, 163, 174, 180, 186, 205, 235-6
Elsie, 142
Emefo, 45
Emenyonu, Ernest, 48, 199, 173, 222, 245
Empire Day, 195
England, 11, 122, 161, 235

English, 108, 195, 198, 213, 214-5, 221-5, 229-30, 232, 238-40, 244-5
  in Achebe's novels, 240
  language, 108, 214, 216, 241, 244-5
  novel, 5
  pidgin, 228-31, 238
  Queen's, 230
  renaissance, 6
  way of life, 244
Enoch, 94-5
Enugu, 219
Equiana, Olaudah, 99
Eru, 27, 186
Eunice, 211
Europe, 63, 160, 240, 244
European, art, 243
  culture, 240
  language, 110
  names, 77
  thought, 7
  tradition, 5
  writers, 246
Europeans, 2
Evil Forest, 22, 24, 101-4, 233
Ezeani, 38, 42, 70, 84-5, 248
Ezeudu, Ogbuefi, 23, 39-43, 62, 68-9, 99, 109
Ezeugo, Ogbuefi, 83
Ezeulu, 6, 23-5, 28-30, 33, 35-6, 47-60, 62, 69-70, 79, 86, 90, 93, 95, 97-8, 104-6, 113, 117, 120, 128-138, 161-2, 166-8, 173-4, 181-2, 185-6, 195-7, 201-4, 208, 222, 224, 226-8, 233, 235-7, 244
Ezeulu's family 75, 92, 96
Ezidemili, 29, 55, 57-9, 70, 129, 167, 185

Ezinma, 5, 31-2, 66-7, 151-7, 159, 224
Ezukanma, Ezekwesili, 69

fable, 156
faggots, 133-5
Fanon, Frantz, 2, 239
fate, 15-6
Festival of the Pumpkin Leaves, 97-8, 132; *see also* New Yam Feast/Festival
fiam, 196
Finnegan, Ruth, 109
Firor, Ruth A., 32-3
folk songs and chants, 176-8
folk stories, 144-5, 174-5, 215
   Achebe's uses of, 145
folktales, 1, 4, 6, 78, 81, 112, 144, 172, 219, 228; *see also* African folktale
folkways, 4-9, 35, 87, 111, 242-3, 251-2; *see also* Igbo folkways
Fraser, Robert, 36-7
French, 210-1
Furmanov, Dmitry, 6

Galloway, Mr. Justice William, 218
Germanic tribes, 32
Ghana, 2
Ginikanwa, 67
goddesses, 24-8, 41-3, 47, 54-5, 57, 60, 70
gods, 9-10, 13, 24-30, 32, 34-6, 46-7, 50, 70, 78-9, 82, 114, 137, 234, 238, 242
   types, 60
Goodcountry, Mr., 28, 62, 94, 186, 209, 234
Government Hill, 133, 154, 161
Great Britain, 215

Greek tragedians, 5
Green, Mr., 6, 63, 122
Griffiths, Gareth, 122-6

Hardy, Thomas, 5
Harvard degrees, 71
Heart of Darkness, 122, 245
Henchard, 5
hero(es), 5, 17, 36, 47, 65, 71, 80
Historical Validity of the Fictive Creations, 247-51
Homiletic Songs, 186-7, 189
Humanism, 6
Hungarian folk song, 6
Hymes, Dell, 214

iba, 31
Ibadan, 219, 245
Idemili, 26, 49, 57, 60, 93, 196, 209
Ifeoma, 75, 91, 206
Igbo, 3-4, 16-7, 22-3, 26, 31, 35, 54, 60-1, 78, 90, 93, 95-6, 98, 106, 108, 125, 128, 169, 175, 177, 186, 190, 190, 195, 227-8, 234
   audience, 97
   authors, 245
   belief, 18, 21-2, 27
   characters, 24, 217, 239
   Christian converts, 62
   colonization of, 200
   community, 82, 220
   cosmological belief(s), 68, 223
   cosmology, 7, 9, 14, 19, 24, 60
   culture, 3, 8, 49, 61-2, 109, 176, 238, 240
   customs, 23, 30, 103, 152
   divination, 33

drama, 90
folk beliefs, 23, 223
folk material, 251
folk stories, 175
folkways, 4-7, 159, 175, 185, 225, 243, 247, 251-2
judicial system, 104
language, 5, 221, 238
maxim, 143, 251
names, 66, 75, 77
novels, 216, 223
oral tradition, 177
traditional religion, 7-9, 24, 233, 235
religious practices, 12, 25
trinity, 5
world view, 22
Igbo Ideas of the High God, 10
Igboland, 19, 62, 120, 156, 238
Iguede, 109
Ijele Mask, 96
Ikedi, Chief James, 73
Ikemefuna, 33-4, 39-43, 45, 68, 83, 92, 120, 135, 147-9, 151-3, 164, 185, 193, 195, 220
Ikenga, 11
Ikezue, 178
ikolo, 97, 106
ilo, 91, 93, 98-9, 101
ilu, 133
imagery, 215-21, 238
Imo, 94
Innocent (Innocenti), 189, 192
institutions, 4
interpretative perspective, 251-2
Ire village, 152
iyi-uwa, 22, 154-5

Jalio, Mr., 72
Jane, Elizabeth, 5

jigida, 225
Jones, Eldred, 239
Joseph, 161, 191-2
Josiah, 140-1, 249-250

Kiaga, Mr., 150
Killam, G. D., 56
King, Bruce, 226
Kinship groups, 103
Kola nut(s), 21-2, 116, 158, 220-1
kotma, 199-200, 250; *see also* court messengers

Lagos, 83-4, 121, 126, 142, 161, 171, 189-192, 218-9, 229, 249
high court of, 218
Law Court, 121
life, 210
Language, 5
Language and Imagery, 214-6
Language and Style, 215
Legends, 145, 168-9, 175
Lenist; *see* Marxist/Lenist dimension
Leper, 133-4, 136
Leprosy, 134, 152, 237
Lewis, Mary Ellen B., 173-4
Lindfors, Bernth, 23, 90, 108, 124-8, 132, 134-5, 140, 172-4, 185, 240, 246
Literal Translation and Phraseology, 221-6
Literary tradition, 8
Literature, 8
    Commonwealth, 2
    Igbo, 5
    political purposes of, 3
    Western and Soviet traditions in, 3
Locusts, 162-3

Lullabies, 201-4

Madubuike, Ihechukwu, 83
Maduka, 152
Mahood, M. M., 201-3
Mali, 2
Man of the People, A, 1, 9, 62, 71-2, 80, 113, 128, 138, 143, 156, 183-4, 197, 211, 218, 220, 225, 228, 230, 232, 236, 248-9
Marxist/Lenist dimension, 6
Mary, 187-8
Matefi, 54-5, 96, 174
Max, 211
Mayor of Casterbridge, The, 5
Mbaino, 38, 83, 119, 179, 185, 193
Mbanta, 20, 29, 41, 43, 67-8
Mbari house, 3
Mbiti, John S., 26
Medium of Expression, Choice of 244-5
Mgbafo, 64, 100-1,103-4, 248
Mgbeke, 64
Mgbokwo, 64
Mgborie, 64
Micah; see Nanga, Chief M.A.
missionaries, 44-5, 151, 196
mmo, 58; see also egwugwu, ndichie
Morning Yet on Creation Day, 25, 36,61
Moses (Mosisi), 189, 192
moral code and ethics, 9
moralist, 4
Munonye, John, 245
myths, 4, 154

Naaman, 236-7

names, 61
  allusive, 77
  categories, 62
  dedicatory, 64
  metaphoric, 74
  philosophical, 66
  praise, 68
  other, 82
naming, 61, 63, 66
Nanga, Chief the Honorable M. A., 62, 71-2, 80, 113-4, 139, 143, 183-4, 198, 230-1, 236
Nathaniel, 81
native authority, 198
ndichie, 70
Ndulue, Ogbuefi, 69, 152
Nettl, Bruno, 178
New Yam Feast/Festival/Harvest, 53-4, 62, 91-2, 136; *see also* yam
Nigeria, 62-3, 71-2, 82-3, 121, 128, 140, 150, 165, 171, 184, 196, 219, 228, 244
  Eastern, 188
Nigerian Civil War, 83
Nigerian college graduates, 31
Nigerian Military Coup (1966), 184
Nigerian societies, 210, 247, 249, 251
Nigerians, 7, 154
Nkwo, 64, 104-5, 169
Nnadi, 192-3
Nneka, 68, 76
No Longer at Ease, 1, 6-7, 9, 18, 25, 34, 62, 80-1, 84, 121-2, 125, 148, 150, 160, 171, 187, 189, 191, 195-6, 210-12, 216, 218, 220-2, 225, 228-30, 236, 248

nso-ani, 48, 60
Nwafo, 50, 64, 196
Nwaka, 29, 50-1, 59, 61, 69, 76, 79, 93, 133-4, 167, 174, 182, 185-6, 226, 233-4
Nwakibie, 13, 20, 68, 76, 78, 82, 116-7, 119
Nwanku, 228
Nwankwo, 64
Nweke, 64
Nwodika, John, 161, 197
Nwofia, 68
Nwoga, Donatus, 2, 26
Nwoye, 18-9, 34, 62, 65, 107, 146-53, 185, 193, 236; see also Okonkwo, Isaac
nza, 78, 80, 120, 145, 220
Nzekwe, Onuora, 245

obi, 106-7, 151, 196
Obi of Okperi, 73; *see also* Ikedi, Chief James
Obiageli, 68, 196, 201-4
Obiako, 13
Obiechina, Emmanuel N., 86-7, 100, 221, 226, 252
Obierika, 6, 37, 39, 41-2, 44, 62, 67-8, 76, 120, 135, 151-3, 163, 165, 168-71, 236, 250
Obika, 54-5, 75-6, 85-6, 132, 136-7, 181, 206-7
Obiora, 206
ochu, 20, 67
Odili, 80, 113-4, 139-40, 142, 156, 183, 198, 225, 230-1, 236, 250
Oduche, 49-50, 52-4, 62, 96, 129-33, 171, 223, 236
Odukwe, 101-2
Ofoedu, 207-8

Ofoka, 53, 202-3
Ogalanya, 93, 95
ogalu, 95
ogaranya na ogbenye, 182
ogbanje, 22, 76, 153-6, 180, 207-224
ogbazulobodo, 54-5, 76, 136
ogbu opi onwu, 79
Ogbuefi, 69, 83-4, 116
Ogoro, Chief Kalu, 26
ogwogwo, 196-7, 203
ogwu, 94
Ogwugwu, 25, 36, 46
Okafo, 64, 178-80
Okara, 221
Okeke, 64
Okeke, Josiah, 236
Okonkwo, 5-6, 16-20, 24-5, 29-47, 55, 62, 64-70, 74, 76-82-3, 96, 98, 107, 110, 114-20, 124-5, 130, 135, 143-8, 150-4, 161, 163-8, 170-1, 179-80, 182, 185-7, 202, 205, 212-3, 217, 224, 233, 236, 243, 250-1
Okonkwo, Isaac (Nwoye), 18-9, 62, 148, 150, 161, 187, 189, 237
Okonkwo, Obi, 18-9, 34-5, 81, 84, 120-8, 161, 187-92, 195, 212-3, 222, 230, 236-7, 249
Okoye, 64-5, 80, 115
Okperi, 35, 47-8, 50, 52, 58, 73, 79-80, 135, 161, 167, 202, 226
Okuata, 32, 74, 76, 182, 206
Olu, 169
omenani, 30
Onenyi, Okeke, 31
Onwuma, 66

Onwumbiko, 66
Oracle of the Hills and the Caves, 33, 39, 42; *see also* Agbala
oracles, 12-3, 22, 24-28, 32-5, 39, 43, 50-1
oral tradition, 251
osu, 18-9, 33-4, 121, 123, 189-91, 213, 236-7
  definition of, 33-4
Osugo, 118-9
Osukwu, Otasili, 195-6
Otakagu, 85-6, 94
Otakekpeli, 86
Oti-anya-afu-uzo, 31
Otiji-Egbe, 72
outcasts, 33-4, 121; *see also osu*
Oxford degrees, 71
Oye, 64-5, 104-5
Oyilidie, 74
ozo, 69, 91, 152, 170; *see also egwugwe, ndichie*
Ozoemena, 66

Pacification of the Primitive Tribes of the Lower Niger, The, 6
pagan cult, 19
palm-oil, 111-3, 158
palm wine, 21-2, 57, 65
Panegyric Songs, 178, 180
pan-Igbo nature goddess, 60
p'Bitek, Okot, 2
People's Organization Party (POP), 71, 142-3
personal god, 79, 166; *see also chi*, gods
Peter, 62; *see also* Oduche
Pevear, Richard, 58
phraseology, 221-2; *see also* Literal Translation and Phraseology
priestesses, 24, 33, 70, 224

priests, 4, 24, 28-29, 33, 36, 38-9, 47-53, 55-9, 70, 137-8, 203
Prime Minister, The, 71
Progressive Alliance Party (PAP), 142-3
proverbs, 1, 4, 81-2, 111-6, 118, 120-1, 129-31, 134-6, 139, 142-3, 177, 215, 238
Proverbs as Imagery, 226-8
proverbial imagery, 141
Protestants, 195-6
Pryse, Elizabeth, 222
python, sacred, 30, 54, 57, 130, 134, 196, 207, 209

racial dogmatism, 6
ram, 43, 105-6, 208
Ramadan, Cathy, 148-50
Random House College Dictionary, The, 33, 37
reincarnation, 17-8, 20, 22-4, 54, 68, 149
Religious Terminology and Allusions, 232-7
Republic of Nigeria, first, 184
Rise of the Igbo Novel, The, 173
rituals, 7, 88, 90, 93, 97, 106, 243; *see also* Igbo rituals
Roscoe, Adrian A., 99
Rotimi, Ola, 89, 92

sacrifice(s), 12, 22, 35, 47, 55, 60, 132, 150, 182, 217
  of human beings, 27
Samalu, *see* Odili
Sartre, Jean Paul, 239
Savage, Dr. Mary, 77
Schweitzer, Albert, 3
second burial, 2
Second World War, 72

Seege, Pete, 180
Senghor, Leopold Sedar, 2, 175
Shelton, Austin, 113, 133, 138
shrew, 53, 105
Simon (Simonu), 189
Smith, Rev. James, 45, 62, 95, 164-5
social commitment, 7
society, 6, 21, 3244, 220; see also Igbo societies
Song of the Heart, The, 191-2
Songhai, 2
Songs, bridal, 204-6
　general, 209-13
　panegyric, 178
　play, 192-3
　work, 199-201
Soviet traditions, 3
Soyinka, Wole, 155
spirit being, 17
spirits, 82, 97
spirit world, 18, 20, 97
stratification of society, 182
struggle for independence, 1
stylistic and technical devices, 8
Sunday, 198
supernatural force, 9
Supreme God, concept of, 10-12
　see also Chukwu, Chineke
swelling disease (dropsy), 24
Syria, host of, 236

tale, see animal tales
Tale of the Kind and the Unkind Girls, 173
tales, Igbo trickster, 156, 162
Ten Commandments, The, 237
Things Fall Apart, 1, 5-7, 9, 16-8, 20, 22-3, 25, 27-30, 33-4, 52, 60, 62, 64-8, 70, 76, 78, 82-5, 93-6, 99-100, 103, 107, 109-11, 114-6, 118, 120-1, 124-6, 130, 134-5, 138, 142-3, 148, 155-6, 162, 168, 170, 178, 185, 193, 196, 199, 207, 213, 215, 217, 220-1, 225, 232-3, 238-40

Third World Countries, 214
Tillyard, 6
Timothy, 141
Tortoise, 81, 137, 156-62
totem, 30, 209
tradition, 5, 8
Trial of Obi Okonkwo, The, 100
tribalism, 128
tribes, 6, 122-3
twins, 24, 33, 121, 248

Uchendu, 20-1, 41, 45, 67-8, 83, 163, 165-6, 186-7
Uchendu, Victor C., 10, 82-3, 127
udala, 51, 105, 136
Udeozo, Ogbuefi Anichebe, 69
Udo, 25, 36
Udo, Ogbuefi, 38, 69
Ugoye, 173-4
Uka, Kalu, 90
Ukpaka, Nweke, 208
ukwa, 30
Uli, 94
uli, 95, 157, 252
Ulu, 27-9, 33, 35, 48-60, 69, 84, 97, 104, 120, 135-8, 167, 182, 202-3, 222, 237
Ulysses, 58
Umuachala, 28, 82, 84
Umuagu, 28, 82, 84
Umuaro, 28-9, 33, 35-6, 47-8, 50, 52-7, 59, 69, 78-80, 82, 84-6, 88, 93, 95-6, 117, 129, 133-6,

166-7, 169, 185-6, 196-7, 204, 207-9, 225-6, 228, 239
Umuazu, 82, 84-5
Umuezeani, 28, 82, 84-5, 206
Umuike, 168-9
Umuisiuzo, 28, 82
Umunna, 45, 82
Umunneora, 28, 82-3, 93
Umuofia, 5-7, 18, 20, 31, 36-8, 42-7, 64-5, 67-8, 81-5, 94-6, 101-4, 106, 108, 114-6, 119, 121-2, 124-8, 135, 146, 151, 154, 161, 163-5, 168, 170-1, 179, 185, 188-90, 192-3, 196, 199, 205, 239
Umuofia Civil Servants, 125
Umuofia Progressive Union, 84, 121, 127-8, 229, 249
Umuogwugwu, 28, 82
Umuru, 169, 199
Unachukwu, 45
Unachukwu, Moses, 208
University of Massachusetts, 245
University of Washington, 3
Unoka, 15, 17, 33, 40, 114-5, 119, 149, 153
Uyanwa, Okagbue, 76, 154
uziza, 201
Uzowulu, 100-4, 248

Voice, The, 221
vulture(s), 81, 148-51

Warrant Chief, 48

Week of Peace, 31, 38, 40, 77, 120, 145
Weinstock, Donald, 148-50
West African, 155
  novels, 86
  societies, 145
  writers, 221
Western, Education 63, 121
  perspectives, 6-7
  societies, 91
  system, 250
  traditions, 3
white clay, 21, 30
white man 11, 24, 29, 35-6, 44-5, 47-9, 52, 131, 133-5, 141, 152, 163, 171, 213, 226, 238, 240, 247
White man's religion, 29, 34, 195
Wintabota, *see* Winterbottom, Captain T.K.
Winterbottom, Captain T.K., 47-8, 63, 72-3, 77, 129-31, 133-4
Wren, Robert M., 7, 17, 75, 172, 195-7
Wretched of the Earth, 239-40
Wright, Mr., 200, 208

Yahweh, 49
yam(s) 39, 47, 53-4, 59, 69, 106, 116-7, 158, 163, 181, 201, 234
yams, sacred, 28, 35
Yoruba, 210